Supply Chain Management

Edited by

Jayashree Dubey
M.L. Sai Kumar

Institute of Public Enterprise (IPE)
Osmania University Campus, Hyderabad

in association with

New Century Publications
New Delhi, India

NEW CENTURY PUBLICATIONS
4800/24, Bharat Ram Road,
Ansari Road, Daryaganj,
New Delhi-110 002

Tel.: 23247798, 65396605
Fax: 011 - 41017798
E-mail: indiatax@vsnl.com
www.newcenturypublications.com

Editorial office:
34, Gujranwala Town, Part-2,
Delhi - 110 009

Tel.: 27247805, 27464774

First Published – June 2007

ISBN: 81-7708-142-x (*10 digit*)
978-81-7708-142-8 (*13 digit*)

Published by New Century Publications and printed at Singhal Print Media, New Delhi -110 005

PRINTED IN INDIA

Foreword

Indian economy is on an unstoppable growth path. The service sector is booming, thanks to the business process outsourcing and the world class Indian IT companies. Organized retail is a booming sector with thousands of crores of rupees being spent on construction of malls for establishing retail stores. Indian manufacturing industry in the past laid emphasis on the philosophy of self-reliance. Early efforts such as the setting up of ITIs, polytechnics, engineering and science institutions, national laboratories and a large number of public enterprises were all done with a view to provide employment opportunities and also to provide basic goods to the citizens. The strategic objectives of Indian manufacturing have changed significantly with globalisation and also with the continuous economic reforms by India. Currently, attracting FDI, employment for low-skilled as well as skilled labour, producing goods both for export and internal use, increasing supply chain efficiencies and reducing wastes are some of the objectives. For manufacturing to contribute 25-26 per cent to GDP, it requires careful planning and execution.

Manufacturing is perceived to be less glamorous and we do not have enough industry and academic interface in the sector. If we have to target a double-digit growth rate, and if we want manufacturing to play a larger role in the global market, the industry and the academicians should work together. The present volume on *Supply Chain Management* will provide an opportunity for discussion among researchers and also between the academia and the industry. I congratulate Dr. Jayashree Dubey and Professor M.L. Sai Kumar for bringing out this volume and also Professor R.K. Mishra, Director, Institute of Public Enterprise (IPE), Osmania University Campus, Hyderabad, for his support.

May 25, 2007

Professor N. Viswanadham
INDIAN SCHOOL OF BUSINESS (ISB)
Hyderabad

The Book

Competitive environment of modern times is forcing the firms to shift focus from inside the corporate walls to collaboration with outside trading partners. Enhanced communication technology has redefined how businesses work together, raise customers' expectations and place new demands on supply chain performance. Internet has allowed companies to come up with highly innovative solutions that accelerate the widespread adoption of core principles of supply chain management. Companies that make use of e-business to redefine supply chain integration achieve significant increase in their efficiency and competitive edge over their competitors. The next few years will see an explosion of e-enabled supply chain management as visionary companies develop new paradigms of e-business for the future.

This book focuses on concepts, principles and real life experiences which improve understanding of the Supply Chain Management (SCM). Available information has been analysed and synthesised across many disciplines, such as purchase and supply management, marketing, organisational dynamics, logistic and transportation management, information technology, strategic management, and operations management.

The book is designed to contribute to the existing body of literature available on supply chain management. It consists of 28 papers authored by scholars in the area. This work, which is replete with new concepts and practices, will commend itself to all categories of readers, particularly academicians, researchers and students of management, economics and commerce.

Editors' Profile

Dr. Jayashree Dubey is currently Assistant Professor (Production and Operations Management) at Institute of Public Enterprise (IPE), Osmania University Campus, Hyderabad. Dr. Jayashree, MBA (Marketing & Finance), Ph.D. (Management) and BE (Electricals) has more than ten years of academic and research experience in the area of production and operations management. She has also been associated with the Distance Learning Programme Division of BITS, Pilani and was a visiting faculty at National Thermal Power Corporation (NTPC). She has handled a major research project of the Ministry of Small-scale Industries, Government of India. Apart from research assignments, she has published articles in the above areas in journals of national and international repute.

Professor M.L. Sai Kumar is presently Head, Information Technology Division at Institute of Public Enterprise (IPE), Osmania University Campus, Hyderabad. He has also been the Coordinator for PGDBM programmes at the Institute. Professor Sai Kumar was conferred the award of "International Man of the Year for IT Education" by the International Biographical Center, Cambridge. Apart from academic pursuits, he has trained several IAS and IPS officers in IT applications. He has conducted several workshops for the corporate sector in areas like software engineering, e-commerce and project management. Being a visiting faculty to various universities, he is also member of recruitment boards of various public and private sector organisations. In his career of over three decades, Professor Sai Kumar has authored several books and published numerous papers.

Editors' Note on the Book

Supply chain management (SCM) is the process of planning, implementing, and controlling the operations of the supply chain with the purpose of satisfying requirements of the customers as efficiently as possible. Supply chain management spans all movement and storage of raw material, work-in-process, inventory, and finished goods from point-of-origin to point-of-consumption.

Competitive environment of modern times is forcing the firms to shift focus from inside the corporate walls to collaboration with outside trading partners. Enhanced communication technology has redefined how businesses work together, raise customers' expectations and place new demands on supply chain performance. Internet has allowed companies to come up with highly innovative solutions that accelerate the widespread adoption of core principles of supply chain management. Companies that make use of e-business to redefine supply chain integration achieve significant increase in their efficiency and competitive edge over their competitors. The next few years will see an explosion of e-enabled supply chain management as visionary companies develop new paradigms of e-business.

Firms are linked in networked supply chain due to the increasing global cooperation and vertical disintegration. The main strategy is to coordinate effectively the entire supply chain, from upstream to downstream activities. The main theme of managing supply chain activities is to gain competitive advantage. This book focuses on concepts, principles and real life experiences which improve understanding of the Supply Chain Management (SCM). Available information has been analysed and synthesised across many disciplines such as purchase and supply management, marketing, organisational dynamics, logistic and transportation management, information technology, strategic management, and operations management.

Supply chains have generated lot of interest lately. It may be because organisations have now realised that long lasting success cannot be achieved without giving due importance to supply chains. However, managing supply chain is a tough task and optimising the supply chain is a challenge. This is due to the intertwined nature of supply chain. Even a slightest mistake at any stage of supply chain can create havoc for the organisation. Sometimes, even the best managed companies fail to grasp the impact of supply chain glitches. The effect is so disastrous that the recovery costs affect the bottom-line of corporates significantly.

Hence, a new and fresh thinking is required for supply chain management. This is necessary because rules of business have changed drastically. Companies have to coordinate the strategic, tactical and operational decisions to optimise the performance of supply chain. In a globally competitive environment, to make profits and to survive, it is important for the companies to link all their upstream suppliers and downstream distributors into an integrated supply-chain network. The implementation of supply chain management is not about reinventing the business. From an organisation's point of view, supply chain management concepts are especially tricky because they go against the mantra of decentralisation, which many companies adopted to spur innovation among business.

The present volume is designed to contribute to the existing body of literature available on supply chain management. It consists of 28 papers authored by scholars in the area. The editors place on record their deep appreciation and gratefulness to each of them for their worthy contributions. This work, which is replete with new concepts and practices, will commend itself to all categories of readers, particularly academicians, researchers and students of management, economics and commerce.

We are thankful to the anonymous editors of M/S New Century Publications, New Delhi, for their efforts to standardise and improve the texts of different contributions.

June 10, 2007
Hyderabad

Jayashree Dubey
M.L. Sai Kumar

List of Contributors

A. Azad	Lecturer, Department of Manufacturing Engineering, College of Engineering, Guindy, Anna University.
A. Duraikannan	Assistant Professor, SSM School of Management, C/o SSM College of Engineering, Komarapalayam, Tamil Nadu
Alok Jha	Faculty in the Area of Data Analytics and Market Research, Institute of Public Enterprise (IPE), O.U Campus, Hyderabad.
Ashvini Ravi	Assistant Professor, Department of Management Studies, R.M.D Engineering College, Anna University, Chennai.
Bhavya Singh	Seshadripuram Institute of Management Studies, Yelahanka, Bangalore.
B. Krishna Reddy	Professor, Department of Business Management, Osmania University.
B.L. Sairam	Assistant Professor, SSM School of Management, C/o SSM College of Engineering, Komarapalayam, Tamil Nadu
C.N. Sundaresan	Reader, Department of Chemistry, Sri Sathya Sai Institute of Higher Learning, Bangalore.
Deepthi B.S.	Seshadripuram Institute of Management Studies, Yelahanka, Bangalore.
G. Chamundeshwari	Xavier Vignana Jyothi Institute of Management, Secunderabad.
G. Deepika	Assistant Professor, Vivek Vardhini School of Business Management, Jambagh, Hyderabad.
G. Nirmala	Department of Computer Applications, R.M.D Engineering College, Anna University, Chennai.

G.V.R.K. Acharyulu	Associate Professor, Apollo Institute of Hospital Administration Jubileehills, Hyderabad.
J. Suresh Reddy	Assistant Professor, Department of Business Management, Osmania University PG College, Mahboobnagar.
K. Guruswamy	Professor, Department of Business Administration, K.S.R. College of Technology, Tiruchengode, Tamil Nadu
K. J. Paulose	Professor, SCMS, Cochin.
K. Narashiman	Assistant Professor, Department of Chemical Engineering, Alagappa College of Technology, Anna University.
Kalavathi V.	Seshadripuram Institute of Management Studies, Yelahanka, Bangalore.
Kishore Kumar Morya	Faculty of Information Technology and Operations Management, ICFAI Business School, Jaipur.
Koilakuntla Maddulety	Assistant Professor, National Institute of Industrial Engineering, Mumbai.
M. Viswanathiah	Alliance Business Academy, Bangalore.
Manimala K.	Xavier Vignana Jyothi Institute of Management, Secunderabad.
Mihir Dash	Alliance Business Academy, Bangalore.
N. Sivakumar	Lecturer, Department of Commerce, Sri Sathya Sai Institute of Higher Learning, Bangalore.
P. Sailaja	Faculty in the Area of Marketing, Institute of Public Enterprise (IPE), O.U Campus, Hyderabad.
P.O. Subash	M.S. Ramaiah Institute of Management Bangalore.
Priya Deshpande	Assistant Professor, Vivek Vardhini School of Business Management, Jambagh, Hyderabad.

R. K. Mishra	Director, Institute of Public Enterprise (IPE), O.U. Campus, Hyderabad.
R. Balajivignesh	Lecturer in Management, School of Management, Janakiammal College of Arts and Science, Kovaipudur.
Rohit Kumar Mishra	Junior Research Fellow (UGC), Department of Business Administration, Sambalpur University, Sambalpur.
S. Baskaran	Lecturer, SSM School of Management, C/o SSM College of Engineering, Komarapalayam, Tamil Nadu
S. Chandrasekaran	Professor, Department of Information Technology, R.M.D Engineering College, Anna University, Chennai.
S.R. Subba Rao	Professor PGDBM, Xavier Vignana Jyothi Institute of Management, Secunderabad.
Shital Jhunjhunwala	Assistant Professor, Institute of Public Enterprise (IPE), O.U. Campus, Hyderabad.
Sudeep Kumar Mandhania	Consultant – Pharmaceuticals and Life Sciences Domain, Infosys Technologies Limited, Hyderabad.
T. Sudha	Research Scholar, Department of Business Management, Osmania University, Hyderabad.
T. Mathew	Lecturer in Marketing, Lala Lajpatrai Institute of Management, Mumbai.
V.B. Narsimha	Assistant Professor, Department of Computer Science and Engineering, University College of Engineering, Osmania University, Hyderabad.
Vaishali Agarwal	Senior Lecturer, Management, Indian Business Academy, Greater NOIDA.

Contents

1

Basics of Supply Chain Management

Rohit Kumar Mishra

1. Introduction

The concept of supply chain management (SCM) has become popular from many directions including quality revolution, notion of material management and integrated logistics. The origins of supply chain management are unclear. However its development starts along the lines of physical distribution and transport (Croom et al. 2000). Another one can be found in the total cost approach to distribution & logistics. Both approaches show that focusing of a single element in the chain cannot assure the effectiveness of whole system (Croom et al. 2000). Supply chain management is originally introduced by consultants in 1980s and has gained tremendous attention. (La Londe 1998). A typical supply chain is generally a network of materials; information and services that linked with the characteristics of supply, transformation and demand. The term SCM has not only used to explain the logistic activities and the planning and control of materials and information flow but also used to describe strategic inter organizational issues (Harland et al. 1999,Thorelli 1986). Many a subject area such as purchasing and supply, logistic and transportation, marketing, organizational behaviour, network management, strategic management, management information system and operation management has contributed to the explosion of SCM literature. In this paper we examine and consolidate over various articles. This study may be the most comprehensive analysis of the multidisciplinary, wide ranging research on SCM.

2. Elements of SCM

There are three driving forces, which lead to the development of SCM. Companies have undertaken various initiatives and approaches to address an assortment of issues related to their supply chains. These approaches and initiatives classified into four streams of research efforts namely strategic purchasing, supply chain management, logistics integration and supply network co-ordination.

2.1 Strategic Purchasing: Purchasing has a passive role in the organization. In the year 1980s, purchasing has involved in the corporate strategic planning process. By 1990s both academics & managers were giving much more attention to strategic purchasing. The ability of purchasing to influence strategic planning has increased due to the rapidly changing competitive environment (Carter & Narasimhan 1996). The perspective of strategic purchasing is also consistent with general strategy literature (Carr & Smeltzer 1999). Strategic purchasing has also a proactive long-term focus. The strategic recognition is evidenced by a recent action taken by US National Association of Purchasing Management (NAPM), founded in 1915. Contemporary purchasing is now best recognized as a critical unit of SCM (Gadde & Hakansson, 1994, Fung 1999).

2.2 Supply Management: In supply management the buyer supplier relationship is emphasized. Since suppliers have profound and direct impact on cost, quality, time and responsiveness of the buying firm. Hence the management of business and relationship with other members of supply chain is referred as SCM.

2.2.1 Communication: Effective inter-organizational communication could be characterized as genuine and involving personal contact between buying and selling personnel (Krause & Ellram 1997). Poor communication was often a fundamental weakness in the interface between a buying firm's efforts to achieve increased level of supplier performance. In their 10 case studies of buying firms in UK, Galt and Dale (1991) revealed the importance of two-way communication with suppliers and its potential positive effect on buying firms competitiveness.

2.2.2 Supplier Base Reduction: The traditional practice of firm contracting with multiple suppliers was based upon following things:

- Competition is the basis of economic system.
- Purchasing must not become source dependent.

Multiple sourcing is a risk-reducing technique (Newman 1989, Shin et al. 2000). Many firms are reducing the number of primary suppliers and allocating a majority of the purchased material requirements from a single source (Spekman 1988, Kekre et al. 1995). This action provides multiple benefits. They are as follows:

1. Fewer suppliers to contact in the case of order given on short notice.
2. Reduced inventory management cost.
3. Volume consolidation & quantity discount.
4. Increased economies of scale based on order volume and the learning curve effect.
5. Reduced lead times due to dedicated capacity and work in process inventory from the suppliers.
6. Reduced logistic cost.
7. Co-ordinate replenishment.
8. Improved buyer supplier product design relationship.
9. Improved trust due to communication.
10. Better customer service and market penetration.

Moreover supply base consolidation sets the stage for future development of the chosen suppliers.

2.2.3 Long-term Relationship: The long-term planning horizon is crucial characteristics of modern supply chain relationship. The advantages of long-term relationship are as follows:

1. Share risk and reward.
2. Maintain the relationship over a longer period of time.

The long-term relationship with the supplier will become a part of well managed chain and have an effect on the competitiveness of the entire supply chain. The terms partnership and partnership sourcing have used to refer the closer and longer relationship with suppliers.

2.2.4 Supplier Selection: Selecting suppliers for specific goods and services is a critical decision for most organizations since supply performance can have a direct impact on the business. In practice however a much wider set of concerns are involved (Croom 2001). Dickson (1996) states that the abilities to meet quality standards and deliver products on time as well as performance history are the most critical determinants in choosing suppliers. So quality is the most important criteria. Helper (1991) showed that importance of quality criteria has increased the most while the importance of price increased the least during the period. It has also found that companies place more importance on consistency and least importance on price. On the whole quality, on time delivery, uninterrupted supply, trustworthiness, integrity, commitment and characteristics are considered for selecting supplier. Those suppliers who are unwilling to share information on cost, quality and production can be screened out.

2.2.5 Supplier Involvement: Supplier involvement may range from giving minor design suggestions to being responsible for complete development, design and engineering of specific part of assembly. Aleo (1992) discussed Kodak's early supplier involvement programme that involved suppliers in new R& D effort. Kamath and Liker (1994) also examined Japanese product development practices and identified a variety of roles that suppliers may play. Mabert et al. (1992) found supplier involvement to be an important to part of the strategy in five out of six firms. The effective integration of suppliers into new product can yield such benefits as reduced cost and improved access to and application of technology.

2.2.6 Trust and Commitment: Firms exchange essential information and engage some suppliers- customers in long-term contract have become the root level of supply chain integration (Spekman et al. 1998). SCM is built on a foundation of trust and commitment. Trust is conveyed through faith, reliance, belief or confidence in the supply partner. Trust is the sense of performance in accordance with intention and expectations. Commitment means the trading partners are willing to devote energy to sustain the relationship. In many cases, commitment makes it more difficult for partners to act in ways that might adversely affect overall supply chain performance. With commitment, supply chain partners become integrated into their major customers' processes and more tied to their goal.

Trust comes in various forms such as cognitive trust and calculative trust. The calculative trusts have a significant impact on buyer-supplier relationships and consequently supply chain performance. Hill (1990) argues that contrary to the theory of transaction cost economics (TCE) that opportunism generally characterizes exchange. The relationship based on cooperation and trust is the key to survive in the market place. Further a high level of inter-organizational trust, that enhanced supplier performance, lowered costs of negotiations and reduced conflict (Zahar et al. 1998).

3. Logistics Integration

Logistics has traditionally been defined as the process of planning, implementing and controlling the efficient flow and storage of goods, services and related information as they travel from point of origin to point of consumption. In logistic domain, transportation, warehousing, purchasing and distribution are included. The traditional approach of logistic integration across functional boundaries with in a firm is termed as "internal integration". A more recent approach of logistic integration across firm boundaries is termed as external integration (La Lone, 1998). Enterprise logistic integration is the extent to which a firm implements both external and internal integration. It can be characterized by integration of logistic activities across functional departments with in the firm (Stock et al.). This notion of enterprise logistic integration reflects the growing importance of logistics as a co-coordinating mechanism among multiple units of the enterprise and ultimately as a source of customer value and competitive advantage.

3.1 Internal Integration: Internal integration is the degree to which firms are able to integrate and collaborate across functional boundaries to provide better customer service (Kahn & Mentzur, 1996). The management of logistic activities involves other functions namely marketing, finance, purchasing and production. Coordination is required with in the firm (Ballou et al. 2000). It is widely argued that task interdependence is the catalyst for interdepartmental integration (Ellinger, 2000). Customer satisfaction is dependent on the output of more than one worker or one functional area. Benefits will be realized by company that operate their logistics processes as an integrated system rather than by optimizing functional subsystems. Numerous empirical studies suggested that collaborative cross-functional integration is positively associated with performance (Stank et al. 1999). Collaborative behaviour is based on co-operation rather than on compliance. Its success is contingent upon the ability of individuals from interdependent department to build meaningful relationships.

3.2 External Integration: External integration is the integration of logistic activities across firm boundaries. It reflects an extension of manufacturing enterprise to encompass the entire supply chain, not just an individual company as the competitive unit. Managers are co-coordinating with companies beyond their own, seeking new ways to lower costs or improve service through mechanism such as vendor-managed inventory and just in time scheduling. Collaboration is needed across enterprise boundaries interacting with external suppliers, carrier partners and customers. Logistics is a boundary-spanning role with these external customers as well. Morash et al. (1997) identify customer service, quality, channel distribution and total cost minimization as major boundary spanning interface capabilities. Higher level of external integration is characterized by increased logistic related communication, greater coordination of the firm's logistics with those of its suppliers and customers.

4. Supplier Network Co-ordination

A sizeable number of researchers have adopted the mathematical modeling approach in their study of SCM. Under this approach a common goal is to optimize the planning and coordination of three fundamental supply chain stages: procurement, production and distribution. Each of the three stages may be further comprised of multiple facilities in various locations in different countries. For example researchers have concentrated on the optimal order quantity (EOQ) and quantity discount inventory model. Various form of production-inventory-distribution has also been widely studied through many problems in these areas formulated as dynamic programming, integer programming, and non-liner programming etc. (Goyal 1998, Lau & Lau 1994).

Most of the supply chain modeling research is an extension or integration of the traditional problems or (1) production planning and inventory control and distribution and logistics. Depending on the scope of supply chain issues researchers choose to address the decision variables used in their models could include demand variability, production scheduling, inventory level, distribution centers, manufacturing plants, number of products types etc. The methodology adopted in the modeling approach is then determined by the decision variables considered and the objective of the study. Simulation method has also been adopted for analyzing more complex problem that includes a larger number of decision variables where optimal solution may not be possible.

The study of bullwhip effect is the noticeable contribution of the modeling approach in providing additional insight into supply chain dynamics. Forrester's visionary work refine the supply chain natured tendency to amplify, delay and oscillate demand information and demonstrate that rational, independent decision making, increased order lead time and simultaneous ordering by retailer increase demand amplification (Forrestor 1958). The magnitude of bullwhip effect reduction through information sharing and physical co-ordination is still not understood.

The mathematical modeling approach is excellent in providing insight and understanding well defined supply chain setting which involves few decision variables and highly restrictive assumptions. The result of much supply chain modeling research is mathematical that suffers from unrealistic assumption and lack of generality. Most principle behind mathematical model is shaped by the empirical studies in (1) strategic purchasing (2) supply management (3) logistic integration.

5. Supply Chain Performance

An effective performance measurement is essential for SCM. Because it provides the basis to understand the system, influences behaviour through out the system and provide information about the result of the system to supply chin members and outside stakeholders. Researchers have found that measuring supply chain performance in and of itself leads to improvement in overall performance.

5.1 Financial Performance: Financial performance has been the dominant model in empirical strategy research (Venkatraman & Ramanujam 1987). The main things like sales growth, profitability, earning per share etc. should examine thoroughly. The inadequacies of using solely financial performance measure in manufacturing and supply chains however have been well documented in the academic literature. It has been further argued that every manager knows that there are important limitations in relying exclusively on financial measures of performance. Kaplan (1998) contended that companies have relied on summary financial measures and thus ignored the powerful opportunities for continuous improvement that a well-constructed set of non-financial measures can offer.

5.2 Operational Performance: A broader conceptualization and more effective business performance should include indicators of operational performance in addition to those of financial performance. This is mainly because non-financial measures can overcome the limitations of just using financial performance measures (Chen and Lee 1995). There are many advantages of using non-financial measures including the fact that non-financial measures are urgent than financial one. They are more measurable and precise. They are consistent with company's goal and strategy. These categories of performance reflect competencies in specific areas of supply chain including cost, delivery, speed and quality, reliability and flexibility. Operational performance measures provide a relatively direct indication of the efforts of the various supply chain construct.

6. Measuring Supply Chain performance

Time-based performance measure has recently received substantial attention in SCM. For example researchers have considered different aspects of time-based performance relative to various stages of over all value delivery cycle and have proposed several measures to evaluate them (Jayaram et al. 1999). The key dimension of time-based performance relative to various stages of over all value delivery cycle and have proposed several measures to evaluate them. The key dimension of time-based performance includes delivery, speed, new product development, time, reliability/dependability, new product introduction and manufacturing lead-time. In addition customer responsiveness has also been recognized in the agility literature as a key aspect of time based performance. Rapid confirmation of orders and rapid handling of customer complaints are found to be two key indicators of customer responsiveness.

To address supply chain performance in a more systematic way, several new frame-works have recently been proposed. Beamon (1999) argues that supply chain measurement system must involve three types of performance measures. It is clear that supply chain measurement system that consists of either financial or operational measures alone is generally inadequate. Most studies have adopted financial and operational measurements to gauge the improvement and performance of focal firm. The notion of SCM however entails measuring the performance of the entire supply chain rather than just the performance of the individual supply chain partners. The essence of SCM implies that it is the combined performance of the integrated supply chain that is of paramount importance.

Several researchers have started to propose measurement of over all supply chain performance including assessing the extent to which supply chain relationship are based on mutual trust, changes in average volume of inventory held and frequency of inventory turnover across supply chain over time. The adaptability of the supply chain as a whole is to change customer needs (Bello & Gilliland 1997). In their seminal work Kaplan & Norton also proposed a "balance scorecard" approach for supply chain performance measurement. Their approach incorporates both financial and operational performance measure that is used at various level of supply chain including supply chain, organizational, functional and team levels. There is an opportunities as well as a challenge for researchers to develop new performance measures for the entire supply chain that would be stimulants for improved supply chain practice.

7. Theoretical Research Framework

SCM is an integrated approach to the planning and control of materials, services, and information flow that adds value for customers through collaborative relationships among supply chain members. The theoretical research framework is developed to guide research effort and provide insight for managerial practice that helps better understand the framework. Supply chain is composed of a network of interdependent relationship developed and fostered through strategic collaboration with the goal of deriving mutual benefit (Miles & Snow 1986). Although complementary to the resource-based view, the relational view considers the network instead of individual firm as the unit of analysis and thus provides a more coherent support to SCM.

Supplier involvement is a critical element of strategic buyer-supplier relationship because many researchers have demonstrated that supplier involvement can provide multiple benefits such as reduced cost and improved quality of purchased materials, reduced product development, time and improved access to and application of technology. Cross-functional teams have been proved very effective in meeting the challenges of successful supplier integration for new product development and other strategic initiatives. SCM is built on a foundation of trust and commitment. Trust contributes significantly to the long-term stability of the buyer-supplier relationship. Committed partners also dedicate resources to sustain and try to achieve the goal of relationship. So buyer-supplier relationship enforced by strategic purchasing and based on trust and commitment foster sharing of information ranges from Research and Development (R&D) to product design and production plan (Ellram & Carr 1994).

8. Supply Chain Initiatives and Supply Chain Performance

Superior buyer-supplier relationship leads to improved performance of both supplier and buyer. For example supply base reduction has been found to provide multiple benefits including better time based and cost based performance. Cross-functional teams have been identified as important contributors to the success of supplier selection and supply chain performance (Burt & Doyle 1993). Supplier involvement has also found to provide multiple benefits. Supplier performance is a key determinant of buying firm's competitiveness. Extant research has also demonstrated that supplier performance is one of the determining factors for the company's operational performance. This framework suggests a mediating role of supplier performance in facilitating the link between strategic purchasing guided by supply management and buyer performance (Davis 1993).

9. Conclusion

Supply chain literature has focused on the importance of one or limited elements of supply chain. Consequently understanding the true dynamics of SCM is far more complex. The complex network of inter-related activities in supply chain makes it challenging to managers to describe and comprehend how these activities are related and how they influence each other. The scientific development of coherent SCM disciplines requires advancement in development of theoretical models to further enhance our understanding of supply chain phenomena. The analysis shows that the area is devoid of clear theory. The relative importance and interrelationship among the various supply chain initiatives as well as direct or mediating effects of these activities and constructs of supply chain performance have been hardly explored. It is hoped that future research effort will investigate profoundly complex and extremely important issue, attending to the complexity brought about by the large number of related and interdependent supply chain activities.

References

Aleo, Jr, J.P., (1992), Redefining the Manufacturer-Supplier Relationship, Journal of Business Strategy, Vol. 13, pp. 10-14.

Ammer, D.S., (1989), Top Management's View of the Purchasing Function, Journal of Purchasing and Material Management, Vol.25, pp. 16-21.

Ballou, R.H., Gilbert, S. M and Mukherjee, A., (2000), "New Managerial Challenges from Supply Chain Opportunities, Industrial Marketing Management, Vol. 29, pp.7-18.

Beamon, B. M., (1998), Supply Chain Design and Analysis: Models and Methods:, International Journal of Production Economics, Vol. 19, pp. 275-292.

Bello, D.C. and Gilliland, D.L, (1997), The Effects of Output Controls, Process Controls, and Flexibility on Export Channel Performance, Journal of Marketing, Vol, 61, pp. .22

Carr, A. S and Smeltzer, L. R., (1999), The Relationship of Strategic Purchasing to Supply Chain Management, European Journal of Purchasing and Supply Management, Vol.5, pp.43-51.

Carter, J. R. and Narasimhan, R., (1996), Is Purchasing Really Strategic?, International Journal of Production Distribution and Materials Management, Vol.32, pp. 20-28

Chen, K. C.W. and Lee, C. W. J, (1995), Accounting Measures of Business Performance and Tobin's Theory, Journal of Accounting, Auditing and Finance, Vol.10, pp.587-609.

Choi, T.Y. and Hartley, J.L., (1996), An Exploration of Supplier Selection Practices Across the Supply Chain, Journal of Operation Management, Vol.14, pp. 333-343.

Chopra, Sunil, Meindle, Peter. 92005) Supply Chain Management Strategy, Planning and Operation, Pearson Education Private limited, New Delhi.

Davis, T., (1993), Effective Supply Chain Management, Solan Management Review, Summer Volume, pp.35-46.

Dickson, G.W., 91996), An Analysis of Supplier Selection Systems and Decision, Journal of Purchasing and Materials Management, Vol.2, pp.5-17.

Ellinger, A. E., (2000), Improving Marketing/Logistics Cross-functional Collaboration in the Supply Chain, Industrial Marketing Management, Vol.29 ,pp. 85-96.

Ellram, L. M. and Carr, A. S, 91994), Strategic Purchasing: a History and Review of the Literature, International Journal of Physical Distribution and Material Management, Vol. 30, pp. 10-18.

Forrester, J., (1958), Industrial Dynamic, Harvard Business Review, pp. 49-58.

Freeman, V. and Cavinato, J. L., (1990), Fitting Purchasing to the Strategic Firm:, Processes and Values, Journal of Purchasing and Materials Management, Vol.26, pp. 15-20.

Fung, P., (1999), Managing Purchasing in a Supply Chain Context: Evolution and Resolution, Logistics Information Management, Vol. 12, pp. 362-366.

Gadde, L. E. abd Hankansson, H., (1994), the Changing Role of Purchasing: Reconsidering Three Strategic Issues, European Journal of Purchasing and Supply Management, Vol1m pp. 27-35.

Galt, J. D. A. and Dale, B. G., (1991), Supplier Development: a British Case Study, International Journal of Purchasing and Material Management, Vol. 27, pp. 19-24.

Goyal, S.K., (1998), A Joint Economic Lot Size Model for Purchaser and Vendor: A Comment, Decision Sciences, Vol. 19, pp. 236-241.

Hakansson, H. and Eriksson, A.K, (1993), Getting Innovations Out of Supplier Networks, Journal of "Business to Business Marketing, Vol.1, pp. 3-34.

Harland, C. M., Lamming, R. C. and Cousins, P. D., (1999), Developing the Concept of Supply Strategy, International Journal of Operations and Production Management, Vol. 19, pp. 650-673.

Helper, S. R., (1991), How Much Has Really Changed between US Automakers and Their Suppliers, Sloan Management Review, Spring Volume, pp 77-82.

Hill, C. W. L., (1990), Cooperation, Opportunism, and the Invisible Hand: Implications for Transaction Cost Theory, Academy of Management Review, Vol. 15, pp. 500-513.

Jayaram, J., Vickery, S.K. and Droge, C., (1999), An Empirical Study of Time-based Competition in the North American Automotive Supplier Industry, International Journal of Operations and

Production Management, Vol.19, pp.1010-1033.

Kamath, R. R. and Liker, J.K., 91994), A Second Look at Japanese Product Development, Harvard Business Review, Vol. 72, pp.155-170.

Kaplan, R.S., (1988), One Cost Systems is no Enough, Harvard Business Review, Vol. 66, pp. 61-66.

Kekre, S., Murthi, B.P.S. and Srinivasan, K., (1995), Operating Decisions, Suppliers Availability and Quality: An Empirical Study, Journal of Operations Management, Vol. 12, pp. 387-396.

Khan, K. B., and Mentzer, J. T., (1996), Logistics and Inter-departmental Integration, International Journal of Physical Distribution and logistics Management, Vol. 26, pp.6-14.

La Londe, B.J., (1998), Supply Chain Evolution by the Numbers, Supply Chain Management Review, Vol. 2, pp. 7-8.

Lascelles, D. M. and Dale, B. G., (1989), The Buyer-Supplier Relationship in Total Quality Management, Journal of Purchasing and Material Management, Vol. 25, pp. 10-19.

Lau, H.S. and lau, A. H..L, (1994), Co-ordinating Two Suppliers with Offsetting Lead Time and Price Performance, Journal of Operations Management, Vol. 11, pp. 327-337.

Mabert, V. A., Muth, J.F. and Schmenner, R. W., 91992) Collapsing New Product Development Times: Six Case Studies, Journal of Product Innovation Management, Vol. 9 pp.200-212.

Miles, R. E. and Snow, C. C., (1986), Network Organizations: New Concepts for New Forms, California Management Review, Vol. 28. pp. 62-73.

Mohanty R.P., Deshmukh, S.G., (2004), Essential of Supply Chain Management" Jaico Publication, New Delhi.

Morash, E. A., Droge, C. and Vickery, S., 91997), Boundary Spanning Interfaces between Logistics, Production, Marketing and New Product Development, International Journal of Physical distribution and Logistics Management, Vol. 27, pp.50-369.

Newman, R. G., (1989), Single sourcing: short term savings versus long term problems, Journal of Purchasing and Material Management, Vol. 25, pp. 20-25.

Shapiro, F., Jeremy. (2002), Modeling the Supply Chain, Thomson Asia Private Limited, Singapore.

Shin, H., Collier, D. A. and Wilson, D. D., (2000), Supply Management Orientation and Supplier/Buyer Performance, Journal of Operations Management, Vol. 18, pp. 317-333.

Spekman, R. E., (1988), Strategic Supplier Selection: Understanding Long-term Buyer Relationships, Business horizons, Vol. 31, pp. 75-81.

Stock, G.N., Greis, N. P. and Kasarda, J. D., (2000), Enterprise Logistics and Supply Chain m Structure: The Role of Fit, Journal of Operations Management, Vol. 18, pp. 531-547.

Taylor, David., Brunt, David., (2001), Manufacturing Operations and Supply Chain Management: The Lean Approach, Thomson Asia Private limited, Singapore.

Thorelli, H, (1986), Networks between Markets and Hierarchies, Strategic Management Journal Vol. 7, pp.37-51.

Venkatraman, N. and Ramanujam, V., (1987), Measurement of Business Economic Performance: An Examination of Method Convergence, Journal of Management, Vol. 13, pp.4-12.

Waters, Donald. 92004), Logistics: An Introduction to Supply Chain Management, Palgrave Macmillan, New York.

Zaheer, A. and Venkataraman, N., (1995), Relational Governance as an Inter-organizational Strategy: An Empirical Test of the Role of Trust in Economic Exchange, Strategic Management Journal, Vol.16, pp. 373-392.

2

Supply Chain Management (SCM) and Enterprise Resource Planning (ERP)

R. Balajivignesh

Introduction

A supply chain is a network of facilities and distribution options that performs the functions of procurement of materials transformation of these materials in to intermediate and finished products and the distribution of these finished products to customers.

ERP (Enterprise resource planning) is as a software solution that addresses the enterprise needs taking the process view of the organization, to meet the organizational goals tightly integrating all functions of an enterprise.

Logistics automation is the application of computer software and/or automated machinery to improve the efficiency of logistics operations.

Vehicle Tracking Systems are electronic devices installed in vehicles to enable vehicle owners or third parties to track the location of a vehicle.

Supply Chain Management

Supply Chain Functions: A supply chain performs twp distinct types of functions (Fischer, 1997):

1. Market mediated functions – its purpose is to ensure that the variety of products reaching the market place matches what the consumers want to buy.
2. Physical function – it includes converting raw materials into parts, components, and finished goods and transporting all of them from one point in the supply chain to the next.

The above functions incur different costs. Market costs arise when supply exceeds demand and the product has to be marked down and sold at a loss or when supply falls short of demand resulting in lost sale opportunities and dissatisfied customers. Physical costs are the costs of production, transportation and inventory. The main aim of supply chain is to find out and monitor these components of cost.

Enterprise Resource Planning

ERP: It is an industry term for the broad set of activities supported by multi-module application software that helps a manufacturer or business, to manage all the parts of its business . ERP facilitates integration of company-wide information systems with the potential to go across companies.

Evolution of ERP: In the 1960's inventory control assumed prime importance and most of the software at that time were designed to help in inventory management. Typically, these were handled by tools called BOM processors (Bill of materials). The focus shifted in the 1970's to Material Requirement Planning (MRP) as the complexity of manufacturing operations increased. The tools to support these continued to evolve by adding further functionalities to meet the increased requirements. Then in the 1980's the concept of Manufacturing Resources Planning (MRP-II), which was nothing but extension of MRP to shop floor and Distribution management activities, grew in importance.

However, in the early 1990's, increased complexity of businesses and the need to integrate all the functions within an enterprise to sustain in the dynamic environment lead to development of ERP (Enterprise Resource Planning) tool. ERP was extension of MRP II to cover the range of activities within any enterprise. Additionally it addressed technology aspects like client/server-distributed architecture, RDBMS, object oriented programming.

Why ERP?

1. Helps in reduction of organization's operating costs can be reduced.
2. Integrates all parts of an organization

3. Increases the efficiency of operations as a result of this integration
4. Integration of information systems which enables seamless flow of information across
5. the organization.
6. Enables consolidation of different software in the organization
7. Helps in better customer service

How ERP Became Important for SCM: Traditionally ERP tools were not considered for SCM and resultantly, the information flow between various members of the supply chain was slow. This was because until the late 1990's the concentration of organizations was on improving the internal efficiency alone. Therefore, ERP systems also supported only such functionalities and the systems across the supply chain were disparate.

The organizations however, soon realized that although internal efficiency is important, its benefit would be limited unless complemented by increased efficiency across the supply chain. They also realized that, seamless flow of real-time information across the supply chain, was key to success in the emerging market scenario which was characterized by galloping advancements of technology, shorter Product life cycle etc. Therefore, organizations started integrating ERP applications with SCM software. This ensures that the efficiency was achieved across the supply chain and there is a seamless flow of information. ERP in such scenario becomes a vital link in the integrated supply chain as it serves as the integrated planning and control system.

In summary, ERP applications help in effective SCM in the following ways

1. Share data: They can create opportunities to share data across supply chain members, which can help managers in making better decisions. They also provide wider scope to mangers of supply chain by making available much broader information.
2. Real-time information: ERP systems can provide real-time information, which can be of great help in supply chain

decisions. For example, ordering raw materials can be based on the inventory details provided by the ERP systems.

Reinforcing ERP in SCM

Integrating ERP and SCM Systems: ERP systems offer tremendous benefits by integrating functions across the organization. They help in automating the business processes and enable reliable information capture and retrieval. SCM systems offer capabilities to integrate various entities making up the supply chain and facilitate seamless flow of information between all the supply chain partners. Given the intra-organizational and inter-organizational advantages offered by ERP and SCM respectively, integration of both the same can help in deriving substantial leverage and the potential of such integration is quite huge.

Integration of ERP and SCM is a very tough task as each member in the supply chain may have different hardware, software and it is very difficult to insist that your company's supply chain partners maintain same systems. It would however be ideal if all the parties involved could agree up front to abide by open standards. This would help easier integration. In the following lines we will try to study some of the approaches to integration.

ERP-ERP Linkage: As per this approach, ERP systems of the supply chain partners are interlinked to each other directly so as to enable seamless flow of real-time information. This might be possible when the ERP systems are sophisticated enough to include the necessary functionality to support SCM (inter-enterprise integration).

If all of them use the same system (i.e. same vendor's) then the integration of the same would be easy. However, if they are different, in such a case necessary middleware software would have to be developed which can enable connectivity and integration of the disparate systems so that there is consistent and seamless information flow.

ERP-SCM System Linkage: As per this approach, the

integration of supply chain is through the linking of ERP and SCM systems. This may be resorted so as to capitalize on the strengths of the two systems (ERP and SCM). For this purpose, sophisticated middleware interface software, which enable sharing of data and processes are used. These software help in linking the ERP and SCM systems at the points where they have overlapping features. For example, I2 technologies use SAP's ALE (Application Link Enabling) to exchange data between SAP R/3 and its SCM product 'Rhythm.' There are also some specialized software called Specialized Integration Software, which allow ERP and other systems to share processes and data. This software allows integration by simply choosing the sending application (e.g. SAP, Baan) and a receiving application (Like Rhythm, Manugistics) and the process to be linked.

Extending ERP

Logistics Automation: Logistics automation systems can powerfully complement the facilities provided by these higher level computer systems. The focus on an individual node within a wider logistics network allows systems to be highly tailored to the requirements of that node.

Components of Logistics Automation

Fixed Machinery

- Automated cranes (also called automated storage and retrieval systems): provide the ability to input and store a container of goods for later retrieval. Typically cranes serve a rack of locations, allowing many levels of stock to be stacked vertically, and allowing far high storage densities and better space utilisation than alternatives.
- Conveyors: automated conveyors allow the input of containers in one area of the warehouse, and either through hard coded rules or data input allow destination selection. The container will later appear at the selected destination.
- Sortation systems: similar to conveyors but typically have higher capacity and can divert containers more quickly. Typically used to distribute high volumes of small cartons to a

large set of locations.

- Typically all of these will automatically identify and track containers based upon barcodes, or increasingly, RFID tags

Mobile Technology

- Radio data terminals: These are hand held or truck mounted terminals which connect wirelessly to logistics automation software and provide instructions to operators moving throughout the warehouse. Many also have in-built barcode scanners to allow identification of containers.

Software

- scheduling order fulfilment, assignment of stock to outgoing trailers. Integration software: This provides overall control of the automation machinery and for instance allows cranes to be connected up to conveyors for seamless stock movements.
- Operational control software: provides low-level decision making, such as where to store incoming containers, and where to retrieve them when requested.
- Business Control software: provides higher level functionality, such as identification of incoming deliveries / stock and

Benefits of Logistics Automation: A typical warehouse or distribution center will receive stock of a variety of products from suppliers and store these until the receipt of orders from customers, whether individual buyers (e.g. mail order), retail branches (e.g. chain stores), or other companies (e.g. wholesalers). A logistics automation system may provide the following:

- Automated goods in processes: Incoming goods can be marked with barcodes and the automation system notified of the expected stock. On arrival, the goods can be scanned and thereby identified, and taken via conveyors, sortation systems, and automated cranes into an automatically assigned storage location.
- Automated goods retrieval for orders: On receipt of orders, the automation system is able to immediately locate goods and retrieve them to a pickface location.

- Automated despatch processing: Combining knowledge of all orders placed at the warehouse the automation system can assign picked goods into despatch units and then into outbound loads. Sortation systems and conveyors can then move these onto the outgoing trailers.

A complete warehouse automation system can drastically reduce the workforce required to run a facility, with human input required only for a few tasks, such as picking units of product from a bulk packed case. Even here, assistance can be provided with equipment such as pick-to-light units. Smaller systems may only be required to handle part of the process. Examples include automated storage and retrieval systems, which simply use cranes to store and retrieve identified cases or pallets, typically into a highbay storage system which would be unfeasible to access using fork-lift trucks or any other means.

5.4 Vehicle Tracking Systems: Vehicle Tracking Systems are commonly used by fleet operators for fleet management functions such as routing, dispatch, on-board information and security. Other applications include monitoring driving behavior, such as an employer of an employee, or a parent with a teen driver.

When managing a fleet of vehicles, knowing the real-time location of all drivers allows management to meet customer needs more efficiently. Whether it is delivery, service or other multi-vehicle enterprises, drivers now only need a mobile phone with telephony or Internet connection to be inexpensively tracked by and dispatched efficiently. Asset Tracking Companies needing to track valuable assets for insurance or other monitoring purposes can now plot the real-time asset location on a map and closely monitor movement and operating status.

References

Managing ERP Implementation, (1998), The Economic Times, 22 January, pp.9

Raj Kumar Prasad and Sandip Sahay, Supply Chain Management, 2003, Effective Executive, pp. 19-24

Rupesh Goel, 2005, Materials Management Review, Volume:1, Issue:5, pp. 21-22

Sahay B.S (2000) Supply Chain Management for 21st Century, New Delhi, Macmillan

Sahay B.S (2004) Supply Chain Management for Global Competitiveness, New Delhi, Macmillan

Sarika Kulkarni, Ashok Sharma, Supply Chain Management, 2005, Tata McGraw Hill, New Delhi.

3

E-Healthcare: Transforming Hospital Supply Chain

G.V.R.K. Acharyulu

Introduction

Health care emerged as one of the major activities concerning the human beings in the recent past (Changing life styles, awareness, habits) irrespective of age, income, region, religion, caste, culture and so on. The need for effective health services is the order of the day. As a result, hospitals are absorbing tremendous amount of resources. Globalization has opened up new opportunities and there is a cut-throat competition among hospitals in offering services to patients of different ailments at reduced rates. The needs, priorities and expectations of the patients from time to time have to be captured and the hospital services are to be redesigned accordingly to enhance the hospital supply chain efficiency of its operations. Adoption of appropriate technology, utilization of highly skilled and specialized professionals add to the competitive advantage.

The Internet has the potential to transform healthcare. Web-based technology is going to become a conventional medium for consumers to connect with healthcare organisations and with other members. However, if for no other reason, it is in the healthcare industry's best interest to understand and embrace technology to ensure that the coming changes lower costs improve quality and increase access for patients.

Healthcare providers, consumers and retailers are utilizing the Internet as a way to enhance communication and knowledge between and within the many areas of healthcare. Numerous practical Internet applications – for example , patient education and support, promotion of one's practice and improving patient outcomes and satisfaction-are emerging as a way of improving care, reducing costs and meeting consumer demands.

Consumers use the web to search for the latest medical research and evaluated treatment data and to interact directly with healthcare providers online. The accessibility and availability to log on at any hour of the day or night and from almost any location is one of the most important aspects of online health assistance. Currently, there are an estimated 15,000 Interne sites that are devoted to medicine or health

E-Commerce and Supply Chain Management

Electronic Commerce and Supply Chain Management focuses on systems and processes to support the flow of information within and between organizations which occurs in the context of procurement, manufacturing, sales, and distribution of goods, information and services.

Electronic commerce has rapidly become one of the primary tools of conducting business throughout the world. One of the advantages offered by E-Commerce is the ability to increase the business transactions, and reduction of operating costs. Supply Chain Management refers to order taking, and order fulfillment, distribution of products, services, or information. With the influence of the Internet the focus of Supply Chain Management is provided all of the consumer good or products in order to improve the customer satisfaction

Role of E-Commerce in Health Care

Today's managers are faced with major challenges such as staff shortages, rising health-care costs, and current market pressures for new and advanced technologies and delivery methods. These challenges, among others, have a significant impact on the quality, efficiency, and cost of providing health care and laboratory services. Given the current health-care and laboratory environments, managers must seek innovative ways to improve quality patient care, while at the same time reduce the cost of services provided. To this end, e-commerce could have a significant impact on the cost, efficiency, and quality of the overall management and delivery of health-care services. Efficiency gains within the healthcare arena have been attributed to the application of information technology and, most specifically, the Internet. E-commerce, as a relatively new technology, if deployed properly, could enhance the management of laboratory and patient-centered databases. Moreover, the sensitive issue of patient information will be escalated with the advancement of e-commerce. It is to be noted that the impact of e-commerce, also referred to as e-health, in creating improvements in the delivery of health services across the spectrum of care for health providers, laboratory managers, consumers, and funding organizations.

Health care lends itself to the application of e-commerce strategies because of its size, the current inefficiencies of a paper-based system, and the critical need for up-to-date information. Consumers demand improved access to quality health-care information and services, while physicians want to track their patients over multiple care sites and have access to information about the latest diagnostic and treatment options. The industry as a whole, faced with increasing demand and rising costs, must improve its efficiency.

E-health promises to create improvements in the delivery of health services for health-care providers, consumers, and funding organizations and agencies. E-health is changing the way providers search for and retrieve medical information, communicate with their patients, and manage acute and chronic conditions. Web-based disease management programs are an important part of the e-health revolution, and are designed to alter the delivery of care through the use of technology to monitor patients daily to determine their health status, remind them to take their medications, and handle problems before they become more serious. These programs collect data without patients having to come to the office or go to the hospital, allow patients to communicate with their physician and s h a re information with others with the same condition, and have the potential to improve quality as well as control costs.

E-Healthcare

E-healthcare connects medicine, business and information technology in an innovative manner by greatly facilitating information exchange and therefore supporting healthcare transactions. Information passing is at the core of e-healthcare functionality: providing all healthcare-related information anytime, anyplace, to anyone necessary in a timely and usage-oriented manner. By sharing information, e-healthcare has the ability to integrate existing and support new kinds of healthcare services.

In analogy to supply chain theory, information integration applies to two dimensions:

- **Horizontal Integration**: Information exchange within the same level of care (e. g. connecting information from previous to current general physicians related to one patient)
- **Vertical Integration**: Information exchange between different levels of care (e. g. connecting information from preventive, stationary and post-incident care related to one patient)

Both kinds of information integration could ensure information passing across individual treatment paths, and across geography. This goal requires the collaboration of medicinal practice, business, legal, and information technology.

E-Healthcare is integration of functional, institutional and processual views on both individual and collective healthcare under particular consideration of information and communication technology. In other words, e-healthcare considers the electronic support of healthcare functions (what services are provided?), participating institutions (by whom are these services provided?) and underlying processes that connect institutions and functions (how are these services provided). Functional elements also include service billing and payment, and therefore commerce. This definition deliberately takes a very broad view on e-healthcare. Key to the success of future solutions will lie in multidisciplinary approaches, taking into account a multitude of aspects.

Patients are the heart of healthcare, which is why most hospitals continue to seek ways to increase revenue by growing market share. In an age of consumerism, patients are choosing-shopping even-for physicians and hospitals in unprecedented ways. They place high premiums on accessibility, security, flexibility, quality and, above all else...personalization. Accordingly, in order for any hospital or clinic to remain competitive and survive, a patient-centric model of care will need to prevail.

In order for hospitals to successfully migrate through tumultuous change and into a new paradigm, they will need to strategically plan and implement technology solutions in phases. The diagram on the following page depicts these phases and the milestones that can help chart the evolution to fully integrated and profitable patient care.

Infrastructure

A robust, scalable and tightly integrated IT infrastructure lays the groundwork for the deployment and operation of all current and pending technologies. Planning ahead and building now will give hospitals the ability to integrate new processes, solutions and business models—efficiently and cost-effectively.

Business Transformation: Given that technology by itself lacks business focus, business transformation is an essential component of any IT roadmap- applying strategy and change-management methodologies to help harness the full benefits of health-care technology solutions. As a result, hospital and clinic constituents will learn how to conduct day-to-day operations in a different, more empowered way. User-friendly technology solutions and interfaces will be optimized and operations streamlined and integrated as part of a large hospital network that spans each aspect of a vast health-care system.

Standardization: Planning and deploying new technologies in synch with evolving, widely adopted standards is the key. IT standards (especially relating to wireless) as well as publicly enforced mandates, will come to a head - designating the ideal time to adopt change and technology on a mass and enterprise wide scale.

Integration: The convergence of infrastructure, transformation and standardization is enabling the integration of processes, business models, data, devices and technologies across an ever-expanding network of healthcare.

Virtualization: Advances in technology and medicine are poised to fulfill their promise. Much of healthcare is virtual, meaning patients can receive and manage much of their health-care from the comforts of home, without ever physically being in the same room with their physician. Care delivery will be optimized and remote at the same time,

Converging Technology and Imagination: Imagine remote diagnosis-from the safety of one s own home, in the back of an ambulance, or at the scene of an accident. Imagine virtual consultations and teaming among all members of a patient's healthcare team-doctors, nurses, therapists and caregivers. Imagine performing remote surgery in the U.S. or across the globe enabled by telemedicine and robotics. Imagine a diabetic patient monitoring her blood sugar level by simply impressing her finger on a PDA .Imagine "data globes" that one day will allow doctors to manually examine their patients from a far. The possibilities are endless and spectacular.

Trends in E-Healthcare

The rise of the Internet has introduced powerful new electronic tools that may enable health organizations to create a new business model. Currently, there are several areas in which the Internet may prove to be of use in healthcare.

Online Health Advice: One can obtain medical information online and learn more about how to deal with one's medical problems as well as buy products through the Internet to help alleviate discomfort. Consumers use the Web to obtain healthcare information when they are trying to diagnose symptoms or cope with a major, chronic illness.

Internet Pharmacy: Consumers can save money on their medications by ordering them online. Healthcare organizations can prepare prescription and non-prescription medications that are tailored precisely to a patient's specific needs. Consumers no longer have to stand in long queues or wait for their prescriptions to be filled.

Electronic Medical Records (EMR): The Internet allows physicians to check patient information from their home or office, view laboratory reports and X-rays online, and access other physicians' libraries and medical education programmes. The rapid evaluation method is a useful tool to collect relevant information and to present it quickly to decision-makers in a form that is understood easily.

Telemedicine: The Internet provides the medium for telemedicine applications - such as video consulting and teleradiology - that have matured to become essential healthcare services. Others - such as telepathology - remain the subjects of intensive research efforts. Telemedicine uses telecommunications to deliver health care, often over great distances, with the possibility of cost savings particularly in remote and rural areas. It is a multi-disciplinary undertaking requiring expertise from telecommunications, health care and information technology sectors.

Online Registration and Scheduling: Online registration and scheduling can minimize time spent on the telephone or waiting in long queues at the reception desk. Pre-admission information and virtual tours can reduce patient anxiety and help both the patient and family to prepare for hospitalization. In addition, the increased monitoring of patients via Internet-enabled sensors and home diagnostics can improve the individual's experience after discharge and increase his or her compliance with treatment recommendations. In addition, e-mail via the Internet will provide individuals with the value of interpersonal communication with their physician.

Electronic Patient Record (EPR): One of the most

important trends is the mover toward a universal electronic patient record. It could be defined as electronically stored health information about any individual uniquely identified by an identifier. This entails capturing, storing, retrieving, transmitting and manipulating patient-specific health care-related data, including clinical, administrative and biographical data.

Radio Frequency Identification (RFID): Radio-frequency-based applications in healthcare are opening up new avenues. It is the next wave in the evolution of computing. As health care in India is a sunshine industry and growing annually at a rate of about 13%(ET Intelligence report 2001), RFID will continue to make inroads via track-and-trace solutions, first as asset and inventory management tools, then gravitating toward personnel, patient, and clinical monitoring devices. High-end asset tracking, location tracking, and anti-counterfeiting are the futuristic areas for active RFID. As volume of consumption drives down unit costs, workflow and business process efficiency will become key drivers of RFID implementation. Electronic inventory tracking of medicines and supplies, online scheduling of operating rooms and staff, and using RFID to enhance bed management can further drive down the costs of healthcare by increasing efficiencies

Smart Cards: Smart cards can provide basic medical information, such as lists of drug sensitivities; current conditions being treated, the name and phone number of a patient's doctor and other information vital in an emergency. Smart cards can also carry vital medical history and details about insurance coverage. For example, complex services such as remote diagnostics and health-related decision-making can be integrated efficiently with a Smart Card's patient record to provide added treatment alternatives to improve the overall quality of health services.

Telesurgery: Another important trend is the move toward Telesurgery. A provision of surgical care over a distance, with direct, real-time visualization of the operative field through Telepresence Surgery to transmit the surgeons actions at a surgical workstation to the operative site at the remote surgical unit, with haptic (force feedback) input to transmit to the surgeon the tactile environment of the operative field. Telerobotics using a robotic arm, and telementoring where an experienced surgeon acts as a preceptor for a remote inexperienced surgeon by observing the surgeon via interactive video.

E-procurement: This is procurement of materials and items related to healthcare through online from the suppliers. The process follows :User logs on to market place via browser, authorized products in on-line catalog, order entered via browser to exchange, system generates electronic PO & sends to supplier, supplier sends electronic order acknowledgement and delivery conformation, receiving reports delivery via browser to exchange,

Access to Information: When a patient's up-to-date medical record is available at the point of care, physicians and clinicians are able to make more educated decisions, resulting in improved outcomes and fewer errors. Not only that, but productivity improves when caregivers are able to update and access records electronically, versus searching for patient charts. At every point of care, information is recorded via networked personal digital assistants (PDAs) and electronic patient charts using perfected speech recognition technology. During his short stay, the patient is monitored remotely via video, and has continuous access to his care team, thanks to the robot orchestrating these details.

Real-time Medical Information: The future of hospitals and clinics depends largely on empowering all aspects of healthcare-creating an environment in which physicians and nurses can access patient information in real-time, from any device and location., where referrals, authorizations and insurance claims are transmitted and processed electronically, prescriptions are written and renewed online, new therapies come to market in months not years and consumers control their electronic medical records and grant viewing permission to those who need it. Technologies are operating primarily as a form of mobile video telephones, allowing real-time, one-on-one communication among patients, doctors, healthcare managers, nursing staff and patient families. Using these devices cuts travel costs, empowers doctors and nurses, and improves staff training, which in turn reduces liability risk and employee turnover.

Wireless Technology: Wireless technologies will be responsible for enabling PDAs and the electronic, point-of-care entry of all medical information by any member of a patient's care team. It will also power mobile video devices that allow remote care and 24x7 data and care access. Wireless systems, including laptops linked to PCs, will track patients' vital signs, admission information and patient histories. Wireless solutions are designed to connect a highly mobile hospital workforce with large amounts of disparate data across multiple locations and constituents and provide remote access to networked, real-time information. This means hospitals can bring data to the point of care-enabling physicians to examine the latest lab reports, access electronic medical records and enter prescriptions electronically on a handheld device.

E-medicine: Web-based Preventive Disease Management

The use of data warehouses will automatically trigger alerts and reminders for patients to perform and record care sequences, such as weighing themselves or monitoring their blood glucose levels. A collection of home care monitoring devices will record, store and update personal health records (PHRs) and notify providers electronically. This growing trend should ease congested physician schedules, while at the same time alleviating the incidence of many of today's illnesses. Hospitals, physicians and pharmaceutical companies will also join forces to deliver "e-medicine" programs and bolster consumer loyalty.

Digital Imaging Systems: Within the field of radiology, innovations in digital imaging have led to the development of the Picture Archival and Communication System (PACS). Current PACS products allow completely digital acquisition, transfer, interpretation, storage and transmission of medical images. Solutions centered on PACS continue to surface, with greater storage capabilities, archiving power, speed and flexibility — a trend that will continue. As hospitals migrate to a new paradigm, many may look to leverage robust, in-house digital imaging capabilities as a means to differentiate them and generate a new, reliable revenue stream.

Software Solutions: Software capabilities will continue to enhance the delivery of data from hospital information systems and other channels, such as PACS, directly to the desktop or any mobile computing device. Clinicians will access lab results, patient data, statistics, analysis, voice recordings and medical images from virtually anywhere, via a Web browser and a security-enhanced connection to their organization

Robust software solutions are designed to enable health-care organizations to improve data integrity and billing accuracy, reduce clinical errors and eliminate many of the manual processes that keep physicians from spending more time with patients. Of course, HIPAA compliance will be maintained by preventing unauthorized access to patient information, displaying only data that is relevant to a specific query-in real-time, not replicated.

Web Applications: Web-based applications provide rapid access to real-time medical information, regardless of platform and programming language boundaries. From a doctor's schedule to the cataloging of medical images to tracking participants in new drug trials, these solutions help enable highly personal, intelligent computing experiences. Using Web services, patients can initiate much of their own care, while at the same time providing healthcare providers with continuous, real-time access to their medical information.

Grid Computing: Distributed networks offer computing power as a utility. These new technologies, such as high-performance Linux "grid" computing, enable the sharing of expensive, ultra high-speed and high-capacity resources and can be woven into the fiber of hospital networks. Grid computing can also provide a lower-cost solution to growing bandwidth and storage requirements inherent in burgeoning medical imaging systems.

Conclusion

In the near future, traditional ways of providing healthcare services may become obsolete. Virtual hospitals may be one way of utilizing high-tech Internet applications, for example, telemedicine, electronic medical records (EMR) and video-conferencing, to utilise time effectively and, at the same time, be cost-effective. Those embracing this technology will ensure that they will be on-board the new wave of coming changes in the healthcare field. As healthcare costs continue to rise nationally and globally in light of demographic trends and health status indicators, providers, suppliers, and payers will continue to look for innovative ways to become more efficient while maintaining and improving quality of care . Use of the Internet in innovative ways will continue to develop. E-health, like e-commerce, is transforming healthcare supply chain. Standards have to be adopted to protect the privacy and confidentiality of patient-specific medical information. Private organizations have created net- works and standards to monitor the accuracy of medical information exchanged on the Web. As e-risks are minimized, the growth and reach of e-health will continue. The development and implementation of a forward-looking web enabled healthcare solutions can guide hospitals and clinics as they reinvent themselves into next-generation patient care networks and position themselves for a profitable and healthy future.

4

Information Technology in Supply Chain Management

V.B. Narsimha

The new millennium is in the midst of explosive change witnessing intense competition amongst the domestic as well as the international players. Little wonder then, *e-Enabled Supply Chain Management* is fast emerging as a core strategy that organizations worldwide are adopting for sustainable business advantage. In this era of Information a firm's supply chain should operate at speed of thought and this is possible only by enhanced *e-speed* communications and information sharing with their critical partners. Internet and associated technologies promise to revolutionize inter-enterprise business processes by enabling seamless information exchange between business partners. High volumes of data can be transferred at low cost, and even minor business partners can exchange information in an economical manner.

Supply chain management consists of the coordination of demand and supply of products and services between a suppliers' supplier and a customers' customer. It involves the flow of product, information, and money between the 'trading partners' of a company's 'supply chain'.

Importance of IT in Supply Chain Management

The Internet wave and emergence of e-business has highly influenced traditional supply chains by enhancing Coordination and Communication between the partners. The enabling technologies like EDI, Intranet, Extranet, Electronic Market Places, ERP, DRP, Warehouse management system, CRM , CPFR etc has tremendously improved the integration among the buyers and sellers. The wonder letter 'e' has removed the roadblocks of information sharing making the firm smarter everyday. Rapid evolution of the digital marketplaces or hubs which allows buyers and sellers to transact in a single intelligent, multidimensional marketplace that connects multiple trading exchanges and making the sharing of information at a wink of an eyelid.

E-business has enhanced both Supply Chain efficiency and responsiveness by sharing real time information regarding inventory, shipment status and other key information like product design, product availability and demand between the partners. The e-Supply Chain will have customers and suppliers seamlessly linked together, throughout the world, exchanging information almost instantly. As a result of e-speed information sharing the companies are adopting pull strategy instead of push strategy. Fast access to relevant supply chain information can pay-off handsomely in lower product acquisition costs, lower procurement transaction, less inventory, higher quality decision-making, shorter cycle times, profitable means of disposing unused excess inventory and better customer service.

Today's managers must make decisions in "real time," an organization is exposed to higher risk and may suffer penalties, such as losing a valuable customer or mission-critical supplier, if decisions are wrong. Therefore, it is imperative that they have all the information they need—quickly and accurately. Information and communications technologies are revolutionizing the scope and scale of e-supply chain infrastructures. Online data exchange is transforming business practices, allowing managers to capture and track complex data more effectively. Orders and various products related to that order can easily be traced. It is also possible to exchange information among entities within the value chain, thus greatly improving customer-provider relationships.

Effective supply chain management can impact and improve upon virtually all business processes, such as data accuracy, operational complexity reduction, supplier selection, purchasing, and warehousing and distribution. Other benefits include as under.

- Quicker customer response and fulfillment rates.

- Greater productivity and lower costs.
- Reduced inventory throughout the chain.
- Improved forecasting precision.
- Fewer suppliers and shorter planning cycles.
- Improved quality and products that are more technologically advanced.
- Enhanced inter-operational communications and cooperation.
- Shortened repair times and enhanced equipment readiness.
- More reliable financial information.

It is important that systems be designed to enhance open and rapid communication and sharing of information across the supply chain and within the organization. Intelligent application of information technology can also eliminate duplicative data entry, provide real-time status information, and help organizations move past a myopic view of their processes to view themselves within the context of larger missions and goals.

Supply Chain Management Software

Supply chain management software is possibly the most fractured group of software applications on the planet. Each of the five major supply chain steps previously outlined composes dozens of specific tasks, many of which have their own specific software. Some vendors have assembled many of these different chunks of software together under a single roof, but no one has a complete package that is right for every company. For example, most companies need to track demand, supply, manufacturing status, logistics (i.e. where things are in the supply chain), and distribution. They also need to share data with supply chain partners at an ever increasing rate. While products from large ERP vendors like SAP's Advanced Planner and Optimizer (APO) can perform many or all of these tasks, because each industry's supply chain has a unique set of challenges, many companies decide to go with targeted best of breed products instead, even if some integration is an inevitable consequence.

It is worth mentioning that the old adage about systems only being as good as the information that they contain applies doubly to SCM. If the information entered into a demand forecasting application is not accurate then you will get an inaccurate forecast. Similarly, if employees bypass the supply chain systems and try to manage things manually, then even the most expensive systems will provide an incomplete picture of what is happening in a company's supply chain.

Relationship between ERP and SCM

Many SCM applications are reliant upon the kind of information that is stored in the most quantity inside ERP software. Theoretically you could assemble the information you need to feed the SCM applications from legacy systems (for most companies this means Excel spreadsheets spread out all over the place), but it can be nightmarish to try to get that information flowing on a fast, reliable basis from all the areas of the company. ERP is the battering ram that integrates all that information together in a single application, and SCM applications benefit from having a single major source to go to for up-to-date information. Most CIOs who have tried to install SCM applications say they are glad they did ERP first. They call the ERP projects "putting your information house in order." Of course, ERP is expensive and difficult, so you may want to explore ways to feed your SCM applications the information they need without doing ERP first. These days, most ERP vendors have SCM modules so doing an ERP project may be a way to kill two birds with one stone. Companies will need to decide if these products meet their needs or if they need a more specialized system.

Applications that simply automate the logistics aspects of SCM are less dependent upon gathering information from around the company, so they tend to be independent of the ERP decision. But chances are, you'll need to have these applications communicate with ERP in some fashion. It's important to pay attention to the software's ability to integrate with the Internet and with ERP applications because the Internet will drive demand for integrated information. For example, if you want to build a private website for communicating with your customers and suppliers, you will want to pull information from ERP and supply chain applications together to present updated information about orders, payments, manufacturing status and delivery.

Installing Supply Chain Management Software

Before the Internet came along, the aspirations of supply chain software devotees were limited to improving their ability to predict demand from customers and make their own supply chains run more smoothly. But the cheap, ubiquitous nature of the Internet, along with its simple, universally accepted communication standards have thrown things wide open. Now, you can connect your supply chain with the supply chains of your suppliers and customers together in a single vast network that optimizes costs and opportunities for everyone involved. This was the reason for the B2B explosion; the idea that everyone you do business with could be connected together into one big happy, cooperative family.

Of course, reality isn't quite that happy and cooperative, but today most companies share at least some data with their supply chain partners. The goal of these projects is greater supply chain visibility. The supply chain in most industries is like a big card game. The players don't want to show their cards because they don't trust anyone else with the information. But if they showed their hands they could all benefit. Suppliers wouldn't have to guess how many raw materials to order, and manufacturers wouldn't have to order more than they need from suppliers to make sure they have enough on hand if demand for their products unexpectedly goes up. And retailers would have fewer empty shelves if they shared the information they had about sales of a manufacturer's product in all their stores with the manufacturer. The Internet makes showing your hand to others possible, but centuries of distrust and lack of coordination within industries make it difficult.

Over the last few years most companies have gotten over the trust issue. In many cases "gotten over" is a euphemism for "have been bullied into sharing supply chain information from a dominant industry player." Want to sell your goods in Wal-Mart? Better be prepared to share data.

The payoff of timely and accurate supply chain information is the ability to make or ship only as much of a product as there is a market for. This is the practice known as just-in-time manufacturing, and it allows companies to reduce the amount of inventory that they keep. This can cut costs substantially, since you no longer need to pay to produce and store excess goods.

Supply Chain Collaboration

Let's look at consumer packaged goods for an example of collaboration. If there are two companies that have made supply chain a household word, they are Wal-Mart and Procter & Gamble. Before these two companies started collaborating back in the '80s, retailers shared very little information with manufacturers. But then the two giants built a software system that hooked P&G up to Wal-Mart's distribution centers. When P&G's products run low at the distribution centers, the system sends an automatic alert to P&G to ship more products. In some cases, the system goes all the way to the individual Wal-Mart store. It lets P&G monitor the shelves through real-time satellite link-ups that send messages to the factory whenever a P&G item swoops past a scanner at the register.

With this kind of minute-to-minute information, P&G knows when to make, ship and display more products at the Wal-Mart stores. No need to keep products piled up in warehouses awaiting Wal-Mart's call. Invoicing and payments happen automatically too. The system saves P&G so much in time, reduced inventory and lower order-processing costs that it can afford to give Wal-Mart "low, everyday prices" without putting itself out of business.

Roadblocks to Installing Supply Chain Software

Supply chain automation is uniquely difficult because its complexity extends beyond your company's walls. Your people will need to change the way they work and so will the people from each supplier that you add to your network. Only the largest and most powerful manufacturers can force such radical changes down suppliers' throats. Most companies have to sell outsiders on the system. Moreover, your goals in installing the system may be threatening to those suppliers, to say the least. For example, Wal-Mart's collaboration with P&G meant that P&G would assume more responsibility for inventory management, something retailers have traditionally done on their own. Wal-Mart had the clout to demand this from P&G, but it also gave P&G something in return-better information about Wal-Mart's product demand, which helped P&G manufacture its products more efficiently. To get your supply chain partners to agree to collaborate with you, you have to be willing to compromise and help them achieve their own goals.

If selling supply chain systems is difficult on the outside, it isn't much easier inside. Operations people are accustomed to dealing with phone calls, faxes and hunches scrawled on paper, and will most likely want to keep it that way. If you can't convince people that using the software will be worth their time, they will easily find ways to work around it. You cannot disconnect the telephones and fax machines just because you have supply chain software in place.

There is a diabolical twist to the quest for supply chain software acceptance among your employees. New supply chain systems process data as they are programmed to do, but the technology cannot absorb a company's history and processes in the first few months after an implementation. Forecasters and planners need to understand that the first bits of information they get from a system might need some tweaking. If they are not warned about the system's initial naiveté, they will think it is useless. In one case, just before a large automotive industry supplier installed a new supply chain forecasting application to predict demand for a product, an automaker put in an order for an unusually large number of units. The system responded by predicting huge demand for the product based largely on one unusual order. Blindly following the system's numbers could have led to inaccurate orders for materials being sent to suppliers within the chain. The company caught the problem but only after a demand forecaster threw out the system's numbers and used his own. That created another problem: Forecasters stopped trusting the system and worked strictly with their own data. The supplier had to fine-tune the system itself, and then work on reestablishing employees' confidence. Once employees understood that they would be merging their expertise with the system's increasing accuracy, they began to accept and use the new technology.

Extended Supply Chain

The extended supply chain is a clever way of describing everyone who contributes to a product. So if you make text books, then your extended supply chain would include the factories where the books are printed and bound, but also the company that sells you the paper, the mill where that supplier buys their stock, and so on. It is important to keep track of what is happening in your extended supply chain because with a supplier or a supplier's supplier could end up having an impact on you (as the old saying goes, a chain is only a strong as its weakest link). For example, a fire in a paper mill might cause the text book manufacturer's paper supplier to run out of inventory. If the text book company knows what is happening in its extended supply chain it can find another paper vendor.

Impact of Globalisation on Supply Chain Management

Just in time manufacturing isn't the only way companies have used their supply chains to reduce cost. Manufacturing in developing countries is substantially cheaper than in the U.S. because of the low cost of labor. It isn't as easy to set up real-time data sharing with a factory in, say, China as it is with a factory you own in the United States. And the sheer distance that overseas goods need to travel – not to mention the number of vessels they need to travel on – in order to reach the U.S. increases the chance that they will get delayed. The bottom line is that foreign manufacturing brings back a lot of the uncertainty that supply chain systems were designed to eliminate. The good news is that technology capable of tracking shipments throughout the world is getting better. The bad news is that a lot of this technology is still pretty expensive, that some of the places you would want to deploy it don't have the necessary infrastructure in place, and well, there isn't a piece of technology out there that can make up for the whim of a Chinese Customs official. Furthermore, labor costs in some places are so low that IT automation and monitoring projects may add more to costs—in terms of software, hardware and still-precious (and unreliable) bandwidth—than they save in productivity. Hence, some low-tech or commodity products may not be worth monitoring at all until they hit a ship in a foreign port.

In the meantime, the best bet is to use whatever systems you can to gain as much visibility into the global supply chain as possible. It may be impossible to replicate the just in time model on a global scale, but by applying whatever technology you can, and by choosing the supply chain partners who have the capability to share data with you, you can get many of the benefits of just in time while paying low foreign prices.

Emerging Technologies and Supply Chain Management

The most notable is Radio Frequency Identification, or RFID. RFID tags are essentially barcodes on steroids. Whereas barcodes only identify the product, RFID tags can tell what the product is, where it has been, when it expires, whatever information someone wishes to program it with. RFID technology is going to generate mountains of data about the location of pallets, cases, cartons, totes and individual products in the supply chain. It's going to produce oceans of information about when and where merchandise is manufactured, picked, packed and shipped. It's going to create rivers of numbers telling retailers about the expiration dates of their perishable items—numbers that will have to be stored, transmitted in real-time and shared with warehouse management, inventory management, financial and other enterprise systems. In other words, it is going to have a really big impact.

Another benefit of RFIDs is that, unlike barcodes, RFID tags can be read automatically by electronic readers. Imagine a truck carrying a container full of widgets entering a shipping terminal in China. If the container is equipped with an RFID tag, and the terminal has an RFID sensor network, that container's whereabouts can be automatically sent to Widget Co. without the truck ever slowing down. It has the potential to add a substantial amount of visibility into the extended supply chain.

Supply chain management (SCM) is the process of planning, implementing, and controlling the operations of the supply chain with the purpose to satisfy customer requirements as efficiently as possible. Supply chain management spans all movement and storage of raw materials, work-in-process inventory, and finished goods from point-of-origin to point-of-consumption.

Today's competitive environment is forcing the firms' shift its focus inevitably outside the corporate walls and collaborate with its trading partners. Increased communications technology has redefined how businesses work together, raising customer expectations and placing new demands on supply chain performance. The Internet has allowed companies to come up with highly innovative solutions that accelerated the widespread adoption of these core supply chain principles. Companies that make use of e-business to redefine supply chain integration will achieve significant increases in efficiency and gain tremendous competitive edge over their competitors. In the next few years, we will see an explosion of e-enabled supply chain management as visionary companies develop new paradigms of e-business for the future. Hence, the battleground of the next decade is clearly going to be e-enabled supply chain versus e-enabled supply chain instead of battle between firms versus firm.

References

Ala-Risku, T., Kärkkäinen, M. and Holmström, J. (2003), "Evaluating the applicability of merge-in-transit: A step by step process for supply chain managers", International Journal of Logistics Management, Vol. 14, No. 2, pp. 67-81.

Aurамo, J., Kauremaa, J. and Tanskanen, K. (2005), "Benefits of IT in supply chain management – an explorative study of progressive companies", International Journal of Physical Distribution & Logistics Management, Vol. 35, No. 2, pp. 82-100.

Bagchi, P.K. and Skjoett-Larsen, T. (2002), "Integration of information technology and organizations in a supply chain", The International Journal of Logistics Management, Vol. 14, No. 1, pp. 89-108. 12

Closs, D. and Savitskie, K. (2003), "Internal and external logistics information technology integration", International Journal of Logistics Management, Vol. 14, No. 1, pp. 63-76.

Haag, S., Cummings, M., McCubbrey, D., Pinsonneault, A., & Donovan, R. (2006), Management Information Systems For the Information Age (3rd Canadian Ed.), Canada: McGraw Hill Ryerson

Handfield and Bechtel, 2001; Prater et al., 2001; Kern and Willcocks, 2000; Bowersox and Closs, 1996; Christopher, 1992; Bowersox, 1989

Kaushik K.D., & Cooper, M. (2000). Industrial Marketing Management. Volume29, Issue 1 , January 2000, Pages 65-83

Rolf G. Poluha, Application of the SCOR Model in Supply Chain Management. Youngstown, NY 2006,

5

Developing Supply Chain Competencies

Kishore Kumar Morya

Supply Chain: Battleground Redefined

Supply chains are tough to manage, even the greatest of the companies could not grasp the impact of the supply chain glitches. The effect is so disastrous that recovery cost them billion of dollars. Companies that did not take the corrective measure eventually went into oblivion. In May of 2001, Cisco Systems[1] had to write off the inventory of $2.2 billion, the largest inventory write-down in the history of business. Cisco could not read the demand pattern accurately. That year's booming Internet market propelled the demand of Cisco's product to high trajectory. Cisco was not having its own manufacturing facility and passed on the anticipated demand to its contract manufacturers. These contract manufacturing, besides taking the orders from the Cisco also looked upon the demand independently, and added more inventory expecting further high demand. This resulted into huge pile of inventory that was never been ordered.

Kmart Corporation [1], which was retail giant before the emergence of Wal-Mart & Target, could not recover from the failure of its supply chain system, and sunk into bankruptcy. It had invested US$ 1.4 billion for overhauling, but it could not rejuvenate the system, it was too late for Kmart to realize the mistakes done.

Nike [2], world's largest shoe company had to suffer from the wrong supply chain decisions. In February 2001, the company lost $ 100 million in sales in the previous quarter. The company had implemented an IT based system supplied by i2 Technologies to manage its supply chain properly, but end up blaming i2 Technologies for the failure.

What is the conclusion that one can derive out of the above examples? It can be derived that if the companies have not given due attention to their supply chains, they are heading towards wrong side of the business. Another important thing is that these companies are most successful in their respective fields. So, what are the reasons behind these failures? Definitely, somewhere managers have not understood the importance of supply chain in the success of the organizations. When managers were asked about the contribution of supply chain in company's overall performance, their response was rather of unprepared ness. According to Matthesen [3] it is largely because most company executive do not have a supply chain background, and they tend to view the supply chain as 'a black box' that they don't understand or have limited visibility into.

Most of the managers see supply chain as a traditional distribution system, which is headache of a production manager or a logistics manager. Main tasks that are involved in supply chain were seen to be distributing finished products to warehouses, distributors or dealers, and retailers. Generally distributors and Dealers were used to work in isolation and customers were never considered as an important part of the supply chain. This was the time of 70s and 80s. But this view of supply chain is out of the context in today's fast changing business scenario, these changed have occurred due to following reasons:

1. Unprecedented advancement in the field of information technology and arrival of Internet.
2. Customer driven markets which are highly fragmented, resulting in broader selection of SKUs (Stock Keeping Units) aimed at specific consumer segments, different price points, shorter product life-cycles, and less predictive demand patterns.
3. Increased cost competencies based on global rivalry
4. Increased pressure from shareholders to reduce working capital
5. New models of supply chains such as based on global outsourcing

6. Increased complexities in supply chains due to increased applications of advanced technologies

Managers are obsessed with Kotler's 4 Ps of marketing. Most of the energies of the managers are consumed in framing products and promotion strategies. Companies invest millions of dollars to innovate products and adding newer and newer features to the existing products. Celebrities are romped in for endorsing the products. But, innovations, adding features and using celebrities increase cost thereby increasing pressure on company's bottom line. To balance the cost, companies resort to the strategies of increasing price of the product. The fourth P of the marketing mix 'Place' gets little attention, and even when a company recognizes the importance of 'Place' it ends up in making some adjustments in dealers and retailers positions.

The strong competitors because of the advanced technology available can match product innovations and adding features to the existing products. Celebrities are ever eager to endorse the products. Then, where can managers identify opportunities to reduce the cost? This new avenue is Supply Chain. But, supply chain cannot be treated as a tangible product, either it cannot be treated as an individual organization. Supply chain is an idea, and managers need to bring novelty to the supply chain. I called supply chain as an idea because traditional distribution system is known as logistics management and it functions on set rules, but supply chain is not restricted to set rules. This is rightly exemplifies by Dell Computers and Zara. Business experts rate Dell Computers supply chain as one of best supply chains. Dell thought of selling PCs online when no other company could even think of. Zara got tremendous success because of its unconventional supply chain mechanism. There are number of companies which are bringing newer ideas in managing supply chain. In India, ITC brought in e-Chaupal to reach directly to rural people. The point I want to make it that to get success in today's highly competitive business field companies have to think out of the box, and supply chain is that area where, if they acquire competitive advantage it is very tough for competitors to replicate.

Supply chains exist in every type of business activity. Most of the managers do not want to accept it. Managers believe that the main activity of a firm is to manufacturer products and sell those products to customers. Yes, definitely true, but manufacturing products and then delivering those products involve very large number of tasks. These tasks are highly interdependent and performed by different entities. Earlier these tasks or activities were not given much attention by business executives. Primarily, this area was concern of operations managers, distributors and it was traditionally known to be 'logistics or distribution management." But in recent times IT revolution and then arrival of Internet brought unprecedented changes in the ways and means of doing business. This also brought new terms like CRM, ERP, HRM, etc, which have changed the philosophy of the managers to view business activities. Customers became the focal point of business. Addressing the need of the customers became the motto of the organizations. Thus, all the firms that took part in satisfying the need of the customers were classified as links of a chain and the chain became the Supply Chain and managing this became Supply Chain Management.

Forrester [4] knew this 40 years ago, when he proposed a theory of management that recognized the integrated nature of organizational relationships in executing business activities particularly in context to distribution channels. He argued that organizations couldn't exist in isolation; by their inherent nature they are intertwined, so he proposed system approach to explain the performance of the functions such as research, engineering, sales and promotion. He demonstrated this by a computer simulation of the order of information flow and its influence on production and distribution performance for each channel member, as well as the entire channel system. More recent replication of this phenomenon includes the "Beer Game" simulation and research covering the "Bullwhip Effect." Predicting what would be the shape of future of business, Forrester suggested that after a period of research and development involving basic analytic techniques "there will come general recognition of the advantage enjoyed by the pioneering management who have been the first to improve their understanding of the interrelationships between separate management functions and between organization and its markets, its industry, and the national economy. Forrester identified key management issues and illustrated the dynamics of factors associated with what we call today supply chain management.

What is Supply Chain?

Defining a supply chain is rather easy, it is a set of firms that take part in moving the materials from source to destination, in the process transformation of materials take the shape of finished products. The source may be one or many suppliers, or services providers, even other firms and destination may be customers, consumers, and may be companies. I would not try to develop a new definition of supply chain, rather I will select from some of the best definitions of supply chain.

Christopher [5] (1992) defines a supply chain as the network of organizations that are involved, through upstream and downstream linkages, in the different processes and activities that produce value in the form of products and services in the hands of ultimate consumers. Here upstream means flow of things towards suppliers like flow of information such market demand originate from customers and flow towards manufacturer and than suppliers, and downstream means flow of things towards distributors, customers such as finished products move towards customers or end users.

"A supply chain is a worldwide network of suppliers, factories, warehouses, distribution centers, and retailers through which raw materials are acquired, transformed, and delivered to customers." (Mark S. Fox, Mihai Barbuceanu, and Rune Teign, 2000).[6]

The supply chain is viewed as a single process. Responsibility for the various segments in the chain is not fragmented and relegated to functional areas such as manufacturing, purchasing, distribution, and sales. Supply chain management calls for and in the end depend on strategic decision-making. "Supply" is a shared objective of practically every function in the chain and is of particular strategic significance because of its impact on overall costs and market share. Supply chain management calls for a different perspective on inventories, which are used as a balancing mechanism of last, not the first resort. A new approach to systems is required-integration rather than interfacing. Houlihan [7] (1988)

Supply chain activities are intertwined in nature and cut across each area of decision making in business. If we look at the decision making process of a business we find three levels: (a) strategic, (b) tactical and (c) operational.

The strategic level decisions are pertaining to supply chain network- selection of suppliers, facility location, facility layout, and transportation routes, warehouse decisions etc. Tactical decisions are plans such as MRP, and scheduling of the activities at the plant. Operational level decisions are day-to-day execution of the plans and schedules. Tactical level and operational level decisions are primarily distributed across the supply chain. Today's business demanding that there should be coordination of decision making at each level to optimize the performance of the supply chain. But the volatile nature of markets makes this difficult: materials do not arrive at time, production facilities fails, workers are on strike or ill, delivery dates are not met, customer change or cancel orders and so forth.

Managing these complexities properly in it is a big task for managers, so when I say be different, it may actually backfire and instead of bringing freshness and novelty, it may crippled the whole supply chain. In my view, being different is a matter of attitude, you look at the same things in different way and you try to do them differently and by doing that you don't forget that it should actually enhance the performance of the supply chain. This point of view is rightly strengthened by the companies like Dell, Toyota, Zara, Nokia, ITC and likewise.

Supply Chain is a network of different types of links. Strength of the Chain lies in the relationship between the links.

Companies are now realizing the relevance and role of these links in success of the businesses. Toyota and Honda have redefined the relationships with suppliers, particularly in North American market. In North American market Toyota and Honda developed trust among the same suppliers who were supplying to Detroit's Big Three for over 15 years. Why these suppliers became less interested in supplying to the Big Three (GM, Ford, Daimler Chrysler) and slowly switched to Japanese companies? The reasons are reflected by the utterance of the following statements from the suppliers:

"The Big Three set annual cost-reduction targets for the parts they purchase. To realize those targets, they will do anything. They have unleashed a reign of terror, and it gets worse every year. You can't trust anyone in those companies."

-Director [8], interior systems suppliers to Ford, GM, and Chrysler, Oct. 99

"Honda is a demanding customer, but it is loyal to us. American automakers have us work on drawings, ask other suppliers to bid on them, and give the job to the lowest bidder. Honda never does that."

-CEO [9], Industrial Fasteners suppliers to Ford, GM, Chrysler and Honda, April 2002

"Toyota helped us dramatically improve our production system. We started by making one component, and as we improved, Toyota rewarded us with orders for more components. Toyota is out best customers."

-Senior executive [10], supplier to Ford, GM, Chrysler, and Toyota, July 2001

These utterances suggest that suppliers are discontent with the treatment meted out to them by the biggest automobile companies of the America, and if opportunities provided, these suppliers will not blink for a moment to switch over to other companies, and that is exactly what happened in the US auto market. Toyota and Honda capitalized this opportunity and offered new business experience and relationship based on trust. The natural conclusion we could now see in the US market. Toyota and Honda are creating new dimensions of doing business in US market, which was once considered to be citadel of GM, Ford, and Chrysler. What I am trying to derive out of this that suppliers are one of the vital link in the process of transforming the raw materials into finished product and delivering that product to customers. In other words suppliers are partners of the business, and organizations need not to be convinced that in today's scale driven, technology intensive global economy, partnerships are the supply chain's lifeblood. Organizations business success is increasingly relying on their suppliers. Suppliers play an important role in deciding the cost of production, therefore firms are seeking avenues to reduce cost, improve quality, and develop new processes and products faster than their rivals' vendor can. Similar observations and arguments can be explained pertaining to distributors, wholesalers, dealers and retailers.

Realisation of the importance of links of supply chain is not the end of it; actually this is the starting point for the organizations to develop an optimal supply chain. So, what to be done to create an optimal supply chain? Let's us understand it from the customers' perspective. Customers want a right product, at the right place, at the right time, and at a minimum cost. If a company is not fulfilling any of the above said parameters then it is a tough task for that company to survive for a longer period of time. Here the next step of developing an optimal supply chain starts. Underlining the role of supply chain partners,

Companies need to develop processes that execute the objectives of delivering right product, at right place, at right time with minimum cost, always. There are number of companies, which have developed truly optimal supply chains. They could do so by thinking and acting differently. Here I am taking supply chains of two companies for the purpose of explaining my point, these companies are: Dell Computers, Zara.

Dell Computers

Business Experts nominated Dell Computer's Supply Chain as one of the best supply chains in the world. Dell was relatively new company in the PC markets, in the presence of giants like IBM, HP. Michael Dell (CEO and Chairman) based its business model on delivering customized PCs to end users directly, according to their needs and at the earliest. So, Dell started taking orders by telephones. When Internet arrived, Dell was the first company, which started the concept of selling PCs online. It takes the customers orders online through its website, assembled the configurations asked by the customers, and ship CPUs from its plant to customers directly. It has contract with Sony to supply monitors. But Dell does not ask Sony to deliver monitor to its plants, but rather tells Sony to ship the monitor directly to customers. Besides this, Dell has an integrated system placed with logistics companies such as UPS and FedEx, so that the CPUs from its assembly plant and Monitors from the Sony reach at customer's door at the same point of time, and this is repeated each time with each customer. You can visualize that if the number of orders is in thousands it becomes a formidable task for the company to be on schedule at each time it delivers the products to the customers.

In 1975, a small entrepreneur, Amancio Ortega faced with a difficult situation. Amancio Ortega was in lingerie business and was supplying to one big supplier. One day supplier cancelled the lot from the Ortega because of some unsited problem and distributor also mentioned to Mr. Ortega that he was not in a position to purchase the lot in near future. Mr. Ortega was having high stock of the products and if it had not sold he would be out of the business. So to save the losses he opened a small shop near his house and started selling the products. For a couple of days, sales were not great, but as the words of mouth spread that shop became highly popular.

Today, there are about 600 Zara's stores and it contributes over 80 per cent of the ∈4 billion Inditex Group's total sales. [11] What is the mantra of Zara's stupendous success? Ortega is the person who thought of making cloth as a perishable product- no different than yogurt and bread-to be consumed, rather than stored in closets. Nobody could think that before Ortega, and this is how you become successful if you are different from the crowd.

Key Success Factors for Zara

Zara has followed some untraditional ways in managing its customers, managing its supply chain and managing the brand. Zara is very quick in customer response. When a new idea of fashion generated at any of the fashion show Zara expert designers transform the idea into reality within two months and introduce the latest trends clothes at Zara's store in next two months. Zara also keep track of its customers. Marketing Executives roam around in Zara's store and take customers tips to change the design of the clothes. The main success mantra for Zara is the fast and speedy response to customers and to achieve that they have identified there critical success factors. These are the following.

- Zara continuously keep track of latest trends in the markets and this decides the production.
- Zara delivers products twice in a week, instead of weekly delivery, which is followed by others.
- Marketing Research.
- Ready raw material base.
- Multifunctional quick decision-making.
- Vertical integration to ensure controls over supply chain, and proximity.
- Technology.
- Cost control, despite flexibility.
- Technology and Infrastructure.

Zara creates deliberate scarcity of the products at stores. Conventional supply chain concept says that a product should be available at the place where customers come to buy that product, but Zara does not do that, in fact at Zara's stores customers wait for days to buy their prized products. Why Zara has done that? The strategy is that Zara wants to create an image in the customers that Zara's products are scarce one and are highly demanded in the markets, so there is always heavy rush on Zara's stores. Has not Zara think and act differently?

Conclusion

In the changed business setup of 21st century, organizations are competing at new frontiers. Supply chain is one of them. But, knowing that supply chain exists is not sufficient; the important thing is that what a company wants to do with that. One way of developing competencies is that organizations need to bring novelty, some freshness in their supply chain. This requires out of the box thinking and execution of supply chain strategies. Dell and Zara has shown this to the world by being different.

Notes

1. David A. Taylor, "Supply Chains; A Manager's Guide" Pearson Education Inc. 2004
2. David A. Taylor, "Supply Chains; A Manager's Guide" Pearson Education Inc. 2004
3. Special Report, "Creating the Optimal Supply Chain" The Boston Consultancy Group, Knowledge.
4. John T. Mentzer, Editor, "Supply Chain Management", Response Books Sage Publications India Pvt. Ltd., Second Printing 2003, New Delhi
5. John T. Mentzer, Editor, "Supply Chain Management", Response Books Sage Publications India Pvt. Ltd., Second Printing 2003, New Delhi
6. John T. Mentzer, Editor, "Supply Chain Management", Response Books Sage Publications India Pvt. Ltd., Second Printing 2003, New Delhi
7. S. Jaya Krishna, "Supplier Relationship Managements: the strategic Imperative and Advantage," The ICFAI Journal of Supply Chain Management,
8. Jeffrey K. Liker & Thomas Y.Choi, "Building Deep Supplier Relationships," Harvard Business review
9. Jeffrey K. Liker & Thomas Y. Choi, "Building Deep Supplier Relationships," Harvard Business Review.
10. Jeffrey K. Liker & Thomas Y.Choi, "Building Deep Supplier Relationships," Harvard Business Review
11. Devangshu Dutta, "Brand Watch Zara" Images Fashion Forum, 2004

References

A. Gunasekaran & E.W.T. Ngai, "Build-to-order supply chain management: a literature review and framework for development," Journal of Operations Management, Volume 23, Issue 5, July 2005, Pages 423-451

Andel, Tom, "Information Supply Chain: Set and Get Your Goals,"Transportation and Distribution, Vol. 38, No. 2, 1997, pp.33

Anderson, Erin and James A. Narus, "A Model of Distributor Firm and Manufacturer Firm Working Relationships," Journal of Marketing, Vol.54, January, 1990, pp. 42-58

Bechtel, Christian and Jayanth Jayaram, "Supply Chain Management: A strategic perspective," International Journal of Logistics Management, Vol. 8, N0.1, 1997, pp. 15-34

Bowersox, Donald J., "Lessons Learned from the World Class Leaders," Supply Chain Management Review, Vol.1, No. 1, 1997, pp. 61-67.

Bowersox, Donald J., Philip L. Carter, and Robert M. Monczka, " Material Logistics Management," Internal Journal of Physical Distribution and Logistics Management, Vol. 15, No. 5, 1985, pp. 27-35.

Bucklin, Louis P. and Sanjit Sengupta, "Organizing Successful Co-Marketing Alliances," Journal of Marketing, Vol. 57, April, 1993, pp. 285-301

Charles C Poirier, "Supplier Relationship Management: An Advanced Supply Chain Management Techniques," The ICFAI Journal of Supply Chain Management, Vol. II, No. 3, ICFAI University Press, September 2005, pp.14-18

Fisher, Marshall L., "What is the right supply chain for your product?", Harvard Business Review, March-April, 1997, pp. 83-93

Fuller, J.B., J.O'Conner, and R. Rawlinson, "Tailored Logistics: The Next Advantage," Harvard Business Review, May-June, pp. 87-98

John T. Mentzer, William DeWitt, James S. Keebler, Soonhong Min, Nancy W. Nix, Carlo D. Smith and Zach G. Zacharia, "Defining Supply Chain Management," Journal of Business Logistics, Vol. 22 No. 2 2001, pp.1-25

Kasra Ferdows & Michael A Lewis & Jose A.D. Machuca' "Rapid – Fire Fulfillment," Harvard Business Review, under the article: The 21st –century Supply Chain, November 2004, pp. 106-110.

Lee, Hau, "Aligning Supply Chain Strategies with Product Uncertainties," California Management Review, spring, 2002, pp.

105-119

Mihai Barbuceanu, Rune Teigen and Mark S. Fox, "Agent Based Design and Simulation of Supply Chain Systems," IEEE Computer Society Press, 1997, pp. 36-42.

Miguel A. Lejeune and Nevena Yakova, "On characterizing the 4 C's in supply chain management," Journal of Operations Management, Vol. 23, Issue 1, Jan. 2005, pp. 81-100

Peeyush Mehta, "Production Planning and Scheduling in Multistage Batch Manufacturing System," A thesis at IIM, Ahmedabad, 2004

Reuben E. Slone, "Leading a Supply Chain Turnaround," Harvard Business Review, under the article: The 21st –century Supply Chain Part1, October 2004, pp. 116-121

Rune Teigen, "Information Flow in a Supply Chain Management System," Research Thesis, Department of Industrial Economics and Technology Management, Trondhiem, Toronto May, 1997

S. Jaya Krishna, "Supplier Relationship Managements: the strategic Imperative and Advantage," The ICFAI Journal of Supply Chain Management, Vol. II, No. 3, ICFAI University Press, September 2005, pp.7-13.

Shirisha Regani, "Taiichi Ohno and Toyota Production System," Case Folio, A monthly journal of Management Case Studies, Vol. V, No. 3, ICFAI University Press, March 2005, and pp.73-90.

Yossi Sheffi, James B. Rice Jr., "A Supply Chain View of the Resilient Enterprise," MIT Management Review, Reprint, Fall 2005,Vol. 47, No. 1, pp. 41-48

6

E-Choupal: The V2I Model of Supply Chain Management

Priya Deshpande and G. Deepika

Introduction

Because of the Green Revolution, India's agricultural productivity has improved to the point that it is both self-sufficient and a net exporter of a variety of food grains. Yet most Indian farmers have remained quite poor. The causes include remnants of scarcity-era regulation and an agricultural system based on small, inefficient landholdings. The agricultural system has traditionally been unfair to primary producers. Soybeans, for example, are an important oilseed crop and sold by farmers with smallholdings to traders, who act as purchasing agents for buyers at a local, government-mandated marketplace, called a mandi. Farmers have only an approximate idea of price trends and have to accept the price offered them at auctions on the day that they bring their grain to the mandi. As a result, traders are well positioned to exploit both farmers and buyers through practices that sustain system-wide inefficiencies. To reduce these inefficiencies, ITC-one of India's largest exporters of agricultural commodities, has conceived E-Choupal as a more efficient supply chain aimed at delivering value to its customers around the world on a sustainable basis. The company has initiated an E-Choupal effort that places computers with Internet access in rural farming villages; the E-Choupals serve as both a social gathering place for exchange of information (choupal means gathering place in Hindi) and an e-commerce hub. The E-Choupal model has been specifically designed to tackle the challenges posed by the unique features of Indian agriculture, characterized by fragmented farms, weak infrastructure and the involvement of numerous intermediaries, among others.

E-Choupal makes use of the physical transmission capabilities of current intermediaries—aggregation, logistics, counter-party risk and bridge financing—while disintermediating them from the chain of information flow and market signals. What began as an effort to re-engineer the procurement process for Soya beans, tobacco, wheat, shrimp, and other cropping systems in rural India has also created a highly profitable distribution and product design channel for the company—an e-commerce platform that is also a low-cost fulfillment system focused on the needs of rural India. The E-Choupal system has also catalyzed rural transformation that is helping to alleviate rural isolation, create more transparency for farmers, and improve their productivity and incomes.

Production Channels Prior to E-Choupal

There are three commercial channels for soya: traders, government-mandated markets (mandis), and producer-run cooperative societies for crushing in cooperative mills. The system varies among states and districts, as does the percentage of produce going through each channel, but on average, 90% of soya crops are processed through traders and mandis. The operation of the Mandi consists of a number of different stages, from the logistics of transporting grain to the market to quality inspection, auction, bagging and weighing, and payment. Based upon local information within the village, farmers decide in which of the nearby mandis to sell.

Limitations of the Mandi Supply Chain System

- The *mandi* system does not serve the farmer well, and is burdened by inefficiency. Because the farmer does not have the resources to analyze or exploit price trends, the timing of the sale may not result in the optimal price for the crop. Moreover, since the actual sale price is determined at the auction, by the time the farmer gets the price, it is too late to go to another mandi to make his sale.

- Apart from the exploitation of the farmer, there are other inefficiencies in the system. The multiple points of handling in the supply-chain require the produce to be bagged, which takes four to five times longer to be unloaded at the processing plant than unbagged produce. Traders generally do not have the capacity to store and manage different qualities and grades of produce, inhibiting efforts to produce better crop grades. Pricing is set locally at the mandis, and is not reliably tracked or reported nationally, resulting in a lack of information that reduces the opportunity for arbitrage and leads to market inefficiency. In addition, regulatory restrictions tend to limit arbitrage to small geographic areas.
- Not only does the agent inflate the price to trading companies, he also inflates the price at the mandi. Additionally, the trading company establishes a daily price range for its agent to buy within. If the agent's average buy price that day is lower than the low end of the established price, the agent sells the grain to the trading company at the established low price and pockets the difference. If, however, the average buy price is higher than the trading company's established high price, the agent will still buy the produce but will report to the company that since its price was not high enough, no grain could be bought. The agent will store the grain and sell it to the trading company the next day when the established price has been raised to make-up for the previous day's procurement shortfall. Commission agents therefore capture the entire benefit of intra-day price shifts. The agents therefore operate without risk of loss of profit.

As a result of the commission agent structure in the traditional mandi system, ITC had no direct interaction with the farmer. This gap created a range of supply-chain issues, including limiting ITC's knowledge of its crops, suppliers, and supply risks, as well as limiting the company's ability to improve crop quality and quantity by bringing modern agricultural practices to the farmers. The company developed its E-Choupal strategy as a way to communicate directly with the farmer and to bypass the inefficiencies arising out of the agents' intermediation, thereby achieving "virtual vertical integration."

Virtual Vertical Integration (V2I) Model of SCM: An IT-Driven Solution

E-Choupal links the Indian farmer with consumers in local and global markets, by leveraging ITC's time-tested and proven competencies in marketing and distribution. Unlike in the alternative mandi channel (where farmer discovers the price for his produce after he has incurred costs of transportation, therefore ends up selling even if he is not happy with the price), E-Choupal leverages the seamless workflow capabilities of IT to virtually integrate several best-in-class players along the chain and offer the services on a single platform to every farmer. E-Choupal empowers the farmer's decision-making with information. In the process many overheads like multiple transportation & handling, bagging etc., are erased. Thus, through the virtual vertical integration (V2I) model of supply chain management (SCM), E-Choupal secures the scale benefits for India's agricultural economy without displacing the small farmer.

From the conception of the model, an IT-based solution was recognized as fundamental to optimizing effectiveness, scalability, and cost. Information technology is 20 per cent of all the effort of ITC's E-Choupal business model, but is considered the most crucial 20 per cent.

The two goals envisioned for IT are:

- Delivery of real-time information independent of the transaction. In the mandi system, delivery, pricing, and sales happen simultaneously, thus binding the farmer to an agent. E-Choupal was seen as a medium of delivering critical market information independent of the mandi, thus allowing the farmer an empowered choice of where and when to sell his crop.
- Facilitate collaboration between the many parties required to fulfill the spectrum of farmer needs. As a communication mechanism, this goal is related to the commitment to address

the whole system, not just a part of the system.

E-Choupal Supply Chain

The previous day's mandi closing price is used to determine the benchmark Fair Average Quality (FAQ) price at the E-Choupal. The benchmark price is static for a given day. This information and the previous day mandi prices are communicated to the sanchalak through the E-Choupal portal. The commission agents at the mandi are responsible for entering daily mandi prices into the E-Choupal. If and when the Internet connection fails, the sanchalak calls an ITC field representative.

Inspection and Grading: To initiate a sale, the farmer brings a sample of his produce to the E-Choupal. The sanchalak inspects the produce and based on his assessment of the quality makes appropriate deductions (if any) to the benchmark price and gives the farmer a conditional quote. The sanchalak performs the quality tests in the farmer's presence and must justify any deductions to the farmer. The benchmark price represents the upper limit on the price a sanchalak can quote. These simple checks and balances ensure transparency in a process where quality testing and pricing happen at multiple levels. If the farmer chooses to sell his soy to ITC, the sanchalak gives him a note capturing his name, his village, particulars about the quality tests (foreign matter and moisture content), approximate quantity and conditional price.

Weighing and Payment: The farmer takes the note from the sanchalak and proceeds with his crop to the nearest ITC procurement hub, ITC's point for collection of produce and distribution of inputs sold into rural areas. At the ITC procurement hub, a sample of the farmer's produce is taken and set aside for laboratory tests. After the inspection, the farmer's cart is weighed on an electronic weighbridge, first with the produce and then without. The difference is used to determine the weight of his produce.

Hub Logistics: After the inspection and weighing are complete, the farmer then collects his payment in full at the payment counter. The farmer is also reimbursed for transporting his crop to the procurement hub. Every stage of the process is accompanied by appropriate documentation. The farmer is given a copy of lab reports, agreed rates, and receipts for his records. Samyojaks, who are adept at handling large amounts of cash, are entrusted with the responsibility of payment, except at procurement centers near large ITC operations where ITC is handles cash disbursement. Samyojaks also handle much of the procurement hub logistics, including labor management at the hub, bagging, storage management, transportation from the hub to processing factories, and handling mandi paperwork for the crops procured at the hub. For his services in the procurement process, the samyojak is paid a 0.5% commission.

E-Choupal: The Unique 3-D Marketing Channel

On the ground, E-Choupal is proving to be a unique 3-D marketing channel for many products & services consumed by rural India. The marketing dynamics in the backdrop of increasing consumer-centricity of today's world are well known. For example, while superior products and USPs are the necessary starting point for success in the marketplace, experience is becoming a critical differentiator. Process benefits - which make transactions between buyer & seller easier, quicker, less expensive and more pleasant - support this dimension. A third dimension, personalization, successfully employed by a few corporates, will be the only sustainable differentiator in tomorrow's world. Relationship benefits - which reward the willingness of consumers to identify themselves and to reveal their purchasing behavior - lay the foundation for this dimension.

The organic blending of relevant knowledge (e.g. application) and customized information (e.g. local weather), with farmer's purchase transactions, is creating a unique value for him, especially in farm inputs. The Sanchalaks connected to the market leading farm input companies and experienced agricultural scientists through the E-Choupal infrastructure are able to deliver this benefit to the farmer leveraging the power of collaborative networks. A couple of other important process benefits that E-Choupal is delivering to the marketer are:

- Superior demand forecasting & real-time communication, especially valuable in FMCG as well as short-window-demand products, and
- The ability to assemble groups of highly involved customers for credible and focused research as well as to demonstrate product features.

This has been proving a boon in consumer durables. By virtue of its wealth enhancing capability, E-Choupal has been able to build valuable and sustainable relationships with farmers, majority of rural consumers. As the relationships transcend short-term expedient considerations, these people share a wealth of information about themselves, which is then converted into valuable knowledge to market tailor-made credit and insurance products.

Sustaining Commercial Volume

"Virtual vertical integration" can only work if there is a continuous flow of information between the E- Choupals and ITC. Because of the number and physical dispersion of the E-Choupals, this communication must be initiated by the sanchalaks. If their motivation to communicate with ITC diminishes, the channel will still function for procurement, but will lack the vitality to supply risk management, distribution, or product design. Maintaining continuous commercial flow keeps the sanchalak motivated to spend time and money calling the ITC representative to ask about new products, convey village demand, and providing ITC with local updates. An example of the power of local information was seen early in E-Choupal implementation. Sanchalaks thus provide an essential role in the chain of communication.

ITC maintains commercial volumes by sequencing procurement and sales year-round, thereby securing the continuous flow of commission checks through E-Choupals. Purchases and sales have been arranged so that *kharif* (the cropping season that coincides with India's monsoon, July through October) and *rabi* (winter cropping season in irrigated areas) inputs and procurement maintain a steady stream of revenue for sanchalaks.

Scaling the Model

Profitable re-engineering requires the unambiguous understanding of value provided, the circumstances in which they are applicable, and the revenues they are capable of generating. ITC's model identifies three sources of value for the company that can help scale the model:

Crop Specific Intervention: ITC recognized that agrarian systems vary by crop. This means that the inefficiencies in the supply chain, the correction required from E-Choupal, the magnitude and timing of the resulting revenues will differ by crop. For example, the systems, and consequently the E-Choupal models and payback streams, for coffee and shrimp are very different from those for soya.

Low-Cost Last Mile: The same system of physical and information exchange that brings produce from the village can be used to transfer goods to the villages. ITC's current channels reach areas with populations of 5,000 and above. E-Choupals allow penetration into areas with populations less than 5,000. Products such as herbicides, seeds, fertilizers, and insurance policies, as well as soil testing services are sold through E-Choupal. E-Choupal as a distribution channel begins in agriculture but extends well into consumer goods and services. In the traditional channel, comprised of mobile traders and cycle-based distributors, farmers lack the resources to make informed purchasing decisions. More often than not, traders and distributors do not understand the farmers' issues and end up selling them products and services that do not satisfy their needs. With many larger companies hesitating to serve the rural market, farmers often do not have variety in their choice of products and services. This lack of choice means that not only are farmers forced to buy whatever is available, they often must pay a premium for those products.

Intelligent First-Mile: The global resources, best practices, and remunerations that the E-Choupal brings to farmers have encouraged innovation and provided an avenue to see their ideas realized. This illustrates ITC's vision of using E-Choupal as the "intelligent first mile." Farmers are now coming up with products and services that ITC could provide to further improve operations.

ITC's core asset is its knowledge of the customer. By transforming the value chain and setting up a platform for procuring commodities from them directly, they now have a foundation for forging a close relationship with the farmers. This relationship leads to a better understanding of the issues plaguing farmers. Through E-Choupals, hubs, and processing centers, ITC has the ready infrastructure needed to implement an alternative channel for distribution of goods and services to rural India.

In addition, the information infrastructure implemented by ITC can be used to enhance its business decision-making, better manage risk, and identify opportunities for cross-selling and up-selling. The company can leverage detailed transactional data and transform it into actionable knowledge. Data mining and data warehousing will help company executives to better understand the behavior of their customers, identify unfulfilled needs and ways to serve them efficiently. The communication infrastructure compensates for the lack of physical infrastructure needed for marketing products and services in rural India. It enables rapid, low-cost information dissemination and a trusted brand for introducing new products, while minimizing the need for a traveling sales force. Online ordering and order management eliminate the need for physical storefronts. And the IT infrastructure and local sanchalak provide customer intelligence, thus maximizing customer satisfaction and profitability.

Benefits to the Farmers

Prior to the introduction of E-Choupal, farmers' access to agricultural information was incomplete or inconsistent. The only sources of information were word of mouth within the village and the commission agent. E-Choupal allows farmers daily access to prices at several nearby mandis. Some e-Choupal sanchalaks have taken this a level further by accessing external pricing sources such as prices on the Chicago Board of Trade, in order to track global trends and determine the optimum timing of sales.

- Farmers benefit from more accurate weighing, faster processing time, and prompt payment, and from access to a wide range of information, including accurate market price knowledge, and market trends, which help them decide when, where, and at what price to sell. The total benefit to farmers includes lower prices for inputs and other goods, higher yields, and a sense of empowerment
- Through E-Choupal, farmers have access to prices and make the critical decision of when and where to sell his crop. Both factors work together to provide the farmers a better price for their crops.
- Under ITC's system, farmers no longer bear the cost of transporting their crops to the mandi and are instead reimbursed for transport to the procurement hub. The transaction at the ITC hub is also much faster than at the mandi, usually taking no more than two or three hours. Moreover, ITC's electronic weighing scales are accurate and not susceptible to sleight of hand like the manual weighing system at the mandi. The system also does not require produce to be bagged, which avoids the associated loss of produce by intentional spillage. Thus the E-Choupal system has logistical and transaction efficiencies.
- The incremental income from a more efficient marketing process is about US$6 per ton, or an increase of about 2.5% over the mandi system. The system also provides direct access to the farmer and to information about conditions on the ground, improving planning and building relationships that increase its security of supply. Thus there are meaningful net economic benefits to farmers, and it is having a measurable impact on what farmers choose to do: in areas covered by E-Choupals, the percentage of farmers planting soy has increased dramatically, from 50 to 90% in some regions, while the volume of soy marketed through mandis has

dropped by as much as 50%.

The E-Choupal system gives farmers more control over their choices, a higher profit margin on their crops, and access to information that improves their productivity.

Benefits to ITC

The commissions paid to the agents under the traditional system were not excessive, but because of the inefficiencies involved, the true cost of intermediation through the mandi system was between 2.5 and 3% of procurement cost.

- Removal of intermediary manipulation of quality and the ability to directly educate and reward quality in the customer base resulted in higher levels of quality in E-Choupal procurement. This resulted in higher oil yields, which in turn is leading to higher profits for ITC.
- E-Choupals also allows ITC to develop long-term supplier relationships with farmers and attain some degree of supply security over time. Risk is also managed in the E-Choupal system by a far stronger information infrastructure. Sanchalaks and Samyojaks working on behalf of ITC provide excellent bottom-up information on pricing, product quality, soil conditions, and expected yields. This allows ITC to better plan future operations.
- In the mandi system, there was a mark up of 7-8 per cent on the price of soybean from the farm gate to the factory gate. Of this mark up, 2.5 per cent was born by the farmer while 5 per cent was borne by ITC. With E-Choupal, ITC's costs are now down to 2.5 per cent. In absolute numbers, both the farmers and ITC save about US$ 6 per metric ton.

Challenges Faced by E-Choupal

Understanding the constraints imposed by the physical and social environment in E-Choupals operate is necessary to provide the context for understanding the system design.

- **Overcoming Power Constraints:** Power availability in rural India is unreliable and the quality of power is sub-standard.

- **Transportation:** Most E-Choupal villages lack proper roads, limiting vehicle access.
- **Telecom Infrastructure:** Telecommunication infrastructure in villages is poor.
- **Customer Base:** Before the arrival of E-Choupal, most villagers had never seen a computer. ITC realized the importance of appropriate user interfaces. They organized meetings and focus groups of farmers to gather information about potential user groups.

Conclusions

IT-Enabled V2I model of SCM can serve a dual agenda: bridging rural isolation and the resulting disparities of education and economic opportunity, while at the same time creating a potentially large profit opportunity for the organization willing to tackle the inefficiencies. The goal of being self-sufficient in food supply brought Indian agriculture into the mainstream of political and social consciousness. The E-Choupal model shows that a large corporation can combine a social mission and an ambitious commercial venture; that it can play a major role in rationalizing markets and increasing the efficiency of an agricultural system, and do so in ways that benefit farmers and rural communities as well as company shareholders. ITC's example also shows the key role of information technology—in this case provided and maintained by a corporation, but used by local farmers—in helping to bring about transparency, to increase access to information, and to catalyze rural transformation, while enabling efficiencies and low-cost distribution that make the system profitable and sustainable. Critical factors in the apparent success of the venture are ITC's extensive knowledge of agriculture, the effort ITC has made to retain many aspects of the existing production system, including retaining the integral importance of local partners, the company's commitment to transparency, and the respect and fairness with which both farmers and local partners are treated. Emerging areas like telemedicine, E-Governance, education and entertainment will soon ride on the

Internet, web-casting and video conferencing infrastructure of E-Choupal.

Glossary of Terms

Choupal: A Hindi word meaning village gathering place.

Inputs: In an agricultural context, this refers to the range of seeds, fertilizers, pesticides, etc. that are used in the farming process

Kharif: One of the two sowing seasons of Indian agriculture. It refers to the season that coincides with India's southwest monsoon rainfall (July to October). The kharif crop is therefore entirely rainfed.

Mandi: A government mandated market-yard where farmers sell their crops

Rabi: One of the two sowing seasons of Indian agriculture. It refers to the winter sowing season in areas that have irrigation.

Samyojak: The commission agent in his role as a collaborator in the e-Choupal model

Sanchalak: The village farmer who runs the e-Choupal and acts as ITC's representative in the village

VSAT: Very Small Aperture Terminal (VSAT) is the technology used in the e-Choupal to achieve Internet connectivity

References

Evans, Naim, Towill, 1993, "Dynamic Supply Chain Performance: Assessing the impact of Information Systems", Logistics Information Management, Vol 6, No.4, pp 15-25.

Food and Agriculture Integrated Development Action. CII-Mckinsey Report

Ghanekar J, "Trade Liberalisation and the Soyabean Sector in Maharashtra", Indian Journal of Agriculture Economics, 2002.

Jairath M.S, "Institutional *Reforms-A case study of Agriculture Markets in India",* Indian Journal of Agriculture Economics, 2002

National Agriculture Policy 2000, Ministry of Agriculture, Government of India.

Rognes, J, 1995, "Negotiating Co-operative Supplier Relationships: A Planning Framework, International journal of Purchasing and Materials Management, pp 12-18.

Tedia, Jain & Tanweer "*Success Story of Soyabean in M.P.: Information & Management Technology for Soyabean Industries*".

7

Supply Chain Management Operations under Sales Tax/Value Added Tax

T. Mathew

Introduction

Let me first give you a brief outline on VAT system and its impact on a live case, which was faced by our company in Dec 2005. This is an interesting paper for managing the SCM in varying situation of taxation.

There are several plus points in VAT wherein, you tax just the value add, (hence) double taxation can be eliminated. The cascading effect of taxes can be controlled. The business is entitled to the input tax credit (ITC). This would be therefore capturing a broader tax base thus broadening the tax base and hence reducing evasion due to proper self-assessment. This has a reducing effect on the prices of the final product. This would however depend on the nature of the goods and the distribution chain length at the front end and the back end. Normally a relatively long distribution channel would witness a rise in the overall costs unless there is an uniform tax regime throughout the system. Another concern was the co-existence of the central sales tax (CST) with VAT, which could distort the nature of supply chain transactions as well be seen in this case. The continuation of CST would make inter-state sales an unviable option, as stock transferring would get expensive by 4 per cent under VAT. Or the other way to look at this is in order to avoid these expenses there will be a big strain in SCM to provide the services to their customer as such additional costs have to be absorbed by the supplier using appropriate techniques in SCM & Logistics.

VAT as a system of levying taxes on sale of goods and has been introduced nationwide in 21 states of India on April 1,

2005.The only states that have opposed embracing the new system are Uttar Pradesh, Madhya Pradesh, Gujarat , Rajasthan and Tamil Nadu. VAT (Value Added Tax) is a consumption tax that is levied at every point in the distribution chain on the value added at each stage. In the traditional sales tax regime tax was levied at each stage on the total value of goods which in effect led to a cascading of taxes. Below is an illustration outlining the difference in the tax structure under the Sales Tax regime and the Vat system.

We can clearly see that for the same tax rate VAT results in lower taxes which directly impact the end price to the consumer.

The difference arises primarily due to the fact that a dealer under the Vat system does not take into account the tax paid by him as a cost .Earlier he would treat the tax paid on his purchases as a cost, added some value/margin to it and then sold it to the customer on which there would be a further tax. Thus effectively there would be a tax on tax resulting in cascading of taxes. Under the VAT system the dealer would get credit equal to the input tax paid by him on the output tax he pays thus effectively only the value added by him is taxed and since he does not treat the input tax paid as a cost the margin is added to the cost of the input and there is no cascading of taxes as a result.

VAT and CST (Central Sales Tax)

In the existing sales tax system, sale price includes tax paid under the Act, but under VAT, sale price does not include tax paid under the Act. Hence, a dealer will not fix the sale price taking into account the tax paid on purchases. There is provision for set off of tax paid if the goods are exported or sold in course of inter-state trade and commerce. This is applicable to all the State's VAT Law. For example, if a dealer has paid tax Rs. 50.00 on his purchases of goods valued Rs.500.00, and adds value to the tune of Rs. 450.00, under the sales tax system, he will sell the goods in course of inter-state trade at Rs. 1000.00 + CST @4 per cent (Rs. 40.00). Under VAT, he will sell the goods at Rs. 950.00 + CST @ 4 per cent (Rs. 38.00) as he will get input tax credit of Rs.50.00.

CST may be phased out completely within two years. Under VAT, a dealer is likely to get the goods at Rs. 988.00 instead of Rs. 1040.00 and after two years, the goods will be available to the consuming state at Rs.950.00 instead of at Rs. 1040.00.

Pre-VAT Situation

Even before the nationwide implementation of VAT on April 1, 2005 few states of India already had a VAT system in place. Haryana was the first state to do so in April of 2003 when it passed the Haryana Value Added Tax Act .The implications of VAT are that there will be no difference in the tax payments of a company when it comes to sales within the same state. India has a federal structure and most taxes on sales are collected by the consuming state i.e. in which the sale is made. Thus where the sale is made makes a big difference to the tax payments with respect to the rate applicable and other taxes levied on the movement of goods across states such as Inter-state tax and entry tax. In the present tax structure companies design their logistics in order to minimize tax savings rather than maximize operational efficiency. A company that may be well served by having only one warehouse or stockyard may decide to have as many warehouses in the states of its biggest sales in order to escape Inter-state Sales tax.

Post-VAT Situation

Since VAT has not been implemented in each and every state of India the situation has become complicated. Twenty-one states have implemented VAT but they are still at various stages with regard to their implementation programme and it may take up to a year for all of these states to complete the phasing in of the new system. Every state has decided to bring in its own flavor of VAT with varying rates for the same goods even though the white paper on VAT brought out by the government restricts states to only 4 rates 12.5 per cent, 4 per cent, 1 per cent and 20 per cent.

Briefly we would like to inform our case situation involves one of the biggest providers of telecommunication in India, whom we call M/s XYZ Co., Ltd (to maintain confidentiality). They are importing the main components from China with the ancillary components from Korea. They have very wide network all over India. Now under the above tax situations XYZ imports the cargo in Bulk from both China and Korea into India. Logistically this is done with one entry point into India and the coordination would be in such a way that they would require the cargo together and immediately after they place the order (two weeks is the max lead time). The reason being that their final product sales is very much depending on the new technology available and the market promotion activities which are driven by various new schemes availability of money with the common man, new trends/technologies.

Therefore, it is imperative that the logistics must be perfect to arrive into India within their demand forecast range. In case we fail it means possibility of lost sales, technology obsolescence and uncertain future demand prediction. XYZ imports the main component (A) from China and the ancillary component (B) from Korea into India, which would be then distributed to various states based on the demand of their final product. Once transported both A & B is put into their warehouses in that state they are then tested and their engineers assemble the final product on site. Herein lies the problem as each state has a specific demand and the SCM has to be properly monitored so that the right quantities of A & B would reach the right warehouses in the several states requested by the company XYZ.

This is a simple SCM exercise to match the demand projection for the various states. As this demand is very sensitive and cannot be altered, as the future is unpredictable due to promotion constraints and technology obsolescence added to the stiff competition and the price competition prevailing in India.

XYZ being the market leader in their field are very much concerned for the services they provide to their customer and they insist their suppliers follow the standard set by them in terms of delivery schedules and services.

The problem is more complicated when the situation of VAT,

ST prevails in India as the above shipments have to follow exactly the quantity requested for the states and XYZ would be requiring consolidated shipments on time however the system should follow the challenges posed by VAT, ST regulations in India.

In short XYZ insisted that all documentations and shipments must be done in such a way that they would save on the states where VAT is favorable and avoid paying unnecessary high taxes in case of wrong documentation and delivery. Also the distribution channel must be geared to face these challenges.

Having seen the implication of VAT, ST for the customer we now build our case on the import regulations and connect the same with VAT.

Customs operations are a high-risk activity for importers and there are many reasons for this. The rules of the game has changed, and continue to change, putting importers at a high risk of committing errors in what is being declared to customs. The VAT payments made to customs are not always consistent with the VAT declarations submitted to BIR. Most if not all importers look at customs operations as a mere logistics activity, without regard for indirect tax compliance.

Role of Customs Brokers. For importers, customs brokerage is high impact service and is integral to the supply chain. While there are numerous customs brokerage firms willing to provide its service, the selection of a business partner is most important to importers for the following reasons:

- To provide customs clearance and related services (e.g. transport service);
- To ensure complete and correct declarations to customs;
- To ensure compliance with import rules and regulations issued by customs and all other government agencies; and
- To assist the company in providing complete and correct VAT declarations to BIR

This was a new kind of supply chain challenge. The situations demanded a secure and synchronized movement, and delivery of goods - otherwise business could get impacted.

To do them, our company/suppliers would need to remodel its

processes, which is a huge challenge, and prohibitively expensive. In normal course, goods are moved from the factory to the warehouse, and thereon to distribution points across the country. To pull off a logistics operation, which requires synchronization across multiple dispatch and receiving stations, becomes a specialist's job.

A time-definite logistics operation requires an operational team with an ability to coordinate and work across cities through a seamless flow of information (which is often required on a minute-to-minute basis), and an organization that is skilled n providing proper logistics services. Our team members follow one simple rule: complete access and flow of information between each other at every single moment.

Our challenge was to look at the Logistics efficiency to avoid the CST burden we had to work with State boundaries instead of the usual geographical convenience. It was clear that due to the disparate ST situation transportations had to be done on longer routes with uncertain lead times resulting in poor customer service. Added to this problem is the resource spent on paper work and formalities for follow up with various dept on the issue of local taxes.

Our goal was to minimize the tax incidence in the entire supply chain without compromising on business and services to our customer. Ensuring proper documentation using IT can plan this can be achieved. A proper understanding of the tax situation and its implications is vital for the organization, suppliers and distributors to ensure competitive and efficient service.

As a result of good economic growth Company XYZ got very good orders from several customers all over India. The final product is used in the telecommunication field and we were expecting the orders in a week. The final product is basically made up of

Main Component A + Ancillary Component B, however based on the communication network there are various sizes of A, like 2 feet, 5 feet and 7 feet and these requirements are very specific. We denote these as A1, A2, A3 all of which is used with

B to make the final product in short,

A1+B=Final product (A1B)

or A2+B=Final product (A2B)

or A3+B=Final product (A3B)

There is a specific demand for A1B, A2B & A3B from each state in India. As the component A & B are imported its better to ship them together to save on freight. This would be a simple logistical exercise but it turned out to be a big challenge since different states in India have varying tax systems. This challenge is the biggest constraint to the SCM systems, which was imposed on the manufacturers, shipper, transporters and users.

XYZ marketing team had finalized their orders in a week time just before the festive season in India. It was imperative that the shipments must be done promptly in a week to 10 days and material to land into India just before the festival holidays. XYZ has JIT planning and would clear the customs before the holidays and their final equipment would hit the market just in time for the holidays so that they can service their customers. As a logistical challenge this meant we had to hit the bulls eye on target at the first shot. This indeed became more challenging when the whole SC network had to gear up to blend with the VAT/ST regime in India. The orders were so specific that we could not mess up with sending wrong quantities/grades as this would result in increased costs due to transportation back to the right destination from the wrong one and the increases in the tax and the big loss in sales due to missing the festive season with the lurking danger of hanging on to inventory which can become obsolete. The payment terms in this contract were DA 90 days and XYZ had decided to impose the penalty clause of not making for any payment for the material, which is not shipped (arrived to India) within the deadline. As Operations chief we had therefore lot at stake and the company image of XYZ as a market leader in India would suffer. Furthermore, the orders were very substantial so the losses due to SC miss-management would be very substantial.

As demand forecasting is very difficult for such products due to various factors being involved it becomes very difficult to plan production for such huge quantities however the first step we did was to request our supplier from China to keep some stock (around 25 per cent quantity) which was based on past performance and the world trend for the main component A. The principle of commonality was used, as our Chinese maker did not diversify making A1, A2 or A3. Only A was made, this was easily possible as the Chinese maker had one plant only making product A, this is normally sent to the other plants (located several kms away from the main plant). This had its plus and minuses because postponement was easy however shipment would be a problem because of the transportation. Schematically the main component manufacturing would be

The cost saving was possible in the manufacture but the problem was in the shipment.

We had also made a good PR exercise and planning for several scenarios with the logistics providers to gear up on the shipments on priority as several combinations had to be worked out for the shipment of component A. This components freight calculation was based on volume.

A similar exercise was done for the ancillary component B from Korea, however this components shipment was relatively easier as this was a smaller component and the airfreight calculated on weight. Also the manufacturer and shipment was located at one point with the possibility to hold on to 75 per cent inventory at any time (This manufacturer had demand worldwide so they could easily plan their production).

In order for our customers to get the exact shipments as per the requirements of VAT/ST prevailing in the different states it became imperative that the whole supply chain be geared up to the customers requirement. This would be a great service to provide the material in time and without any problem on the costing.

How We Tackled the Issue?

After much brain storming our customer released the order from Kolkata but the shipments were to the various locations like

Orissa, Jharkhand, Bihar, Rajasthan, Punjab, Gujarat, Karnataka, Tamil Nadu & Kerala as per the case above. Some of these states have different VAT/ST rates from the normal. Therefore it was decided that the documentations for each was to be separated at the HAWB level with the "Ship To/Bill To" clause to mention the different addresses for the sates above. This way one set of clean documents would be there with the consignment resulting in very smooth clearance and no problem with the tax authorities.

The plants in China unfortunately were making product A variations at different locations in China. That is A1, A2, A3... all were at different locations but fortunately their PPC was done in such a way that the final sorting was done by cross decking at the Central Warehousing at HO near to the airport for smooth shipment.

What we did was added another colored labeling to each cargo for each state (mentioning the name of the state). This was very good identification for all the personnel throughout the supply chain to identify the cargo as per the state.

Since this labeling was a new activity for only Indian customers peculiar situation our supplier in China had to outsource this label and its lead-time was 2 days. This was a crucial point as will be seen later. This way all personnel handling the cargo like packing personnel, forwarder at the air forwarder, airlines personnel, customs personnel, order customer personnel and even the distributor/retailer network and final customer knows from the package itself the final destination.

We had excellent rapport with the airlines personnel especially Air Brunei, AI, CX, SP & Malaysian Air so that we can get the space and proper freight. This order was coinciding with the festive season in China and also the festive season in India so the air traffic was very heavy. Normally only 2MT cargo is available to Kolkata on these flights and our experience showed that the best two airlines would be AI & Malaysian Air. However the operations is very peculiar at Hong Kong transit point because these airlines first cart the passengers and their excess luggage and during the festive season these flight are full and luggage is huge. Therefore it is imperative that we try to secure space. So, we had around 10MT of material and therefore it had to go on 5~6 flights depending on the space. In case passenger cargo is excess the airlines gives us the balance space available. Our labels are then the only source of identification at the forwarder and the airlines company as to which cargo will be loaded as per the space available with the airlines on a particular day. This was a way to ensure the full lot for a particular state goes as one shipment (which is request of our customer) and this would be split second decision of the forwarder and the airlines as our goods had to be carted to the airport and then would be accepted or not accepted depending on the passengers luggage.

It was imperative to use Consol cargo so that the HAWB can be used for the customs clearance and the MAWB used for banking formalities.

Thus we can say the following are the constraints

- VAT/ST regulations in India.
- Quantity pickup for the airlines.
- Proper labeling for cargo and education throughout the SCM.
- Holiday season both in India & China.

What Actually Happened?

There was a big problem as below

- The labels, which were outsourced in China, arrived late and the cargo could not be attached with the labels however the package of the labels was sent with the lots for each of the states in India. This had a serious problem because the personnel throughout the SCM could not actually see the effect of the color of the labels and had to be told at each stage of the system. This actually defeated the very purpose of labeling. The cargo had to be forwarded to airlines without waiting for it to be stuck on each of the cargo because of the time constraints for shipment and the problem of cargo shut out at the airlines.
- The forwarder in China despite being told the situation of VAT and the need for settling the documents separately for

the states based on HAWB with a single MAWB still did not understand this situation. They made a big mistake buy shipping the cargo NOT as CONSOL but instead as DIRECT which means one HAWB and one MAWB. This also defeated the whole purpose to avoid problems in taxation at India. This was also due to time constraint at forwarder to avoid shut out at airlines and the need for quick shipments.

How We Solved this Problem?

- We had to immediately request airlines to change the manifest from Direct to Consol. This would mean that there would be different HAWB for one MAWB so both the taxation and payment issues can be settled. Since the airlines were just going to go for holidays we had to request the HQ to make the changes on the manifest. Fortunately we knew the normal Consol agents which these airline companies use and had instructed them too to take care on this matter.
- We had to attach the labels at the Kolkata airport before it comes in for customs clearance. This was a huge problem because this cargo responsibility was not taken by anyone due to the above manifest. Fortunately we had a good forwarder personnel who were allowed to enter the special area at airport and fix the labels on the cargo. As this cargo was previously cleared by this forwarder they knew exactly what to paste and where. Furthermore as this was urgent we had to shell out some money, which our supplier in China agreed to pay, as this was their fault.

This is truly a good lesson for us to learn on SCM issues on how to educate personnel to understand clearly and implement the proper instructions given to them.

8

Efficiency of Supply Chain: A Study of Food Sector in India

S.R. Subba Rao and G. Chamundeshwari

Introduction

The food sector in India comprises food items based on agriculture, forestry, dairy, fisheries, meat and marine products. The items reach the consumers through a supply chain which consists of farmers who produce the items down to consumers who are the ultimate users, with a number of intermediate players. Food supply chain plays a key role in the economy with value addition to products, returns to farmers and other players in the intermediary stages, creation of employment opportunities and reduction of wastages. The approaches adopted by those in the supply chain vary, resulting in different levels of efficiency and returns. The paper, initially, examines the existing position of the food sector in India. After giving a conceptual coverage of supply chain management, the supply chain relating to food sector is studied. Then, the efficiency of food supply chain is analysed and the scope from improvement that can be brought about for the benefit of the suppliers as well as the consumers is examined. Some illustrations of the players in the food supply chain are given to highlight the significant role played by them.

Growth in per capita incomes, movement of people to higher income classes, urbanization, food items accounting for about 50 per cent of the total household consumption expenditure, and concern for quality and hygiene are resulting in an increasing demand for processed and ready to eat food. The demand for processed food is mainly confined to metropolitan areas with high potential in other areas. Globalization of trade and high speed logistics services are availed by retail chains in advanced countries which source food supplies from developing countries.

Significance of Food Sector

Out of the total land in India, 52 per cent is cultivable when compared to 11 per cent in the world. Agriculture accounts for 24.2 per cent of the gross domestic product (GDP), 15.2 per cent of exports and employs 58.4 per cent of the work force (FICCI, 2004). India tops in the world in milk production (over 91 million tonnes) and livestock (485 million), stands second in the production of fruits and vegetables (150 million tonnes) and third in foodgrains (212 million tonnes). It produces eggs, poultry and fish significantly. Exports of agricultural products comprise about 12 per cent of the Indian exports (FICCI, 2005). Thus, India has a high share of cultivable land, and agriculture sector contributes notably to GDP.

Though some of the products of agriculture and allied sectors account for a substantially high share in the world production, food processing levels are low in India. Processed food is only 2 per cent in the fruits and vegetables sector, 6 per cent for poultry, and 8 per cent for marine products. Buffalo meat accounts for a notable share of 21 per cent and milk has a higher share of 35 per cent in the case of processing. The sector contributes 13 per cent of manufacturing sector's GDP, and employs over 120 lakh persons. Food processing sector has grown at an annual rate of 7.1 per cent during 1993-94 to 2002-03, which is higher than the growth rates of agriculture and GDP, though the potential is very high as only a very small share of food produce is processed. India aims at tripling the size of the food sector with an additional investment of about Rs. 1,100 billion, during 2005-15, with a rise in the quantum of perishables from 6 per cent to 20 per cent, value addition through processing from 20 per cent to 35 per cent, and share in global trade going up from 1.6 per cent to 3 per cent (FICCI, 2005). With growing population and food accounting for a major share of the total private consumer expenditure, food processing sector has a high potential for growth. Growing incomes, changing habits, and rising tendency for eating outside for convenience are positive aspects for the growth of food processing sector. The scope for growth is more in the case of organized sector, as the food processing sector in India is highly fragmented and unorganized sector accounts for a major share.

Supply Chain: Concepts

Supply chain refers to the planning and control of the flow of total material from suppliers to manufacturers to distributors and finally to the end users (Jones and Riley, 1985). Supply chain management (SCM) involves many independent organisations and develops through intra- and inter-organisational integration and co-ordination encompassing the initial stage to the end user. It includes a two-way flow of materials, services and information, and the related managerial and operational tasks. It aims at providing high value to customers with appropriate resource utilisation, and building competitive advantages (Cooper et al, 1997). Logistics is the process of strategically managing the procurement, movement and storage of materials, inventory and marketing through channels of the organisation, to maximise current and future profitability by fulfilling orders with cost-efficiency (Christopher, 1998). The aspects of SCM, which exclude logistics, take a more holistic approach and put emphasis on the network than on a single entity (Hannu Yrjola, 2002). Thus, the key elements involved in the case of SCM are customer value, competitive advantage and integration and coordination, which are elaborated below.

Consumer needs can be met efficiently with Efficient Customer Response (ECR) which is based on efficient assortment, replenishment, promotions and new product introductions. These are dependent upon product range, pricing, and space management (Rose, 1994).

Competitive advantage to companies comes through enhancement of productivity and value. Productivity advantage accrues by achieving the same results with lesser resources than others. Value emanates from customised products or services, responsiveness and reliability, which require innovation and resources (Christopher, 1998). In the case of supply chain approach at global level, three types of economies, viz., economies of scale, economies of scope and economies of speed should be achieved. Economies of scale accrue through volume which enhances bargaining power and lowers unit costs. Economies of scope refers to the benefits from sharing resources in respect of businesses, products and markets. Economies of speed refers to the ability to respond fast to changing customer needs, and improved performance resulting from better sharing of information (Scharlacken et al, 1997).

Coordination comes through partnership in SCM which requires a continued interaction among companies over time, with sharing of information, risks and rewards (Ellram et Krause, 1994).

Supply chains of a firm and an industry differ, though they may have many common goals such as cost minimisation, better processes and customer service. The differences arise in information systems, nature of coordination and authority, among others (Sharman, 1999). There should be global co-ordination and local management in dealing with global and local activities. Global activities require network structuring, development of information systems, international transportation and sourcing decisions. Local activities relate to customer service and management of warehouses and human resources (Christopher, 1998). The importance of managing information flows increases as the complexity of supply chain grows.

Supply chain may also be looked at from the angle of the flow of material and information from the demand side. Demand information includes volume, geographical location, seasonality, and size of orders and deliveries (Miles, 1994). The estimates of suppliers push the material to the supply chain accordingly. Instead of that, there should be recourse to demand chain management as per customer needs (Bruce, 1997). The nature of demand will vary according to the products and supply chains should in turn be related to the specific product groups individually (Fisher, 1997). The SCM should vary according to the individual product or product group, incorporating therein the nature of customers and their demand pattern (Heikkilä, 2000). An integrated approach among the supply chain entities helps forecasting the demand better.

Forrester, through simulation experiments, found that a 10 per cent variation in demand caused a 50 per cent variation for the manufacturer. Such demand variation amplification is called the Forrester effect (Towill, 1991). Distorted information in the supply chains results in demand variations in an amplified manner which is called the Bullwhip effect (Lee et al, 1997). Cyclic customers order in batches, besides maintaining varying inventory control policies, which distort information (Burbidge, 1989) and it is called the Burbidge effect.

The common reasons for demand amplification in supply chains are demand forecast updating, order batching, price fluctuation and shortage gaming. Demand forecast updating relates to the Forrester effect. Order batching relates to the Burbidge effect. Price fluctuation occurs when the products are offered by the up-stream tiers of the supply chain at less than the normal price to the down-stream tiers who tend to build up inventories beyond the required levels. Shortage gaming arises when the down-stream tiers game with orders. In situations of limited supplies and longer lead times, the down-stream tiers tend to increase inventory with bigger orders to which orders from new suppliers get added. The down-stream tier cancels orders when the demand is fulfilled and target inventories are reached. Such interaction makes the demand to the up-stream tiers distorted (Lee et al, 1997; Hannu Yrjola, 2002).

For retailers, the demand management problems are similar to those in supply chains. For perishable products, the SCM requires movement of goods from the first supplier to the retail chain in a few days. When the number of tiers in the supply chain declines, the number of physical operations on the product will be less, which lessens the time needed for the product to move through the supply chain. It reduces the scope for distortion in information (Lee et al, 1997). Larger retailers negotiate for better terms for bigger orders. With better information flow, retailers pressurise suppliers for reduction in lead times and order sizes. It enhances costs by way of lower vehicle loads and a more complex production process (Fernie et al, 2000).. Then, supply chain cost can come down only with better coordination among suppliers and retailers in fulfilling orders in time and maintaining standards.

Crossdocking improves supply chain efficiency. It refers to avoidance of maintaining inventory in a warehouse by sorting the products received therein and reloading and transporting the same to the stores (Daugherty, 1994). In Vendor Managed Inventory (VMI) the supplier assesses real demand as per information of actual sales and inventory levels in the stores and makes the replenishment decisions about the quantities, transportation and timing. It eliminates the process of ordering and purchase decisions and reduces the distortion of information about demand in the supply chain (Lee et al, 1997). The VMI facilitates better resource utilisation in production and transportation, and reduces inventory. The new concepts in SCM are generally based on modern information technology, viz., automatic product identification, electronic data processing, and decision support systems which need not be sophisticated (Waller et al, 1999). The approaches aim at decreasing information distortion in the supply chain by sharing information with co-operation.

Supply Chain in Food Sector

The food supply chain consists of various players. Logistics is the thread which connects the different components of the supply chain. These aspects are discussed below.

Players in the Supply Chain: The players in the food supply chain consist of farmers who sell produce directly to consumers or to traders or manufacturers, without or after storage of the produce; cold storage units; food processing entities; packaging units; wholesalers or distributors; retail chains or other forms of retailers; hotels, restaurants, caterers; and consumers. It also depends upon the support services rendered by logistics providers (warehouses, cold storage units, transport services etc.);

financiers; insurers and government agencies. The consumers may get the products from the farmers directly or through a combination of the different players in the supply chain.

The supply chain may pass through all the stages referred above or only through some of them. Some farmers may sell the produce on the farm itself to intermediaries. Some may keep a part of the produce for consumption and sell the rest. These approaches provide low returns. If the produce is stored and sold when the market is favourable, the returns will be higher. Processing of the produce will add value to it. Some food items may be processed by the farmers themselves while this function is taken up mainly by the manufacturers. The value addition to the processed foods depends upon the volume and quality of the products, level of technology used and the targeted markets. Wholesalers or retailers procure the produce from the farmers or manufacturers. There could be some intermediaries who obtain the produce from the farmers and supply the same in bulk to the manufacturers or retailers. Thus, the value addition to the produce and the returns that accrue to the various players in the supply chain depend upon the approaches followed in dealing with the produce as referred above.

Many small scale growers of fruits, vegetables and flowers in India get less than 20 per cent of the price paid by consumers, while for milk the producer gets about 70 per cent of the final price. Some items such as onion, potato and tomato face wide price fluctuations (The Tribune, 2001). This indicates that the farmers are a weal link in the supply chain.

Storage: The storage capacity of warehouses in India is about 50 million tons, of which Food Corporation of India with 1700 warehouses accounts for 46 per cent, Central Warehousing Corporation 34 per cent and private godowns 20 per cent. There are 3253 cold storage warehouses having a capacity of 8.73 million tons. The storage facilities are not adequate to meet the demand. Also, the farmers may not be able to avail the storage facilities, though available, due to inability to meet the relative costs. Thus, the benefits of storage facilities accrue to the intermediaries significantly.

Cold Chains: A cold chain comprises pre-cooling facilities at the farm level, cold storage units or warehouses, refrigerated carriers, and automatic handling equipment, with trained manpower. These are meant for perishables which include the farm produce and processed food items. The chain helps maintaining the freshness and quality of the products with temperature controls suitable for the individual products. The chain serves all players in the supply chain i.e., from the level of farmers to that of retailers. Computer operated information systems and traceability of products are vital for an effective operation of cold chains. For export items kept in cold chains, the quality and hygiene standards have to be followed as per the regulations of the importing countries. The business of cold chains depends upon monsoons, pests and diseases which influence the crop production and supplies.

About 30 per cent of the fruits and vegetables produced in India are wasted annually because of cold chain deficiencies such as inadequate cold storage capacity and refrigerated containers, lack of cold storage units near the farms and poor transport facilities, among others. This results in unstable prices and unremunerative returns to farmers. There is high scope for cold storage units in India for perishable items such as meat, poultry, dairy, seafood, vegetables, fruits, cereals, oil seeds, honey, ready to eat snacks, convenience foods, etc. Cold chain logistics providers should use appropriate technology in dealing with the various stages of running these chains to save time, cost and efforts. Their operational costs will come down when there is an increase in the volume of business.

Packaging: Packaging of items plays an important role in contributing to value addition of products and boosting up their sales. Consumers get to know of the products well in terms of nutrition value, expiry date and other details from the information provided on the packages. Attractive packages enhance the sale of farm produce, dairy products, fruit juices, and all food products in general. Packaging business has become highly competitive with different modes of packaging in use.

Retail Chains: Some of the retail chains take up the food processing work to save costs and supply the products at lower rates to customers. They also achieve economies of scale by eliminating the intermediaries which increases their returns. This helps the primary suppliers of the food items to get remunerative prices. Bigger retailers will be able to bear the capital costs and recurring expenses associated with in-house processing activities . Some of them enter into long term contracts with big manufacturers to procure branded items at economic prices. Though, in such cases, the price advantage may lie with the retail chains, the manufacturers get the benefit of selling their products in bulk rather than through a multitude of distribution channels.

Quality and Hygiene: In order to maintain high standards regarding quality and hygiene in the case of food products, each player in the supply chain, from the level of farmers to the final stage of delivery to customers, has to ensure compliance of the relative standards. For this standard practices have to adopted. These cover the content, manufacturing process, storage, packaging, distribution methods and shelf life of products. Standards enable players in the supply chain to improve productivity and get higher returns.

Growth in the world food trade and compliance of the World Trade Organization requirements necessitate high standards in regard to quality and hygiene. Consumers are keen to buy hygienic food in view of the vulnerability to diseases with unhygienic food, and the standards have to be stringently followed in the case of exports. The manual operations on food items affect the quality of food items with implications of hygiene. The sector should focus on quality, health and convenience factors for rapid growth.

Corporate Sector: The corporate sector in India and some multi national units have entered the supply chain in the case of food products. These include entities which procure produce from small farmers (e.g. E-choupals of ITC International Division), those taking up processing activities (e.g. ITC, Dabur, MTR,

Godrej, Amul), wholesaling (e.g. Metro A.G.), retailing (e.g. Hindustan Level), and restaurant chains (e.g. Coffee Day, Saravana Bhavan, Sagar, McDonalds, Pizza Hut, and Qwiky's).

Government Policies: The government procures foodgrains under the Public Distribution System with payment of minimum support prices. The benefits that accrue to farmers with such support from the government depends upon the open market prices, which sometimes may be favourable but the farmers may not be in a position to sell in the market due to infrastructure bottlenecks. Farmers seem to prefer government purchases but face bottle necks in terms of maintaining requisite standards for the quality of the produce. The central and state governments have given priority for the establishment of cold chains. As the investments in these chains are capital intensive and the returns accrue over a long period, incentives are provided for attracting relative investments.

To facilitate growth of food processing sector, the Government of India has taken measures such as significant de-licensing, priority sector status for lending, allowing 100 per cent foreign direct investment except for alcoholic beverages and retailing. It provides duty and tax reliefs. Export-oriented units are provided incentives and concessions such as duty free import of raw materials, intermediates and capital goods. (FICCI, 2005). Foreign investment is expected to improve the position of food processing industry in terms of infrastructure, cold storage, application of technology and so on and this is coming forth to a certain extent.

The Government has been encouraging the establishment of Agri-Export Zones (AEZs), with APEDA as the nodal agency, to source raw materials and to add value to them through processing and packaging. These efforts are meant for exports. The AEZs adopt a cluster approach of identifying potential products, geographical region-wise, and integrating the entire process from production to the final level of consumption. The State Governments identify products having export potential (Economic Survey, 2002-03). Sixty AEZs have been sanctioned so far (www.apeda.com). The cluster approach reduces wastages and would facilitate availability of logistical services in time at lower cost.

Corporate units with credentials can sponsor new AEZs or take over the existing ones, partly or fully. State Governments or corporate sector will manage and co-ordinate services which include provision of pre and post harvest treatment and operations, processing, packaging, storage and research & development, among others. Units in AEZ are entitled for all facilities available to exporters under export schemes (Directorate General of Foreign Trade, 2000).

The Minister of State for Commerce stated that five Ministries perform tasks that basically concern AEZs. Agriculture Ministry deals with horticulture zones, Food Processing Ministry food zones, Commerce Ministry AEZs, Health Ministry medicinal plant zones, and Panchayat Raj Ministry rural business hubs. All these zones have to come under one Ministry (Business Line, 2006).

In sum, the government has been taking various steps for the growth of food processing industry in India. However, coordination is warranted among the agencies involved in the process.

Supply Chain Efficiency: Supply chains in the case of food sector vary from product to product in terms of number of players and value addition at the level of each player. The value added depends upon the handling time or the process period and the costs involved. These are influenced by the availability and quality of infrastructure such as roads, human skills, equipment used, and logistics such as storage facilities, transport network and others.

The efficiency of a supply chain depends upon the way in which the relative activities or processes referred above are conducted such that cost, time and efforts are saved and productivity increases. These cover forecasting supply of and demand for products, sourcing of raw materials and intermediates, production, inventory, orders, distribution, and making the products available to customers. A connecting thread in these cases is the level of technology used, technology-backed information systems and logistics which integrate the various players in the supply chain.

The farmers are the weakest link in the food supply chain. Those who sell produce directly to consumers or to traders or manufacturers immediately after its availability from the field get low returns. Any delay made in the sale of the produce, without storage, will lead to deterioration in its quality and there may even be wastage due to exposure to the environment.

Warehouses and cold storage units enable those who use these services to get better returns. Food processing units add value to the produce. Packaging units will boost up the value of the produce depending upon the quality of packaging. Wholesalers or distributors play a key intermediary role in channelising the products to the retailers and hence enhance the utility value of the products.

Retail chains or other forms of retailers provide the crucial connection by serving as an outlet for the consumers to buy the products. Hypermarkets reduce distribution margins by procuring products directly from manufacturers and big distributors and by paying low unit prices to them as they will be keen to have their products sold in the hypermarkets. Their size will enable them to adopt modern method at stage of their operations i.e. from purchase of products to the final stage of delivery to customers. They give intense competition to the domestic retail chains who will per force improve the quality of their products. Offer them at competitive rates and improve operational efficiency and customer service. Domestic chains have also been increasingly opening big retail stores and some of them have opened hypermarkets.

Retail chains are using scanned bar codes and sensors in their stores. They are mainly meant for bulk purchases and those who purchase in small quantities shop at super markets and smaller retail outlets. They operate with efficient supply chains backed up by high technology and information systems and get products of high quality from the national and global markets. Intra- and inter-firm integration, with sharing of information, would improve the efficiency of supply chains which requires agreements for compliance.

Smaller retail stores, offering food items, use low technology and deal with inefficient supply chains containing many distributors who are located nearby. The more the intermediaries on which the retail stores depend, the greater will be the final price as each of them will have their margins loaded into the their selling price. Thus the smaller stores tend to sell products of low quality at higher prices while retail chains sell quality products at competitive prices. The smaller retail stores have their own niche markets, and have still a hold in smaller cities and other centres down the order. However, their operational costs and profit margins will be high per unit of product when compared to retail chains and hypermarkets.

Hotels, restaurants and caterers use significantly the food materials for preparing the eatable items which will have value addition. The efficiency of these units in the supply chain depends upon the size of the units.

Overall, there are inadequacies in terms of warehouses, cold chains, processing activity, quality packing, transportation and distribution network for marketing the products, and technology to process and preserve food items without loss of quality.

Illustrations of Some Supply Chain Players

IAMC: An Integrated Agro Marketing Complex (IAMC) has been set up at Rai, Sonepat district, Haryana, which is the biggest of its kind in North India. It is in an area of over 400 acres (of which food park occupies 150 acres), costing about Rs. 500 crore. It promotes agri-business in the state and will cater to the needs of food- processing and agro-based industries of the neighbouring states. The food park has infrastructural facilities such as agricultural produce handling systems, grading and sorting centres, cold storages, covered platforms, weigh bridge, loading-unloading bays, quality testing, packaging, warehousing, shipment, transportation, auctioning, marketing and direct sales outlets. It has information network and arrangements for meetings and allied needs. It has facilities for fruit and vegetable dehydration, spice processing, solvent extraction, frozen meat, among others. (CII, 2000).

Nestle: Nestle has a chocolates and milk plant at Moga, Haryana. It proposes to add mineral water to its milk business, at a price of Rs 70-75 for 250 ml. targeted at five-star hotel customers. It has introduced premium mineral water brands (Perrier and San Pellegrino) and a mass-segment brand (Pure Life). It has launched Pure Milk which is "ultra heat treated" milk, in select cities. Its Moga plant procures milk from 77,000 farmers. (CII, 2000).

HAFED: The Haryana State Cooperative Supply & Marketing Federation Ltd (Hafed) makes available agricultural inputs at reasonable prices to farmers through Cooperative Marketing Societies (wholesale) and Primary Agricultural Cooperative and Credit societies (Mini Banks) in the State. It procures foodgrains and oil seeds from farmers at minimum support prices or commercial rates. It has created a long chain of godowns and plinths, including cold storages, for scientific storage of foodgrains and to create buffer for storage of fertilizers in the off season so that continuous supply line is maintained when there is demand for such inputs. It has a chain of processing units which include 13 rice mills, two oil seeds processing mills and plants for barley malt, animal feeds and pesticides. It sells consumer products by procuring raw materials such as paddy, oil seeds, tea and other agricultural produce, directly from the farmers. Quality checks are done at the levels of procurement, production and packing to ensures purity, safety and natural taste of the products. (http://hafed.nic.in/prod.htm)

Herbal Garden and Herbarium: Herbal Garden and Herbarium at Jogindernagar, Himachal Pradesh, is manned by the Department of Ayurveda, Himachal government. It grows medicinal plants and supplies to private individuals and pharmaceutical concerns (Dabur, Jandu, Maharishi Ayurved,

Vaidyanath and others). The herbs include three life-saving ones viz., Taxus baccata, the cancer-curing herb costing over Rs 1 lakh per gram, roots of Podophyllum hexandrum (vankakdi) which cures breast cancer, and Aconitum heterophyllum used for curing acute diarrhoea. (CII, 2000).

Conclusion

To conclude, some of the products in the case of agriculture and allied sectors in India account for a significant share in the world production. Yet, food processing levels are low in India. Growing population, food accounting for a major share of the total private consumer expenditure, rising incomes and tendency for eating convenience foods are positive aspects for the growth of food processing sector. Organized sector has a high potential for growth The government has been taking positive steps in this regard. However, there are inadequacies in respect of warehouses, cold chains, processing activity, quality packing, transportation, marketing and technology. When these deficiencies are attended on a priority basis, the efficiency of the players in the supply chain will go up significantly.

References

Bruce, H. 1997, "Demand Chain Management – The Future Paradigm for the 21st Century", APICS International conference proceedings, pp. 276-278.

Burbidge J.L. 1989, "Production flow analysis – for planning group technology", Clarendon Press, Oxford.

Business Line, 2006, Agri export zones may have single investment window, New Delhi, April 11.

Christopher, M. 1998, "Logistics and supply chain management – Strategies for reducing cost and improving service", Pitman publishing.

Confederation of Indian Industry (CII), 2000, Conference on Agri-infrastructure, "Impact of globalisation on Indian agriculture". held at Chandigarh on December 4.

Cooper, M., Lambert, D. and Pagh, J. 1997, "Supply Chain Management: more than a new name for logistics", International Journal of Logistics Management, Vol. 8, Iss. 1, pp. 1-13

Daugherty, P. 1994, "Strategic Information Linkage" In: Robertson, J. & Copacino, W. "The Logistics Handbook", The Free Press, New York, 1994

Directorate General of Foreign Trade, 2000, Government of India, http://164.100.9.245/exim/2000/agrizone.htm

Ellram, L. and Krause, D. 1994, "Supplier Partnerships in Manufacturing Versus Non-Manufacturing Firms", The International Journal of Logistics Management, Vol. 5, No. 1, pp. 43-53

Fernie, J. Pfab, F. and Marchant, C. 2000, "Retail Grocery Logistics in the UK", The International Journal of Logistics Management, Vol. 11, No. 2, pp. 83-90

Fisher, M. 1997, "What is the right supply chain for your product?"; Harvard Business Review, March-April, pp.105-116

Hannu Yrjola, 2002, Supply Chain Considerations for Electronic Grocery Shopping, Dissertation for the degree of Doctor of Science in Technology, Helsinki University of Technology, Finland.

Heikkilä, J. 2000, "Developing Demand Chain Management: Case Study of the Fast Growing Cellular Networks Industry" Doctor's Thesis, Act Polytechnica Scandinavia, Espoo.

Jones, T. and Riley, D. 1985, "Using inventory for competitive advantage through Supply Chain Management", International Journal of Physical Distribution and Material Management, Vol. 15, No.5, pp. 16-26

Lee, H.L., Padmanabhan, V., and Whang, S. 1997, "The Bullwhip Effect in Supply Chains", Sloan Management Review, Spring.

Miles, R. 1994, "Supplying the demand chain", APICS International conference proceedings, pp. 437-440

Rose, J. 1994, "Spinning the ECR Wheel in Europe", European Retail Digest, Autumn, pp. 4-8

Scharlaken, J. and Harland, D. 1997, "Global Supply Chain Planning: Synchronizing Operations and Logistics with the Pulse of the International

Marketplace", APICS International conference proceedings, pp. 211-217.

Sharman, G. 1999, "Supply Chain Management – challenges for supply chains of the future", Presentation at Helsinki University of Technology, Dec. 2

Towill, D. 1991, "Supply Chain Dynamics", University of Wales, College of Cardiff.

US Foreign Commercial Service (USFCS) and US Department of State (USDS), 2006. Doing Business In India: A Country Commercial Guide for U.S. Companies.

Waller, M. Johnson, M.E. and Davis, T. 1999, "Vendor-managed inventory in the retail supply chain", Journal of Business Logistics, Vol. 20, No. 1, pp. 183-203.

9

E-Payments Enabling E-Financial Supply Chain

Shital Jhunjhunwala

Introduction

The normal operating cycle of most organizations consists of acquiring raw material & other resources, producing the good or service and selling the final output. This link from supplier to final customer (supply chain) has been given substantial importance in the last few years with a view to reduce inventory cost, ensure smooth production process and minimize delivery time to customers. The emphasis on (Physical) Supply Chain Management along with enhanced technological advancement has shown major improvements in material movement. There is another side to the coin. Money has to be collected from the customers and payment has to be made to suppliers of goods and services. This is the financial supply chain management. It consists of two parts. From the buyers prospective this involves purchase-to-pay cycle. From the seller, it is the order to cash cycle. Financial supply chain management is about enabling fast and smooth movement of cash.

Research by Killer and associates suggests that more than $260 billion of Global 2000 companies are blocked in financial supply chain. Better management of the financial supply chain could lead to about saving 10 million in each of these companies by reducing non-productive working capital.

Financial Supply Management in the broader sense covers the following:

- Optimum level of cash to be maintained.
- Efficient collection of receivables.
- Suitable disbursement procedures.

- Strategy for Investing surplus and meeting deficit

In a conservative narrow sense it is limited to speeding up cash received and slowing down cash payments. Intense competition culminating into high pressures on margins has necessitated the need to optimize financial supply chain. Traditional two tools were very popular for reducing receivables float - The Lock Box System & Concentration banking

E-Financial Supply Chain

If globalization means material can be bought and services outsourced from the cheapest source in the world and goods and services can be sold in every nick and corner of the world it also means that money must flow across the globe in the fasted and most efficient manner. Cross border movement of money has increased complexity and risks associated with financial supply chain. Technology has come to our aid once again. E-financial supply is slowly making inroads. E- invoicing and e-payments which till early nineties were considered extremely risky is now gaining acceptance worldwide. Governments of different countries are also taking initiative to provide necessary regulations. According to Alenka Grealish, (Scaling the e-Financial Supply Chain Mountain) while in 2003 only 30 per cent of the top 1000 North American companies were using e-financial supply chain by 2010 about 68 per cent would do so.

ERP software packages like SAP and Oracle have made e-documentation (e-ordering, e-invoicing, etc) not only possible but very effective and economical. What is still in the nascent stages is e-Payments, the most critical aspect of e-Financial Supply Chain management.

E-Payments

E-payment is about automating payment transactions through online mechanism. Electronically-based payment systems have been in operation since the 1960s and have been expanding rapidly as well as growing in complexity. However, in most of the major industrialized countries, an inverse relationship exists between the volume and the number of transactions handled electronically. 'Typically, of business payments around 85-90 per cent or more of monetary value will be processed electronically, while less than 5-10 per cent of the total number of payment transactions will be handled in this way.'[2] Different E-payment methods are available. They are classified into two categories – Account based systems & Electronic Currency Systems.

Account-based Systems

Post-Paid Tokens: Credit Cards: Credit cards have been in use for a very long time and have a large and well established network of users and merchants providing wide spread usage in number of transactions. Unlike offline payment, in online payment physical card is not required. The card number has to be keyed in along with some additional verification and security codes.

Pre-Paid Tokens: Debit Cards: These are similar to credit cards, but payments are directly withdrawn from the bank account and not from an intermediary account.

Mediating Services: To use this service one has to register using a credit card or bank account as the source of payment.

Pay – Pal is a popular US based mediating service. It is a web-based platform for electronic payment processing for online vendors, auction sites and other corporate users. The buyer only needs to know recipients e-mail address, which is verified and linked to a pay pal account. Payment is debited from the users pay pal account.

Internet Banking: Internet banking refers to a system that enables bank customers to access accounts and banking services through a personal computer, mobile or other intelligent device. Two popular kinds of internet facilities are E-cheque & Electronic bill presentation & payment.

E-cheque: An electronic version or representation of a paper cheque, e-cheque allows account holders to pay funds to other account holders within the network. It consists of an electronic payment instruction that is digitally signed using Public/Private

Key cryptographic techniques. The account holder writes an e-check using a computer or other type of electronic device and transmits the e-check to the payee electronically. The payee deposits the e-check, receives credit, and the payee's bank clears the e-cheque to the paying bank. The paying bank validates the e-cheque and then charges the cheque writer's account for the check.

Electronic Bill Presentation and Payment: Electronic Bill Payment is a service that allows you to view as well as pay your bills using Net Banking, Mobile Banking, ATM and Phone Banking services.

Virtual Banks: Virtual Banks require the user to open an account similar to a traditional brick and mortar bank. The account is operated only through an e-mail account. Payments can be sent and received online. The world's first fully functional virtual bank was the "Security First Network Bank" (SFNB). Based at Atlanta, Georgia, USA it began operations on October 18, 1995.

Mobile Payment: The wireless device and its network can be used to make electronic payments. Some options include:

Pay-by-Phone Systems require to call financial institution with instructions to pay certain bills or to transfer funds between accounts. An agreement with the institution to make such transfers is required.

M-banking: GSM/SMS systems are used for contacting and effecting payments with the bank as alternatives to PC-based systems.

Bank-based Mobile Mediation Services: Payments from one GSM mobile to other GSM phones are possible using a Paybox method. The client enters the mobile number together with the amount to be paid and confirmation takes place with a personal Paybox PIN. An automatic reply from Paybox acknowledges the payment. The amount is debited from the customers bank account.

Telephone Bills can also be used to make payments. Ring tones or games are downloaded and the amount is charged in the telephone bill.

Electronic Currency Systems

Electronic Money: Electronic money also known as electronic cash, electronic curiency, digital currency, digital money, scrip or digital cash refers to money which is exchanged only electronically, through the use of computer networks, the internet and digital stored value systems. Electronic Funds Transfer (EFT) and direct deposit are examples of electronic money.

Electronic money means monetary value as represented by a claim on the issuer which is:

1. stored on an electronic device;
2. issued on receipt of funds of an amount not less in value than the monetary value issued;
3. accepted as means of payment by undertakings other than the issuer.

Electronic Fund Transfer (EFT) - Any transfer of funds, other than a transaction originated by check, draft, or similar paper instrument, which is initiated through an electronic terminal, telephone instrument, or computer or magnetic tape to authorize a financial institution to debit or credit an account.

Singapore has a very successful electronic money implementation for its public transportation system (commuter trains, bus, etc), The electronic money, known as EZ-Link by most Singaporeans, is a card the size of an ordinary credit card; it has a smart chip plus a wireless communication module. Passengers just need to tap the EZ-Link when they board the bus and tap the card again when they alight; the bus fare system automatically deducts the calculated bus fare from the EZ-Link value. Recently, McDonalds is setting up EZ-Link payment infrastructure at their fast-food branches all over Singapore's main island. It is believed that in the near future EZ-Link will gain more acceptance as a convenient electronic money solution in Singapore.

E-Purse - Smart Cards: E-Purse holds electronic monetary value on a computer chip on a card, usually smart card. It records the value of each transaction on the card and the monetary value is deducted from the computer chip on the card. They are used for small amounts and rely on specialized hardware and dedicated smartcard readers for authentication.

Virtual Debit Cards: These are pre-paid debit cards that can be re-charged via electronic money systems including e-gold, e-Bullion or via a wire transfer. This system has the advantage of being anonymous since people without bank accounts can use it and more secure since the uses can never be debited more than the value of his prepaid card.

E-Wallets: e-wallets can be to make small online or offline payments . Whenever a purchase is made, the e-wallet balance in the online account decreases by that amount. E-wallets may work by using some form of stored value or by automatically accessing an account you've set up through a computer system connected to your credit or debit card account.

Credit card and debit cards are the most popular methods of payment and are used mainly for micro payments. Internet banking is being increasingly used as an alternate payment mechanism for payment to suppliers. While in Finland credit card, debit card and internet banking is being used almost equally by e-commerce web sites, websites in France, Germany, Italy , Austria and Spain do not use internet banking.

E- Payment Mechanism

The payment mechanisms of three popular e-payment options are described below.

Using a Credit Card: The payment processing arena is like an onion. You just keep peeling back the layers and find that there is more, says Colleene Isaacs, vice president of business services for Segue Systems, a leading provider of credit card clearing services. The biggest thing is understanding that there's more than one party involved, and allowing yourself time.

The participants and elements involved in processing payments are

Acquiring Bank: In the online payment processing world, an acquiring bank provides Internet merchant accounts. A merchant must open an Internet merchant account with an acquiring bank to enable online credit card authorization and payment processing. Examples of acquiring banks include Merchant e-Solutions and most major banks.

Authorization: The process by which a customer's credit card is verified as active and that they have the credit available to make a transaction. In the online payment processing world, an authorization also verifies that the billing information the customer has provided matches up with the information on record with their credit card company.

Credit Card Association: A financial institution that provides credit card services that are branded and distributed by customer issuing banks. Examples include Visa® and MasterCard®

Customer: The holder of the payment instrument—such as a credit card, debit card, or electronic check.

Customer Issuing Bank: A financial institution that provides a customer with a credit card or other payment instrument. Examples include Citibank and Suntrust. During a purchase, the customer issuing bank verifies that the payment information submitted to the merchant is valid and that the customer has the funds or credit limit to make the proposed purchase.

Internet Merchant Account: A special account with an acquiring bank that allows the merchant to accept credit cards over the Internet. The merchant typically pays a processing fee for each transaction processed, also known as the discount rate. A merchant applies for an Internet merchant account in a process similar to applying for a commercial loan. The fees charged by the acquiring bank will vary.

Merchant: Someone who owns a company that sells products or services.

Payment Gateway: A service that provides connectivity among merchants, customers, and financial networks to process authorizations and payments. The service is usually operated by a third-party provider such as VeriSign.

Processor: A large data center that processes credit card transactions and settles funds to merchants. The processor is connected to a merchant's site on behalf of an acquiring bank via a payment gateway.

Settlement: The process by which transactions with authorization codes are sent to the processor for payment to the merchant. Settlement is a sort of electronic bookkeeping procedure that causes all funds from captured transactions to be routed to the merchant's acquiring bank for deposit.

Steps involved in making payment using a credit card are:

- A customer decides to make a purchase on a merchant's Web site, proceeds to checkout, and inputs credit card information.
- The merchant's Web site receives customer information and sends transaction information to the payment gateway.
- The payment gateway routes information to the processor.
- The processor sends information to the issuing bank of the customer's credit card.
- The issuing bank sends the transaction result (authorization or decline) to the processor.
- The processor routes the transaction result to the payment gateway.
- The payment gateway passes result information to the merchant.
- The merchant accepts or rejects the transaction and ships goods if necessary.
- The settlement process transfers authorized funds for a transaction from the customer's bank account to the merchant's bank account"

Using a Pay Pal Account

The players in this include customer, Internet Merchant Account and Payment Gateway.

1. The customer inputs credit card information on the Online Store.
2. The Payment Gateway encrypts data and securely sends it to the Internet Merchant Account.
3. The transaction is reviewed for authorization.

4. The result is encrypted and sent back through the payment gateway.
5. The seller get the results and decide whether or not to fulfill the order

Impediments to E- Payments

The transformation of the Internet from a huge virtual community into a huge virtual economy may herald the age of electronic money - and with it, headaches for traditional banks and regulators.

Efficiency and convenience appear to be the primary motive for use of e-payments. Speed and flexibility of the system is also a key attraction. It is particularly well suited for international transactions where traditional payment mechanisms take long and are likely to involve additional transaction and conversion costs.

However the major issue preventing its universal acceptance is security concerns. In case of any security breach, the users, issuers or the banks may suffer loss. Generally, the secured cards come with built-in security features such as encryption, prescriptions of maximum monetary limits, tamper resistant, etc. Putting limits on the value for individual transactions, use of a PIN for authorizing loading and/or transfer instructions enhances the security features.

Cross border transactions necessitate clear laws regarding clearing and settlement arrangements associated with the e-money products, question of finality of settlement, issues related to bankruptcy of the issuer of the card in case of payments already made or transactions in the pipeline, etc. Lack of universally applicable laws has been a major hindrance to wider use of e-payments.

Initially starting an online payment system could be costly, time taking and cumbersome. Navigating through the website to make a payment can be difficult. The biggest hurdle in the use of online payment mechanisms is confidence in ability to use and trust in the system.

Conclusion

Cross border transactions, decreasing cost of technology, speed of transaction and a 24 hour 365 day facility has lead to development of e-financial supply chain. Though e - financial supply chain has been growing it needs to accelerate at a much faster pace to keep up with global business demands. Comprehensive laws and mitigation of risk of fraud would enhance its use and acceptance. Proper financial supply chain management using e-payment mechanisms can reduce cost of working capital and improve supplier relationship management by providing speedy payments.

References

Directorate For Science, Technology And Industry Committee For Information, Computer And Communications Policy Working Party, On The Information Economy, Online Payment Systems For E-Commerce , April 18, 2006. DSTI/ICCP/IE(2004)18/FINAL.

Electronic Commerce and the Banking Industry: The Requirement and Opportunities for New Payment Systems Using the Internet, Andreas Crede, http://jcmc.indiana.edu/vol1/issue3/crede.html.

E-purse, Sharad Kumar, Surjit Arvind, BTC News, http://rbi.org.in/scripts/BTCDisplay.aspx?pg=BTCNews.html.

Global Supply Chain Management: Front and Center for Treasurers, Paul Simon, JP Morgan.

Scaling the e-Financial Supply Chain Mountain: A Review of Solution Providers Facilitating the Ascent , Report Published by Celent.

10

Radio Frequency Identification (RFID): Redefining the Global Pharma Value Chain

Sudeep Kumar Mandhania

Introduction

Drug counterfeiting is causing major headaches in the pharma industry, with the business of selling fake drugs burgeoning across the globe. The rise in the number of counterfeit drug cases in the US is a case in point. Apart from this, pharmaceutical markets absorb billions of dollars in product returns each year caused by overstocked or outdated products. Faced with some high profile recalls in recent years, the industry is seeking ways to better monitor the international drug supply from "manufacture to medicine cabinet." The numbers are alarming and the stakes couldn't be higher for consumers, pharmaceutical manufacturers, distributors and retailers.

The pharmaceutical industry is looking to RFID as a primary way of solving these problems. RFID technology's ability to ensure the validity of data in the pharmaceutical industry is providing many new opportunities for reducing costs, while improving product quality and drug safety. The Food and Drug Administration (FDA)'s main interest in RFID is as a technology that can keep the drug supply safe and secure. According to the agency, RFID provides the most promising approach for reliably tracking, tracing and authenticating pharmaceutical products, through the use of tags which are both readable and writable; and hence it is recommending widespread use of RFID in the pharmaceutical supply chain at the item level by 2007.

Emerging Role of RFID in Pharma: In addition to anti-counterfeiting, RFID benefits include improved inventory management through the reduction of out-of-stock items and safety stock, a decrease in shrinkage and diversion, and faster, more efficient product recalls. The benefits of RFID go well beyond the fight against counterfeit drugs. The pharmaceutical industry relies upon the integrity of many forms of data throughout the process of drug trials, manufacturing, distribution and retail sale. RFID's ability to uniquely identify each item (often called mass serialization), and securely capture data without line-of-sight throughout the supply chain offers many benefits to the pharmaceutical industry, including:

Operational Efficiency: Expired or damaged products that are either returned or expire in warehouses are the bane of pharmaceutical distributors. At the item level, RFID can provide 100 percent visibility of inventory no matter where it is in the supply chain, making it easier and quicker to move goods to the right place within the channel. The technology can improve productivity in shipping and receiving, reduce touch labor, increase the assurance of shipping and dispensing accuracy, and expand product availability at the retail store, thus reducing customer complaints and charge backs. Having a more accountable supply chain at every point using RFID can dramatically reduce inventory losses and write-offs due to shrinkage.

Brand Protection: Brand protection is paramount for drug manufacturers. A single product-tampering incident can wreak long-term havoc on a company's reputation. It can take months, if not years, for a compromised product to recover market share, requiring significant investments in marketing and public relations to do so. Because RFID tracks the pedigree of each product, it significantly reduces the chances of tampering, thereby adding a valuable protective layer. The technology can positively identify if returns were originally shipped from a particular manufacturer and at what price.

Patient Safety and Regulatory Requirements: The Prescription Drug Marketing Act (PDMA), effective1988, was enacted amid growing concerns of prescription drug diversion and counterfeiting. In pharmaceutical counterfeiting, supply chain is the weakest link. Unlike other industries, product isn't necessarily shipped straight from the manufacturer to the customer. Instead, it goes through primary and sometimes secondary wholesalers to get to the customer. Pharmaceuticals may be transferred up to 10 times before they get to the shelf. This makes goods harder to track and easier to divert. Therefore, PDMA requires that drug wholesalers that are not manufacturers or authorized distributors of a drug must provide a pedigree for every prescription drug they distribute.

For example, before drugs are purchased, Florida requires pedigrees with signatures verifying the name, address and date of all prior sales tracing back to the manufacturer. Paper process is ineffective because it does not prevent counterfeit drugs entering the healthcare system, only assists in investigation and prosecution. It is also cost-prohibitive because it adds a manual process to the millions of transactions that are already time-sensitive. RFID facilitates electronic management and tracking of drug pedigrees, popularly known as e-pedigree. RFID systems include silicon tags containing an electronic product code (EPC), antennas, tag readers and writers at every stage in the supply chain, and information systems. At their simplest, RFID tags emit radio signals that are read by other devices and interpreted as EPCs that identifies a specific item, such as a pallet, a case or even an individual product within a case. Information may include the manufacturer, the product and a serial number. Other information can be added, such as time and date stamps and temperature sensors.

Expiration Management and Product Recalls: In addition to anti-counterfeiting, RFID can track lot and expiration dates, improving expiration management. By zeroing in on individual items and capturing manufacturing data, such as lot number and location information, RFID can significantly reduce the time spent identifying products targeted for recall as well as reducing the likelihood of a mass market recall of branded products. For instance, in the past, a number of brands suffered from mass market recalls as there were no systems in place to uniquely identify the defective products and their location. Since RFID can facilitate unique identification and location of the products, companies need not resort to panic mass recalls.

Challenges to Widespread Adoption of RFID

The appeal of RFID and EPC technology is the ability to uniquely identify individual products throughout the supply chain and create seamless visibility. However, there are concerns among pharmaceutical manufacturers and distributors regarding its implementation and benefits, leading to its delayed adoption in the industry. Some of the biggest hurdles impacting the adoption of RFID include:

Cost and Value Sharing: The biggest obstacle to the spread of RFID is not the cost of its tags (whether it is 20 or 25 US cents) but the cost of the infrastructure it requires, making it unattractive for distributors who usually have tiny profit margins. Yet manufacturers are slowly changing this by making non-adoption a liability issue. All the manufacturer has to do is put a tag on the drug's packaging and therefore has to worry only about the cost of the tag. However, if a mistake occurs, and an RFID tag was available but not read, then the jury in a court takes note when a manufacturer points the finger to the distributor. As the cost of tags is expected to further decrease over time, the biggest issue in RFID implementation now appears to be who pays for adoption throughout the supply chain.

Safety of Technology: Researchers warn that the security breaches that RFID deployers dread most, like malware, worms, and viruses, are right around the corner. Since the technology is still too expensive for mass implementation across the entire drug supply chain, so too much emphasis has been paid to making RFID affordable while neglecting safety. Conventional wisdom suggests that computer viruses cannot spread through RFID tags because their chips have too little memory. But this perception exists simply because RFID exploits have not yet appeared "in the wild", and that RFID installations have a number of characteristics, such as lots of source code and generic protocols and facilities, that make them outstanding candidates for exploitation by malware.

Available Alternative Technologies: Companies that are primarily concerned and focused on combating drug counterfeiting have resorted to alternate authentication technologies. These include measures such as color shifting inks, holograms, fingerprints, taggants, chemical markers embedded in a drug or its label, laser marking technology designed to securely mark transparent materials like glass bottles and vials, and so on. However, it is difficult for manufacturers to use these technologies on a continued basis as counterfeiters adapt rapidly to any particular measure and also because the most effective measures differ by product causing the most effective use of authentication technology to vary by drug product over time. Once these manufacturers take cognizance of the numerous applications and benefits of RFID, it would be a matter of time as they switch over to RFID.

Legislation and Government Policy: Pharmaceutical manufacturers are not clear with the regulatory compliance and legal implications attached to RFID. Either the FDA or the manufacturers need to develop a standard for information, where it will be checked, how detailed the information will be and who carries the cost of implementation. The FDA, however, plans to wait until there is significant market experience to propose policies or regulatory requirements relating to the use of RFID systems. It had designated 2004 as the timeframe in which feasibility studies were to be conducted, with implementation on some products in 2005. By the close of 2007, all pallets and cases, and most packages should be labeled with RFID tags. Because states license and regulate wholesale drug distributors, they have an important role in regulating the drug distribution supply chain and RFID adoption across the drug chain.

Industry Perceptions and Mindset: When RFID was introduced, pharmaceutical manufacturers viewed it as another product ID code system like barcode. They looked at processes where barcodes were being used and tried to replace them with RFID. However, companies need to take a holistic view of the technology and consider the entire basket of applications and benefits it offers, rather than a mere replacement of an existing system. RFID has several advantages over bar codes. Storage of re-programmable data on a silicon chip that can be accessed through a wireless interface is a much more robust solution for automatic identification systems. With RFID, the radio signals are used to both power silicon chips as well as transmit data to and from them. Data can be read from passive, battery-less RFID chips in a range of distances from several inches to up to 30 feet (9 meters).

Before any real-world utilization of RFID capabilities can occur, however, there is an array of unresolved issues involving technology choice, RFID system capabilities, data sharing and privacy concerns that the industry stakeholders must consider and resolve.

- **Technology Choice:** What will be the wireless spectrum, bandwidth capacity, range of operations, and interference protection thresholds that best meet the anticipated scope of uses, data capacity, reliability and error rates for RFID systems?
- **RFID System Capabilities:** Will companies have individual RFID systems or will they rely solely on a shared interoperable user network? Will companies use multiple versions of RFID tags (or multimode tags) for product and/or store packaging levels? In addition, beyond simple product identification and authentication, can the technology be used to identify and protect against product diversion and smuggling?
- **Data Sharing:** What restrictions will be imposed on the sharing of data among the various supply chain participants? How will intellectual property interests in product data recorded on RFID tags be protected?
- **Privacy Concerns:** How will the industry address consumer

privacy issues, which quickly become more problematic depending on whether RFID tags are used on containers provided to consumers?

The next biggest barrier or challenge is the integration of RFID with legacy systems like barcodes and other automatic identification systems. The challenge also includes integration with management systems like enterprise resource planning (ERP) solutions, warehouse management systems (WMS), and fleet management systems. The lack of clearly defined standards, low knowledge and understanding of RFID among employees, competing business priorities, availability of suppliers, and technical limitations of RFID are other barriers that may have caused companies to ease into their RFID investments. Many of these RFID hurdles must be resolved at the industry rather than the company level. Many companies are focusing on the efforts within their own four walls, but collaboration with trading partners drives the greatest savings when it comes to RFID.

Conclusion

The year 2005 has seen development of strong business cases for RFID adoption, the only impediment in achieving a faster return on investment being high tag prices. Hence, it is pivotal for the industry to work towards lower tag prices. The mid 1980's and early 1990's period witnessed usage of tags in the automotive manufacturing industry. However tags were priced at over $25 per piece. Since then, tag prices have come down and were available for as low as 20 cents per tag in 2005. With mandates and regulatory authority directives driving the market, industry participants expect that higher volume orders for tags would lead to further reduction in prices of tags to 5 cents per tag or lower.

The promise of a safer, more accountable and highly efficient supply chain combined with FDA support for the technology is driving interest and demand for RFID in the pharmaceutical industry. Manufacturers, distributors and retailers are poised to take advantage of the technology's many benefits and are in the midst of conducting pilots to better understand and apply the technology to their businesses. An additional growth factor is the compliance with mandates from customers and trading partners. However, more and more organizations are looking to implement RFID solutions for business process improvement reasons that go beyond simple compliance. The participation of the US FDA through its directives regarding use of RFID is also supporting the growth in interest in RFID for the pharmaceutical and healthcare markets.

However, it is important to note that RFID is not a panacea to curb counterfeits from entering the market. Even if all necessary action is taken to secure the supply chain from counterfeits, there are hundreds of thousands of uncertified sources from which medicinal products are acquired, particularly through internet and mail order sales, which are impossible to control and pose the greatest risk for fake drugs entering the market. Implementing a series of strategies to improve the supply chain, including carefully selecting suppliers, fully training their staff in good distribution practices (GDP), streamlining recall procedures and increasing transparency would go a long way in complimenting RFID's role in maintaining supply chain integrity.

While top pharmaceutical companies have embarked on their RFID journey, others sitting on the fence are waiting for them to solve the problems of implementation and cost before they join the bandwagon.

References

Combating Counterfeit Drugs: A Report of the Food and Drug Administration (Feb 2004).

Drug Diversion & Counterfeiting: Emerging Role of RFID" – George Wheeler (Sep 2004).

How Pharma is Tightening its Supply Chain to Avoid Counterfeiting – Gail Dutton, World Trade Magazine (Nov 2004 issue)

Item Level Visibility in the Pharmaceutical Supply Chain: A Comparison of HF and UHF RFID Technologies" - Philips Semiconductors, TAGSYS and Texas Instruments Inc. (Jul 2004).

RFID: Cure for Counterfeit Drugs? – Samuel Greengard, RFID Journal (Oct 2003)

11

Protein Biosynthesis Based Bio-Mimetic Framework of Supply Chain Management

C.N. Sundaresan and N. Sivakumar

Introduction

Nature is the best teacher (Baba, 2000). Several processes and systems involved in business and industry are seen in nature as well. For example:

- Nature produces a plethora of products. Bees collect nectar from flowers and produce honey.
- Nature has evolved highly sophisticated information networks. The brain has millions of neurons, which are interconnected to send and receive information.
- Nature is a good marketer too. Flowers and fruits advertise their presence through striking colours, wonderful smells, shapes and tastes.
- Nature has its own maintenance and repair systems. Through biological succession, older generations of species are replaced with newer and more efficient generations.
- Nature has a technology system par excellence. It uses most efficient techniques to minimise cost and maximise value - with minimum investment and maximum dividend. The hibernation process of both plants and animals in the Tundra forests during winter is a great example of optimisation technique.

Nature also transports, stores, distributes and cleans up its produce. The food produced in the leaves is distributed to all parts of a plant. Animals and insects store their food effectively. The food chain in nature is a highly evolved system by which primary producers (plants) supply food for secondary producers (animals), which in turn supplies tertiary producers. Nature has evolved scavengers (micro organisms), which ultimately clean up the system and recycle all the products produced biologically. In short nature is an extremely efficient supply chain. This paper aims to understand supply chain management from the protein biosynthetic process that takes place efficiently in every cell.

Bio-mimetics in Industry

Bio-mimetics is the method of imitating the processes and techniques used by nature to achieve efficiency, effectiveness and sustainability (Benyus, 1997). The current wave of corporate environmentalism, forced by the threat of global climate change, has lead to a new role for companies. Corporates are being forced to move beyond compliance with regulations to a leadership stance in the green, energy efficient economy of the future. Emulating the patterns and designs and strategies in plants, animals, and ecosystems, is an effective way for corporations to become cleaner, leaner, and more consistently innovative (Bernstein, 2006). This has led to developing bio-mimetic approaches to management functions.

There have been several successful applications of bio-mimetics in the production of a wide variety of products. The following are some well-known applications (Benyus, 1997; Lieckfeld, 1993; Neinhuis and Barthlott, 1997):

- Ceramic tiles have been manufactured by emulating the self-assembly of abalone shells.
- Adhesive tapes have been produced patterned after geckos' (a type of lizard) feet.
- Computer chips have been designed to assemble themselves through crystallization, just as microscopic algae called diatoms assemble their shells.
- Neural networks software has been created based on immune systems in living beings.
- Genetic algorithms have been designed based on the natural selection process to optimise code for designs.
- Fresh water production systems have been developed based

on the reverse osmosis processes employed by the mangrove forests, a salt-water plant that grows along the coastlines of tropical areas

- Self- cleaning facade paint has been produced based on the water- and dust-repellent properties of the lotus leaf.

These successful applications have led to a new wave of bio-mimetics in industry and management.

Literature Review

Bio-mimetics research related to business and industry is of recent origin. McKelvey and Aldrich (1983) have used biological metaphors in the study of organizations. Schwefel and Manner (1990) and Manner and Manderick (1992) have evolved 'heuristics from nature', utilizing analogies from natural or social systems to solve optimisation problems. Colorni et.al (1996) describe the main characters of heuristics derived from nature taking inspiration from physics, biology, and social sciences. The authors deal with the following problems:

- Genetic algorithms with timetable problems.
- Simulated annealing with dial-a-ride problems.
- Sampling and clustering with communication spanning tree problems.
- Tabu search with job-shop-scheduling problems.
- Neural nets with location problems.
- Ant system with travelling salesman and quadratic assignment problems.

A large part of research literature has focussed on bio-mimetics in relation to production processes and systems. Demeester et.al (2003) have researched on what the biological cell can teach about the future of manufacturing. In biological cells, all products and machines are built from a small set of common building blocks that circulate in local recycling loops. Based on this premise the authors explain the cell metabolism as a manufacturing system and show its efficiency in the form of using pull-systems to avoid overproduction, minimising work in process by using bottlenecks to control the release rate, using excess capacity to simplify control, and managing quality at the source. The authors develop an 'organic production system' involving local production, standard components, templates and local closed recycling loops which enhance the efficiency of the production system.

Miller and Miller (1993) specifically study the protein synthetic process in a cell as a production process. They explain this process as the most fundamental of all production processes, which range from the cell level to ultimately the supra-national level. Simsek and Albayrak (2004) have used the functions in a cell to describe production processes in a factory. Terming the process as the 'living factory' model the authors describe holonic manufacturing in terms of nucleus holons, endoplasmic reticulum holons, ribosome holons and Golgi holons named after different parts of the cell for more efficient manufacturing. Similarly, Akturk and Turkcan (2000) have developed a cellular manufacturing design, while Okino (1993) and Ueda (1992) have developed a 'bionic manufacturing system'. Further, Bozinovski et.al (2000) have discussed about 'bio-mimetic autonomous factories' and Vaario (1996) has explained about 'self organisation in manufacturing systems'.

Another research area has been studying successful applications for bio-mimetics in industry. Benyus (1997), Lieckfeld (1993) and Neinhuis and Barthlott (1997) have studied these applications related to production of a wide variety of successful products.

From the technology perspective, Mendez (2002) suggests the use of 'carpe technology', which involves sharing of information and collaboration of several disciplines in technology development. According to the author using technology that blends the knowledge from several disciplines has led to DNA based evolution leading to smarter drugs, nano-technology implants and genetics based correction and optimisation techniques.

Research has also been done to provide a systems perspective to bio-mimetics. Mchugh et.al (1995) have expanded the concept of holons to encompass all components of an enterprise system, leading to a 'holonic-enterprise'. A holonic business enterprise consists of a network of companies (holons), each offering a different core competence that has integrated its operations to serve customers in ways that would have been difficult for each individual company. The authors argue that a holonic enterprise offers many advantages. These include leverage through synergy, speed in decision making and action, flexibility in capacity and product capability, shared risk, faster growth and increased profits, customer capture, reduced requirements for capital, quick recognition and response to failure, and increased ability to deal with inevitable changes in market conditions.

Bio-mimetics related to supply chain management however, has received very scant research attention. Passing reference of the topic has been made in Aurifeille and Deissenberg, (1998), Mendez (2002) and Simsek and Albayrak (2004). The current paper therefore represents indicative research and concentrates on developing a framework for supply chain management through bio-mimetics, especially the protein biosynthetic process.

Overview of the Protein Biosynthetic Process

Proteins are the most dynamic and varied class of bio-molecules. Proteins are polypeptide chains consisting of amino acids. The uniqueness of each cell type is due almost entirely to the proteins it produces. Because of their strategic importance in the cellular economy, protein biosynthesis is a regulated process. Protein biosynthesis is an extra ordinarily complex process in which genetic information encoded in the nucleic acids is translated into the primary structure of proteins. Protein biosynthesis is mediated by the coordinated interplay of more than a hundred macromolecules.

Proteins are biosynthesised based on a set process, as follows (Elliot and Elliot, 2001):

- The DNA in every cell chromosome transcripts and creates an mRNA (messenger RNA) using freely available nucleotide bases.

- The mRNA moves to the ribosome in the cell, where it pairs with a tRNA (transfer RNA). The nucleotide bases on the mRNA and tRNA are recognised in triplets called as codons. The genetic code consists of 64 codons; 61 codons represent 20 different amino acids and three represent 'stop codons'.
- The codons representing amino acids get assembled one after another creating a chain. This process is called protein elongation. This chain of amino acids represents a protein.
- The synthesis of proteins stops with the signal from the 'stop codon'.
- The protein then moves to the Golgi complex, where it is sorted depending on its destination. The Golgi complex is to proteins what a mail sorting office is to a posted mail. The proteins are also packed to enhance their reliability.
- Nascent proteins contain signals that determine their ultimate destination. Proteins are transported to their destinations in appropriately addressed transport vesicles.
- The vesicles are released into the cell's cytoplasm where they migrate to their destinations.
- Some proteins are stored in specified places till wanted. These are released when needed by neuronal or hormonal stimulus.

As can be seen from the above, the protein biosynthetic process is a supply chain. The supply chain aspects of the above process are detailed in the next section.

Supply Chain Aspects of the Protein Biosynthetic Process

The protein biosynthetic process has several supply chain management aspects. These are discussed below:

Every supply chain consists of the following components:

- Suppliers
- Manufacturers
- Distributors
- Customers

The protein biosynthetic process has all these components. Proteins require amino acids, which are supplied by the tRNA. The proteins are manufactured in every cell in the ribosomes. The

Golgi complex distributes the protein to the endusers. The customers of the process are the areas or organs, which ultimately need and use the protein.

A supply chain consists of both pull and push processes. In a pull process, execution is initiated in response to a customer order. In a push process, execution is initiated in anticipation of customer needs. Therefore, at the time of execution of a pull process, customer demand is known with certainty whereas at the time of execution of a push process, demand is not known and must be forecast. Protein biosynthesis includes both pull and push processes. A protein is assembled on the request from a specific organ. This represents the pull process. However, the required free amino acids are always made available even before a request is initiated. This represents the push process in protein biosynthesis.

Distribution Networks: Distribution occurs between every pair of stages in a supply chain. Raw materials and components are moved from suppliers to manufacturers, while finished goods are moved from manufacturers to the end consumers. The protein biosynthetic process has its own distribution network. RNA supplies amino acids to the ribosome for manufacture of proteins using messenger RNA (mRNA), while the Golgi complex supplies the proteins to the necessary places. The Golgi complex sorts out the proteins based on their destinations. The Golgi complex consists of structures called cisternae, which packs the proteins into transport vesicles and releases them into the cell's cytoplasm where the vesicles migrate to their destinations already coded into them.

Inventory Management: Inventory is an important aspect of every supply chain. Inventory is spread throughout the supply chain from raw materials and semi-finished goods to finished goods that suppliers, manufacturers and distributors hold. Inventory management in the supply chain aims at optimising the inventory level without affecting the customer service levels. Adequate inventory ensures that supply chain processes can be decoupled, supply and demand can be balanced and uncertainties can be managed. The protein biosynthetic process has a very efficient inventory management system. The basic inventory in the process is amino acids and manufactured proteins. The amino acids are available in adequate quantity so that protein synthesis can be performed at any time. However, proteins are synthesised only on demand. Thus, an inventory of proteins, which are unused at any point of time, is almost eliminated. The protein biosynthesis process thus ensures that the inventory is optimised without affecting the needs of user organs.

Warehousing: Warehouses are facilities in a supply chain where goods are held or stored. Warehouses provide flexibility to both suppliers and buyers. Warehouses also act as supply chain coordinators. The protein biosynthesis process has some interesting warehousing facilities. This is especially in case of digestive proteins and enzymes. The enzyme needs to be released only when food enters the gut. In this case the proteins and enzymes are stored in secretary granules until wanted.

Information Flows: Information is an important component in a supply chain. Uninterrupted flow of information can increase the efficiency and effectiveness of the supply chain. Information connects and coordinates the various components of a supply chain. Information is useful both at the strategic level and operational level. The protein biosynthesis process has a very efficient information system. All the information for synthesising the proteins is encoded in the genetic material of the chromosomes. The first step in protein biosynthetic is synthesis of mRNA. The initiation of the synthesis of RNA is done using promoters regions in the DNA. Similarly there is a terminator region in the DNA, which stops the transcription process of an mRNA. Similarly in the ribosome where the proteins are actually synthesised there are initiators and terminators. Further, when a cell runs low on nutrients and energy, a ribosome modulation factor is used to deactivate ribosomes from manufacturing proteins. Thus it can be seen that information plays an important role in the protein biosynthetic process.

Reliability and Quality Management: Reliability is defined as the ability of a system or component to perform its required functions under stated conditions for a specified period of time. Quality on the other hand represents fitness for use of a product (Juran and Godfrey, 1998). While reliability is concerned with the performance of a product over its entire lifetime, quality is concerned with assuring reliability through conformance to specifications. Each protein is made using the genetic information stored in the chromosomes. The information in the DNA is first transcribed into an mRNA and then translated into the protein by pairing with tRNA. The quality of translation and production depends on the correct pairing of tRNA with mRNA. Each pairing has a binding energy. This binding energy is proofread by aminoacyl synthetases. In case of wrong pairing, the tRNA diffuses away due to lack of energy. However in case of correct pairing, the tRNA stays due to right hydrogen bonding. The binding energy difference between a correct assembly and incorrect assembly is thus used to achieve quality.

Organisation and Packaging: Packaging is an important aspect of supply chain management. Packaging has two functions. Firstly it is used to display the products and provide information. Secondly packaging is very important in the transportation of goods. Packaging takes place in a complex way in proteins. Proteins are packed and transported in biologically inactive form and converted into biologically active three-dimensional form prior to delivery overseen by molecular chaperones, to their correct destination.

Logistics Management: Logistics plays an important role in supply chain management. It ensures that the goods reach at the right time, in the right quantity and quality and at the right place. Protein biosynthesis has a very efficient logistics system. The initiation tRNA ensures the production of the right protein and the energy binding ensures quality. The Golgi complex ensures that the protein reaches its right destination. Proteins are stored in a few cases till needed and supplied at the right time through the process of hormonal stimuli. Thus logistics management is done efficiently.

Outsourcing: Outsourcing is defined as the contracting of a company's business processes to an outside service provider so that the company can concentrate on its core competencies. In cells the process of outsourcing is best found in mitochondria. Mitochondria are organelles in a cell containing enzymes whose basic function is produce energy through respiration. Mitochondria contain many hundreds of proteins. They even have the capacity to synthesise proteins. However in human cells, only 13 proteins are synthesised inside mitochondria. The rest are produced in ribosomes whose function is to produce proteins. Thus through outsourcing different parts concentrate on their core competencies.

Supply Chain Innovations in the Protein Biosynthetic Process

The protein biosynthetic process has interesting innovations. Many of these innovations are not easily noticeable in current supply chain management systems. These include:

Intentional Redundancy: Supply chain management, as we know today plans for removing redundancies. However in an era of quick changes in customer requirements and infrastructure bottlenecks, a good supply chain would also plan for keeping additional products designs ready to meet any contingencies. These situations can lead to a planned intentional redundancy. The protein biosynthetic process has an inbuilt redundancy. There are only 20 amino acids, which make up proteins. However, there are 64 different combinations of bases to produce these amino acids. The genetic code ensures that different combinations of bases can lead to the samc amino acid. This is technically called 'genetic buffering', whereby the effects of mutations on proteins are minimised. This buffering or redundancy ensures that protein requirements can be satisfied (customer satisfaction) even in case of mutations (infrastructure bottlenecks).

Monitored Pull Process: The supply chain management system has a pull component where products are supplied after the customer's requirement is known. One way to improve the efficiency of these supply chains is to monitor and find certain specific models, which are in greater demand and plan for their production and supply in anticipation of demand. The protein biosynthetic process does exactly this. Some proteins are always needed in larger numbers compared to other proteins. The synthesis of these proteins is initiated by stronger promoters, compared to other proteins. A stronger promoter will initiate synthesis more frequently compared to weak promoters. Thus the protein biosynthetic process is a monitored pull process.

Mutation Resistant Reliability: A product must be reliable even in case of incorrect production processes or the poor environmental conditions in which the product is used. The protein biosynthesis achieves this high level of reliability. The reliability of proteins is created through the process of having several genetic codes for the same amino acid in a protein. For example an amino acid named leucine has six different codes. This ensures that any mutation in a code does not degenerate the protein and enhances its reliability.

Ultra High-speed Supply Chain: Supply chains can provide a strategic consumer advantage through shortened cycles and instant availability (Kulkarni and Sharma, 2004). The protein biosynthetic process has an extremely fast supply chain cycle. In a cell 100 proteins are produced per minute per translocase. There are approximately 500 translocases per cell leading to the production and distribution of around 50,000 proteins per minute. Such a high level of production and distribution leads to almost instant availability of proteins, leading to a highly efficient supply chain.

Wobble Mechanism: One of the unique characteristics of the protein biosynthetic process is the wobble mechanism (Crick, 1966). Under this mechanism even a mismatched pairing of mRNA and tRNA can lead to an amino acid, which is very close to the original amino acid planned to be matched. The wobble mechanism is an example for flexibility in production and supply. Using this mechanism even a temporary mismatch in production and supply can still lead to the customer getting an almost similar product leading to satisfaction.

Zero Wastage: The protein biosynthetic process has no wastage whatsoever. There is no wastage at production and distribution stages. While today's supply chain systems describe 'Zero defect' production and supply, the protein biosynthetic process goes a step ahead to 'zero wastage'. It thus becomes an environmentally efficient and sustainable process.

Auto-programmed Total Supply Chain Management Coordination

The essence of supply chain management is collaboration and cooperation. Close coordination between suppliers and other partners in the supply chain leads to benefits like cost reduction, eliminating excess inventory and increased customer responsiveness. Protein biosynthesis is an excellent case of collaboration. All parts of the system work in close coordination. The coordination is achieved through initiators, proofreaders, terminators, release factors, translocators and transporters all incorporated into the entire process.

Meta-system Control for Overall Supply Chain Efficiency

A supply chain must ultimately satisfy end user needs. It is necessary for each component of the supply chain to understand this overriding mission. If a particular component however works for its own benefit without the end user's or the entire chain's interest in mind, it can only lead to inefficiency and degeneration. This requires an overall meta-system control. This is very well understood in the protein biosynthesis process. Though it may seem that the each organ, which uses the protein, is the consumer, all these are in turn a part of the meta-system of the living being. For example, the liver and the brain respectively require different proteins. But their requirements are subject to the needs of the animal or plant as a whole. Therefore control systems called transcription factors have been created to ensure the benefit of the entire meta-system.

The above are important supply chain innovations of the protein biosynthetic process. These lead to several lessons in excellence, which is covered in the next section.

Lessons and Examples in Excellence

The characteristic features and innovations of the protein biosynthetic process hold important lessons for excellence in supply chain management. These are discussed below:

- **Extended Supply Chain Management:** Supply chain excellence depends on the identification and participation of all partners, players and components in the chain. Many times, supply chains fail because while certain players participate and become efficient, while others remain isolated. When all the members are rightly identified efforts can be taken to improve every component's efficiency. The protein biosynthetic framework includes every component of its supply chain in its system. Every component is made to work to its fullest efficiency. This is seen in the supply chain management efforts of Wal Mart, where before a sourcing decision is made every member in the entire supply chain is clearly identified and their efficiency is improved (Worthen, 2006).
- **Push-Pull Balancing:** For a supply chain to be excellent both the push and pull components of the chain must be coordinated and balanced. If either one of the components works independently of the other, it can lead to inefficiency. In the protein biosynthetic process, both the components are perfectly balanced. A case of excellence in balancing push and pull components can be seen in the case of Dell (Chopra and Meindl, 2004). Dell's supply chain process anticipates customer demands to manage its push process in terms of sourcing components. On the other hand a customer's order initiates the pull process, which is balanced efficiently with component sourcing.
- **Targeted Distribution:** The protein biosynthetic process is an example of distribution excellence. Proteins are not distributed in a random manner. Instead they are targeted to specific locations using tailor made encoded distribution

systems and vehicles. Prahalad (2004) gives the case study of Hindustan Lever, which implemented 'Project Shakti', in order to gain access into the most interior regions of India. In this case Hindustan Lever, used 'Shakti Amma' who distributed the products in her local region.

- **Final Inventory Optimisation:** Supply chain management excellence depends on optimising inventory. This requires monitoring inventory in terms of their need and usage and then evolve an optimum. The protein biosynthesis teaches an important lesson in this regard. While initial inventory in terms of amino acids are available in abundance, final inventory in terms of proteins are made available only on demand. This reduces the need to possess value added inventory. However component inventory of lesser value is always available, leading to a balanced and excellent optimum.
- **Strategic Warehousing:** Warehousing design should be based on strategic considerations. It is necessary to keep them close to strategic consumers, as the protein biosynthetic process does. Harrington (2004) gives the example of Toyota, which excelled in its distribution of its European economy car Yaris, though strategic warehousing.
- **Perfect Quality and Reliability:** Today's supply chain management systems describe total quality management and six-sigma as the important components of ensuring quality. However the protein biosynthetic process goes beyond just total quality. It deals with perfect quality. This is achieved by ensuring that even a difference in coding of nucleotide bases lead to the same amino acid. This is an important lesson for supply chain management. Customers will not tolerate excuses of mistakes. Technologies which will ensure that even a mistaken production and supply process can still lead to the customer getting the right product at the right time, is the ultimate model provided by protein biosynthesis.
- **Competency-based Outsourcing:** Today outsourcing is fashion. Though it is done for cost considerations, firms must

also see understand their core competencies before outsourcing. This is an important lesson to be learnt from mitochondria in protein biosynthesis. As long as only non-core processes are outsourced, it will not lead to any problems. However, if firms outsource even their core processes it will lead to inefficiencies and problems and can lead to loss of competitive advantage. This can be noticed in the case of several US firms, which outsourced their processes to Bangalore, only to take them back as it was not strategically right in doing so (Friedman, 2006). An oft-quoted example in this regard is that of Apple, which closed its operations in Bangalore recently.

- **Instantaneous Supply:** Today's supply chain management systems have evolved just in time methods to ensure that the products are supplied at the time of need. However the protein biosynthetic process is even faster, leading to almost instantaneous supply as the need is being expressed. This is because of the extremely high levels of coordination in the supply chain. Today's models do not compare with this level of efficiency. However the protein biosynthetic process is an indication of the levels of efficiency that can be achieved through information flow and supply chain coordination.
- **Self-integrated Information and Logistics Management:** Firms today use the internet as an important tool for information and logistics coordination. However protein biosynthesis uses its own network for information flows and logistics coordination. The logistics concerns are integrated into the system. TPL (third party logistics) is becoming common in supply chain management today. It is important to ensure that firms select their TPL service providers carefully and integrate their interests too, into the supply chain management system, just like the protein biosynthetic system to achieve excellence.
- **Environmental Efficiency:** Supply chain management systems must aim to be environmentally efficient. The amount of wastage produced during production, distribution

and consumption in today's world is enormous. The environmental implications of these are considerable. The protein biosynthetic process through its 'Zero Wastage' procedure has an important lesson in this regard.

- **Bio-innovative Supply Chain Management:** Another important lesson to be learnt from protein biosynthesis is the need for innovations. The aspects of intentional redundancy, monitored pull process and wobble mechanism all represent innovations, which can be carefully integrated into supply chain management. Unless a supply chain innovates, it can slowly become obsolete and stop serving its purpose.
- **Meta Supply Chain Service and Welfare:** Ultimately it must be understood, that every component in the supply chain must fare well and grow for the entire supply chain to be effective. The protein biosynthetic process is a great example of concern for each component. While each player serves others and the system, the entire system looks after the welfare of each component. Therefore 'giving' becomes more important than 'receiving'. This must be goal of every supply chain management process, leading to welfare of all players. This requires the shedding of feelings of 'me and my' and inculcating the feelings of 'we and our'. This is the most important lesson to be learnt from the protein biosynthetic process.

The above lessons thus delineate how supply chain management systems can be designed to achieve efficiency, effectiveness and excellence.

A Bio-mimetic Framework of Supply Chain Management

The previous sections explained the supply chain aspects, innovations and lessons for excellence using the protein biosynthetic process.

The basic premise of the framework is that supply chain components, which are observed in conventional supply chains, when integrated with supply chain innovations noticed in the protein biosynthetic process, leads to supply chain excellence.

These include:

- Proper identification of components of the supply chain integrated with meta-system control for overall supply chain efficiency leads to meta-supply chain service and welfare.
- Pull and push process integrated with monitored pull process leads to push pull balancing.
- Distribution networks, inventory management and warehousing, integrated with intentional redundancy leads to targeted distribution, final inventory optimisation and strategic warehousing.
- Information flows and outsourcing integrated with auto programmed total supply chain management coordination leads to self-integrated information and logistics management and competency-based outsourcing.
- Logistics management integrated with ultra high-speed supply chain leads to instantaneous supply.
- Zero defect procedures integrated with zero wastage systems leads to environmental efficiency.
- Production process integrated with wobble mechanism systems leads to bio-innovative supply chain management.

The above framework thus aims at achieving supply chain excellence using the innovations in the protein biosynthetic process.

Conclusion

This paper has attempted to provide a bio-mimetic framework for supply chain management based on the protein biosynthetic process. The paper has derived lessons of excellence from the process. If these lessons are seriously incorporated into supply chain management systems, it lead to a new generation of excellence in supply chain management.

Dedication

The authors humbly dedicate the paper to Bhagawan Sri Sathya Sai Baba, The Revered Chancellor of Sri Sathya Sai Institute of Higher Learning, Prasanthinilayam, Andhra Pradesh, India.

References

Aurifeille, Jacques-Marie and Christoph Deissenberg, 1998, *Bio-Mimetic Approaches in Management Science*, Kluwer Academic Publishers.

Aktürk, M.S. and Özkan, S., 2001, 'Integrated Scheduling and Tool Management in Flexible Manufacturing Systems', *International Journal of Production Research*, Vol. 39, No.12, pp. 2697-2722.

Baba, Bhagawan Sri Sathya Sai, 2000, 'Subjugate your ego', *Sri Sathya Sai Speaks*, Vol. 31, Prasanthi Nilayam, Sri Sathya Sai Books and Publications, p. 250

Benyus, J. M. 1997, *Biomimicry: Innovation Inspired by Nature*. New York: Harper Collins.

Bernstein, Amy, 2006, 'Janine Benyus: The Thought Leader Interview', *Strategy+Business*, Issue 44, Fall 2006, pp. 109-118.

Bozinovski, S., Muller, B., & di Primio F., 2000, *Biomimetic Autonomous Factories*, GMD Report 115. Sankt Augustin: German National Research Center for Information Technology

Colorni A., M. Dorigo, F. Ma_oli, V. Maniezzo, G. Righini, M. Trubian Heuristics from Nature for Hard Combinatorial Optimization Problems, *International Transactions in Operational Research*, Vol.3, No. 1, page. 1-21

Crick F.H.C, 1966, 'Codon-anticodon pairing: The wobble hypothesis' *Journal of Molecular Biology*, Vol.**19,** p.555.

Demeester L, K. Eichler and C. Loch, 2003, *Organic Production Systems: What the Biological Cell Can Teach us about the Future of Manufacturing*, Insead Working Paper Series.

Elliot William H. and Daphne C. Elliot, 2001, *Biochemistry and Molecular Biology,* Oxford, Oxford University Press.

Friedman, Thomas L., 2006, *The World Is Flat: A Brief History of the Twenty-first Century*, Farrar, Straus and Giroux.

Harrington, Lisa H., 2003, 'Toyota's Supply Chain Delivers the Yaris', *Transportation & Distribution*, Feb, Vol. 44(2), pp.45-48.

Juran, Joseph M and A. Blanton Godfrey, 1998, *Juran's Quality Handbook*, New York, McGraw-Hill Professional

Kulkarni Sarika and Ashok Sharma, 2004, *Supply Chain Management - Creating Linkages for Faster Business Turnaround*, New Delhi, Tata McGraw Hill.

Lieckfeld, C. P., 1993, Entsalzung, *Bionik - Natur als Vorbild Umweltstiftung*, in R. Witt (ed.), WWF Duetschland, Pro Futura Verlag.

Manner R. and B. Manderick (eds.) 1992, *Parallel Problem Solving from Nature*, North-Holland, 1992.

Mchugh, Patrick; Giorgio Merli, and William Wheeler, 1995, *Beyond Business Process Reengineering: Towards the Holonic Enterprise,* John Wiley and Sons.

McKelvey, B., and Aldrich, H., 1983, Populations, Natural Selection, and Applied Organizational Science *Administrative Science Quarterly, 28(1): 101.*

Mendes, André V., 2002, *Carpe Technology*, https://www.netaonline.org/PD-CarpeMendes603.ppt

Miller, Jessie L., Miller, James Grier, 1993, The Producer, *Behavioral Science*, Jan1993, Vol. 38, Issue 1, pp. 46-57.

Neinhuis, C., & Barthlott, W., 1997, Characterization and Distribution of Water-Repellent, Self-Cleaning Plant Surfaces, *Annals of Botany*, 79: 667-677

Okino, N., 1993, 'Bionic Manufacturing System', in J. Peklenik (ed) *CIRP, Flexible Manufacturing Systems Past-Present- Future*, pp. 73-95.

Prahalad C. K, 2004, *The Fortune at the Bottom of the Pyramid: Eradicating Poverty Through Profits,* Wharton School Publishing.

Schwefel H.P. and R.Manner, 1990, 'Parallel Problem Solving from Nature', *Proc. of PPSN-I.*

Simsek Burak and Albayrak Sahin, 2004, *Living Factory: Back to Koestler in Holonic Manufacturing*, working paper of DAI-Labor, GOR1-1 Franklinstrasse Berlin-Germany, www.ieeexplore.ieee.org.

Ueda, K. 1992, 'A Concept for Bionic Manufacturing Systems Based on DNA', *PROLAMAT* (1992): 853-863.

Vaario, J., 1996, *Self-Organization in Manufacturing Systems,* Paper presented at Japan-USA Symposium on Flexible Automation, Boston, MA, July 7 –10.

Worthen, Ben, 2006, *The ABCs of Supply Chain Management*, www.cio.com.

12

Supply Chain Management Practices in Pharmaceutical Industry

B. Krishna Reddy and T. Sudha

Introduction

Recent globalization and the development of information super highway have brought the countries of the world closer. From a business perspective, the world is one market. The American pharmaceutical industry has played a pioneering role in the development of drug industry through in-depth, timely and useful research and bulk manufacturing of drug products. Although the U.S pharmaceutical industry is enjoying the leadership position, it can no longer be content to focus only on the U.S and European markets.

India being the second largest country in the world in terms of population is attracting attention for future business potential. The purchasing capacity of approximately 300 million middle class individuals cannot be easily overlooked by global pharmaceutical companies. This article analyzes the current information available about the Indian Pharmaceutical Industry (IPI) and the supply chain management practices in some of the pharmaceutical companies.

The Indian pharmaceutical Industry under went a phenomenal change after 1 January 2005, when international patent laws are implemented. India's domestic pharmaceutical companies have experienced a significant increase in Research & Development spending to be competitive in world market. Although Indian pharmaceutical market is very small and does not have enough funding for drug discovery programs, India has well-educated scientists, a well-established computer industry, and technological know-how for the manufacture of the bulk drugs and formulations.

The article reflects the growing importance of pharmaceutical supply chain in an environment which is affected by factors as diverse as:

1. Reduction in storage space in hospitals
2. Dramatic developments in the technology and culture
3. Increasing unit costs of medicines
4. Unrelenting pressures to cut cost.

Global Pharmaceutical Industry

Pharmaceutical products consist of two components –the active pharmaceutical ingredient (API) or bulk drug and the formulation (i.e., a suitable final dosage form). Generally, API's are either produced by chemical synthesis or are of plant, animal, or biological origin. Patents are critical aspects in the development and marketing of pharmaceutical products. A patent can be obtained for a new drug molecule, a new indication for an existing molecule, or a new drug delivery system of an existing product. The World Trade Organization (WTO) has decided to enforce a product patent life of twenty years in all countries. In other words, if drug development and FDA approval takes approximately ten years from the first disclosure of molecule, a pharmaceutical company gets only ten years of exclusivity to market the formulation. The excessive cost of the drug development forces drug prices to remain high while the drugs are protected by the patents. In addition not every project leads to a marketed product, so successfully marketed products must cover the cost incurred for the failed projects.

Drug prices vary from country to country. Citizens of developing countries cannot afford expensive medicines that are under patent. Multinational companies (MNCs) must either choose to sell a product at a low price in these countries or face the challenge of piracy or parallel trade. Types of diseases in Third world countries may vary from those in developed nations. However because of lack of sizable profits from distributing pharmaceutical products in Third world countries, MNCs are reluctant to conduct research to develop new drug molecules to treat these diseases.

With the increase in healthcare consciousness, the pharma industry is growing at the rate of 10 – 15 per cent annually. Most of the activities of Pharmaceutical industry are global in nature. The industry is complex, and dynamic with many multinationals in fray in several countries. The business model followed by many companies in the industry is the centralized research and globalized marketing. In other words, the developing of drugs is in one location and selling activities are spread worldwide. Some major global companies are outsourcing a few stages of the drug development to smaller companies in order to save time and cost. The trend of outsourcing in various stages of the drug development and manufacturing process is increasing. So, there is a blur of geographical boundaries taking place in the pharmaceutical industry with more than one nation being involved in the manufacture of a single finished product.

Indian Pharmaceutical Industry

According to the findings of The Associated Chambers of Commerce and Industry of India (ASSOCHAM) the size of Indian pharmaceutical industry will grow to Rs. 600 billion in 2007-08 to significantly drive its pharmaceuticals exports to regulated markets of US and Europe in Generic drug markets in which US$ 65 billion worth of drugs will go off patent.

The Indian pharmaceutical Industry (IPI) today is in the front rank of India's science-based industries with wide ranging capabilities in the complex field of drug manufacture and technology. A highly organized sector, the IPI is estimated to be worth US$ 4.5 billion, growing at about 9 percent annually. It ranks very high in the third world in terms of technology, quality and the range of medicines manufactured. From simple headache pills to sophisticated antibiotics and complex cardiac compounds, almost every type of medicine is now made indigenously

Playing a key role in promoting and sustaining development in the vital field of medicines, IPI boasts of quality producers and many units approved by regulatory authorities in US and UK. International companies associated with this sector have stimulated, assisted and spearheaded this dynamic development in the past 53 years and helped to put India on the pharmaceutical map of the world.

Indian Pharmaceutical Industry: A Snapshot

- Size of industry (2005) US$ 8.2 billion with over 24000 registered manufacturers.
- Ranks 4th in terms of volume and 13th in terms of value of Global Industry
- R & D focused industry
- Demand is derived from doctors and health care
- Meets almost 95 per cent of the country's Pharma needs
- Provides employment to over 2.9million people
- Mc Kinsey projects US$ 25 trillion by 2010.
- Efficient distribution systems not in place.

SWOT Analysis: SWOT analysis can be gainfully used to the IPI and determine where its greatest opportunities lie. This section examines these factors.

The strengths are:

1. Cost competitiveness
2. Rich Biodiversity
3. Well developed Industry with strong manufacturing base
4. Well established network of laboratories and R & D infrastructure
1. Access to pool of highly trained scientists

The major weaknesses are

1. Low investments in innovative R & D
2. Lack of resources for new Drug Discovery Research
3. Lack of strong linkages between industry and academia
4. Production of spurious and low quality drugs tarnishes the image

The opportunities are

1. Significant export potential
2. Contract manufacturing arrangements with MNC's

The threats are

1. Product patent regime poses serious challenge to domestic industry unless it invests in R & D
2. Drug Price Control Order (DPCO) puts ceilings on product prices, which prevents firms from generating surplus for investment.

According to the SWOT Analysis, Indian Pharmaceutical industry is characterized by efficiency through cost structure and good manufacturing base. However, R & D efforts are yet to become comparable to international levels.

Pharmaceutical Industry in Andhra Pradesh

In India, Andhra Pradesh has been placed in a dominant position by having more than 33 per cent of the market share in bulk drugs in country's total bulk drugs production. Of top Five Pharma companies of India, two are located in Andhra Pradesh. The state accounts for nearly one third of the total bulk drug production of the country. It is considered to be the bulk drug capital of the country. The number of pharmaceutical companies and the skilled manpower has also been increasing in the capital of Andhra Pradesh. The state has distinctive advantages with strong R&D base by having reputed institutions like Indian Institute of Chemical Technology (IICT). The pharmaceutical industry was worth more than US$ 1.6 billion in the year 2005. The changes in the procedures like VAT affected the pharmaceutical industry growth in recent years.

The state has become a hub to the investors to invest in pharma industry by having leading companies like Dr Reddy Labs, Aurobindo Pharma, matrix Labs, Hetro Drugs and Natco Pharma. Dr Reddy Labs have the major market share in the state's pharmaceutical share.

Major players	Revenue in 2005 (in million)
Dr Reddy Labs	19472
Aurobindo Pharma	11757
Matrix Labs	6716

Supply Chain Management

Supply Chain management is the integration of activities along the supply chain linking customer orders, distribution orders, inventory ordering, placement of manufacturing orders, cash flows and ultimately supplier orders. The key objective of supply chain management is to provide customer satisfaction by having the correct product in the correct place at the correct time. The dimensions that contribute to a feeling of overall satisfaction are

- Cost – What customers receive for what they have paid
- Convenience – the effort expended to achieve the purchase
- Confidence in the support and services both included and promised.

The report is prepared by the study conducted in some of the Hyderabad based pharmaceutical companies. The present study is confined to the top 20 pharmaceutical companies located in Hyderabad. Companies are selected based on their turnovers

Objectives:

1. To study the functioning of Supply Chain Management practices of Pharmaceutical Companies in Hyderabad.
2. To study the Areas/functions outsourced in different Pharmaceutical companies.

Both primary as well as secondary data has been collected keeping in view the objectives.

A questionnaire has been developed and administered to managers/senior people in the organization connected with supply chain management department for collection of primary data. Secondary data has been collected through company web sites, annual reports and public information sources.

Awareness about company's supply chain and logistics function.

Yes	58 per cent
No	22 per cent
Part of Sales & distribution	20 per cent

The functions of supply chain management and logistics are rapidly acquiring an identity of their own in Indian industry. The survey reveals that as many as 58 per cent of the respondents said their companies had a clearly defined a SCM function.

When did the company start using SCM function?

< One year ago	40 per cent
1 – 3 Years ago	38 per cent
3 – 5 Years ago	22 per cent

SCM function is still a young process as 40 per cent of all respondents said a SCM focus was formed less than a year ago and as many as 38 per cent revealed that SCM department was recognized between 1 and 3 years ago. Even in large MNC's the change to clear accountability for logistics started recently. The process of streamlining the SCM function started some time the end of year 2000. It was done to leverage on the opportunities that existed in the supply chain process and thus ensuring that the benefits ultimately reach the customers.

The classical case of the right hand not knowing what the left is doing is the single most dangerous action in modern business today. One of the key parameters of successful SCM is the degree of integration between inbound, outbound and plant processes. More integration can lead to better coordination, which can lead to better efficiencies.

SCM head reports to

M.D	55 per cent
Head – Marketing	17 per cent
Head – Finance	17 per cent
Others	21 per cent

One of the basic tenets of a successful supply chain initiative is top managements commitment to it. Recognizing that change is driven from the top, the survey enquired about the organization structure in the company. The data revealed that as many as 55 per cent of the companies surveyed, the senior most supply chain manager who could be held accountable reported directly to M.D of the company, thereby ensuring involvement of top management in the process.

Information desired by supply chain manager

Information is vital for handling the supply chain: but it is interesting to note that information about the supply chain itself is not easy to get. In India, unlike the west where SCM is already an

Cost & Savings	68 per cent
Best Practices	70 per cent
List of Service Providers	38 per cent
Concepts	28 per cent
Case Studies	35 per cent

industry with global giants and a matured publishing business, managers still rely heavily on public sources like newspapers and seminars for getting data on SCM.

Practices followed by service providing companies

Different strategies for different segments	69 per cent
Separate bills for every shipment	68 per cent
E-mail all dispatch details	62 per cent
Customer relationship management	56 per cent
Network wide visibility of information	55 per cent
Payment by electronic means	39 per cent
Link to customers/suppliers ERP	35 per cent
Enterprise Resource Planning	30 per cent
Continuous replenishment programmes	28 per cent
Bar coding	28 per cent
Participation in electronic procurement	29 per cent
Vendor managed inventory	25 per cent
Real time sharing of data from customers/suppliers	19 per cent

Even with the information, respondents wanted more of how the managers undertook cost savings and best practices to attain SCM efficiency.

Clearly the SCM process will benefit from its own distinct functional identity. As the identity evolves, the benefits are likely to become more visible too.

69 per cent of the respondents said that they have adopted different strategies for different segments, 56 per cent of respondents had adopted customer relationship management tools, 30 per cent of respondents had installed a form of ERP and 35 per cent of the respondents have link to suppliers ERP.

However a lot of 'modern-day' practices haven't made much headway in sample study, continuous replenishment programmes, much in favour with auto and retail sectors, find little adoption-with 28 per cent of companies adopting Bar coding, the very basic practice in inventory management is done by 28 per cent of respondents. Just 19 per cent of service providers were linking their real time data with their customers possible due to connectivity, IT infrastructure cost and lack of urgency of such linkage.

Challenges faced by the Pharmaceutical companies (Ranked by respondents)

1.	Attracting and retaining skilled work force
2.	Controlling operating costs
3.	Generic competition
4.	Intellectual property protection
5.	Managing regulatory compliance
6.	Pricing pressures and shrinking margins
7.	Realizing tangible value from strategic alliances and joint ventures, partnering arrangements
8.	Reputation management
9.	Successfully developing innovative drugs and enhancing R&D productivity
10.	Sustaining growth in global markets

Moving up the value chain

Develop expertise to add services to grow	73 per cent
Associate with global MNC's for their Indian operations	45 per cent
Acquire other companies to grow	35 per cent
Invest in assets to improve services	40 per cent

What is the way forward to implement vision and mission of the company? 73 per cent of respondents said that they wanted to add services and options by growing. 45 per cent said that the ventures with MNC's to become part of their network for growth, 39 per cent said they would invest in infrastructure and assets. Acquisition of the companies to add to the portfolio of services is close behind with 35 per cent.

Outsourcing in the Pharmaceutical Industry

Outsourcing- the current mantra of pharmaceutical industry-is being used more strategically as on ongoing part of a company's overall business strategy. Outsourced activities can be in various fields "right from drug discovery till manufacturing of product". Pharmaceutical firms have long outsourced functions such as manufacturing, packaging, clinical trials and sales force mobilization. Biotechnology companies, which have almost doubled in number during the past five years, also contributed to this trend as they seek ways of bringing their products to markets without making capital investments in their own manufacturing facilities.

The following are some of the major benefits of outsourcing

1. Outsourcing reduces overall costs by 30 to 35 per cent.
2. Reduces problems faced during the regulatory process.
3. Improve manufacturing efficiencies.
4. Reduces excess production capacity by divesting facilities.
5. Improves net earnings and cash flow.
6. Faster and cheaper to have discovery work outsourced as it reduces the drug development costs.

7. Divert resources to focus ,on other competencies like marketing.

Need for Outsourcing

Pharma alliance or partnership holds cost benefit advantage by reducing huge amounts of capital outlay for producing latest technology in-house. Outsourcing allows pharmaceutical companies to ramp up the R&D operations at a fast pace with minimum capital outlay. Outsourcing can allow pharmaceutical companies to establish consistency and efficiency across international networks of commercial, supply chain and manufacturing organizations. Outsourcing if managed and executed strategically has every potential to add value and keep the investor community happy.

India today has the largest number of US Food and Drug Administration (USFDA) approved drug manufacturing facilities outside the U.S. The Indian patent act amended on March 2005 opens a new avenue for India into the global pharmaceutical market. Pharmaceutical multinationals have maintained a low-key presence in Indian market due to absence of product patents and rigid price controls. IPI did not receive significant foreign direct investment but introduction of new patent will see multinationals strengthening their presence in the country.

It is a great challenge to successfully manage the outsourcing relationship and generate value. To maintain continuous growth in outsourced work from pharmaceutical companies, outsourcing partners need to confidently retain the proprietary knowledge and meet the regulatory compliance. Outsourcing solves the problems for the pharmaceutical companies and allow them to exploit the potential of new drug discovery technologies. It is not a far fetched dream when the pharmaceutical companies provide their core competencies in marketing and commercialization and outsource partners supply innovative products.

There is a change in the way companies now approach the business. It is not just cutting costs by outsourcing, but the quality of the outsourced work is crucial. Matching inbound and outbound transportation is very important in integrating SCM.

The companies outsource/sub-contract the following functions(areas)

S. No	Function (Area)	Yes	No
1.	Ware Housing		□
2.	Outbound Transportation	□	
3.	Customs Clearance	□	
4.	Inbound transportation	□	
5.	Freight Forwarding	□	
6.	Order fulfillment &distribution		□
7.	Return/ Reverse Logistics	□	
8.	Product labeling/Marketing/packing		□
9.	Consulting Services	□	
10.	Procurement	□	
11.	Inventory management		□
12.	IT Services	□	
13.	Customer service		□
14.	Security Services	□	

References

B..S. .Sahay Supply Chain Management for Global Competitiveness, Macmillan India Ltd, 1999.

Brichacek, "Top 50 Pharmaceutical Companies," Pharm. Exec.21 (4) pp. 62-82 (2001)

D.J. Ausman, "Screening's age of insecurity: High-Throughput Screening hasn't given Us More Drugs. Can Better Data Management Make a Difference?" Modern Drug discovery, May 2001, 33-39

Department of Indian Systems of Medicines and Homeopathy Annual report 199-2000,

Dr. Reddy's Laboratory, "Discovery pipeline and Licensing opportunities,

Gattorna .J.L and Walters .D.W Managing Supply Chain, Macmillan Business, 1996

India Infoline Sector Reports, "Pharmaceuticals: Drug price control order(DPCO),"

Justin Paul, "Business Environment" Tata McGraw-Hill Publication, 2006

M.J. Ahn, "Developing a profitable Market-Share Strategy for Multinational Pharmaceutical Companies in China," J.Pharma. Marketing and management 13(1),p.29, (2000)

M.Szabo-Streit, The Pharmaceutical Market in Hungary, J. Pharm. Marketing and Management 13, 49-61 (1999)

Martin Christopher Logistics and Supply Chain Management, Pearson Education, Asia 2000

Once-a-day formulations May Not Turn Into Big Brands, say Analysts, 26 September 2001,

P.R. Cateora and J.L. Graham, International marketing, (Irwin-McGraw-Hill, New York, 10th edition, 1999)

R.K. Srivastava," How Many Indian Pharma Companies Will Survive after 2005?" 5 march 2002

Raghuram. G and Rangaraj N: Logistics and Supply Chain Management, Macmillan India Ltd 2000

Simchi. D, Levi, Kaminsky Philip and Simchi-Levi. E: Designing and management of Supply Chain, McGraw-Hill, 2000

13

Contemporary Issues in Supply Chain Management

Vaishali Agarwal

Introduction

In the contemporary situation, businesses all over the globe are looking forward to protract competitiveness and attain strategic edge in this global economy. With the initiation of liberalization process since 1991, and thereafter entry of number of large-scale players spoiling consumers like never before; the companies in India have became highly competitive in the last two decades. In today's technology-driven global market place, customer expectations have ascended to very high standards. Innovative technologies and the ever-mounting intensity of competition are forcing organizations to retrace how they do business. The present scenario is a revolution phase, that of competition shifting from industrial age to information age. Days when the benefits were available to the organizations by embedding new technology into physical assets and achieving large scale of economies and scope through mass production of standard products have passed. Today the invincible tool available is information, thus contemporary era is aptly described as information age.

Accordingly, organizations no longer gain sustainable strategic edge by merely deploying new technology into physical assets rapidly. This era requires new capabilities in organizations for competitive success. 'Companies, able to develop customer relationship and loyalty, producing customized high-quality products and services at reasonable prices at the right place and at right time (short lead times) will be successful as more and more homogeneous products are available across markets. Thus to survive in this challenging scenario and to attain strategic edge over others an organization needs to focus on cost saving techniques besides revenue increasing methods and one such measure available to them is SCM. The main reason for this edge, as usual, came from the market place' (Sahay, B.S., Supply Chain Management for Global Competitiveness, Macmillan India, New Delhi, 1999). By 1999-2000, in 'Consumer Durable companies in India, the sales growth had dipped to16 per cent from 34 per cent in 1998, as the overall economy dawdled and consumer attitude turned cautious. Most of the companies had set up excess capacities but as the penetration levels dropped beyond the mid-1990s due to slowdown, this hit all the companies badly with profits after tax disappearing to produce a net loss of Rs. 43 crore in 2000 for these companies. Financing costs jumped from Rs 143 crore in 1995 to Rs. 216 crore in 1996 as new capacities came up and inventories across the chain were financed' (Durables Supply Chain, The ET Knowledge Series, Supply Chain & Logistics, 2002).

Thus the prospects for the Indian companies exist in leveraging their proficiency in Supply Chain Management for contribution to competitiveness. The battleground for the contemporary decade is going to be supply chain versus supply chain instead of battle between firm versus firm.

Evolution of Supply Chain Management

The Indian Industry has become highly competitive in the recent past with the entry of various large scale players exerting multidimensional pressures of increasing expectations of consumers and channel members, shortening product life cycles as a result of day to day innovations and demands of high returns from stake holders have shifted the momentum of competitive advantage from physical distribution to integrated logistics management, finally moving over to supply chain management. The concept of Supply Chain Management has recently crossed the threshold into the corporate limelight as a means to develop a strategic edge over and above competitors after a gradual succession through three different phases (Sahay, B.S., Supply Chain Management for Global Competitiveness, Macmillan India, New Delhi, 1999.)

Physical Distribution Management

The first phase was 'Physical Distribution Management' which can be characterized as inventory push era. It means management of movement, inventory control, protection and storage of raw materials and of processed or finished goods to and from the production line. The system is basically a replenishment system, fraught with inherent inefficiencies like extended credit terms, stock piling, sluggish orders and pipeline inventories. Perhaps more than in any other industry in India, this 'Push system' has worked in consumer durables industry for many years. The industry has faced difficulties like stock held up at various levels- factories, warehouses, dealers and trucks, which in turn reveal a high percentage to sales. The situation is not restricted to India merely even Whirlpool, $8 billion giant in consumer durables, until 1995, utilized its capacities to the maximum using the push system and facing a customer demand with response time equal to four weeks which was later reduced to five days by shifting to forecasting based manufacturing using RAD (Reality applied to distribution) resource planning with software from ilog.

Integrated Logistics Management

The next phase was 'Integrated Logistics Management' where importance of integrating operations within the organization like sales, procurement, manufacturing, ware housing, distribution and transportation was recognized. Basically integrated logistics management is the process that creates value by timing and positioning inventory; it is the combination of a firm's order management, inventory, transportation, warehousing, materials handling, and packaging as integrated through out a facility network. Integrated logistics serves to link and synchronize the overall supply chain as a continuous process and is essential for effective supply chain connectivity. The Industry in India has become highly competitive in the recent past. The emphasis was not just to have personnel, but to have own integrated logistics like a global player, SONY. For example, in the Sony world, there are approximately 100 plants and dealers and 6,000 affiliated parts or material suppliers. Its products and parts are transported among more than 200 countries around the world. It is almost impossible for each plant and dealer to arrange logistics by combining the services of customs clearance agents and warehouse, forwarding and insurance companies. Sony logistics understood this and puts it long accumulated expertise to compete with others. Today Sony logistics has been undertaking logistics services for Aiwa and other electronic companies, and has been earning nearly 20 per cent of its total sales from outside the Sony Group.

Supply Chain Management

The present phase of 'Supply Chain Management' extends the scope to link external partners like suppliers, vendors, distributors and customers. Supply Chain Management is a philosophy of business, based on the idea of partnership. Management of the supply chain is concerned with achieving cost-effective satisfaction of end customer requirements through buyer-supplier process integration. SCM is the close linkage and coordination of activities involved in buying, making, and moving a product. It integrates supplier, manufacturer, distributor, retailer and customer logistics processes to reduce time, redundant effort, and inventory costs. The process integration with the supplier upstream and the customer downstream comes about through sharing of information for mutual benefit of the parts of the supply chain. So SCM is a cross-functional inter-enterprise and intra-enterprise system that uses information technology to help support and manage the links between some of the company's key business processes and those of its suppliers, customers, and business partners. It consists of firms collaborating to leverage strategic positioning and to improve operating efficiency.

SCM has given a new dawn to Indian Industry in terms of Pull System. The Pull system, by contrast of Push System, is based on forecasting and only making to order with some safety stock. In conjunction with the outbound strategy, there is a complementary Just in Time (JIT) arrangement with vendors on the inbound side.

"Two to three years ago, supply chain did not figure too high on anyone's list," says DK Kaushal, General Manager-Logistics, and Samsung India ('Durables Supply Chain, The ET Knowledge Series, Supply Chain & Logistics, 2002). He admits things changed as the markets became more competitive and expanded. Costs, which were earlier passed to the customers, now became vital to control, since prices were going down but costs were going up. He adds, "Tough times caused all players to think more in terms of the supply chain in totality, not in pieces." And thus Samsung brought in supply chain practices from day one in India and a paradigm shift was made from 'Made to Stock' to 'Made to Order' and Regional Distribution Centers were set up, one at regional location for faster delivery of products, leading to greater customer satisfaction and low costs. The following table gives a glimpse of success achieved in a very short span of time:

DK Kaushal, General Manager-Logistics, Samsung India, claims Samsung has the lowest cost of logistics as percent to net sales-just 2.23 per cent in 2001. In 2000, this was 2.33 per cent and in 1999 it was 2.72 per cent as mentioned above in the table. Though the industry norms as per ETIG estimates are around 5 per cent of sales.

What SCM can do?

After Enterprise Resource Planning, the most widely used application to improve supply chain performance is Supply Chain Management. SCM is a business system that integrates company's internal resources to manage and work with the external supply chain. An SCM system is a combination of many applications such as demand, inventory, and transportation planning covering the stages in the supply chain. SAP, BAAN, QAD, Peoplesoft, i2, and Manugistics provide Supply-Chain solutions. Sony, Mahindra, Asian Paints, Samsung, Maruti are some of the companies implementing an SCM solution.

Supply Chain Management helps businesses optimally coordinate the movement of goods and materials through the supply chain enabling accurate and efficient order fulfillment, even though the customer orders are constantly changing.

With SCM, a business can estimate future demand for its products, enabling planners to accurately estimate future need for supplies, and extends to "execution" with the planning of their plants, transportation, and logistics. Since time and service are the major market differentiators, managing asset and information flow across the supply chain is a challenge. SCM maximizes supply chain velocity by optimizing planning and execution. The objective is to enhance the company's performance through improved manufacturing or service capability, market responsiveness, and customer-supplier relationship.

The demands made to a manufacturer by a client are dependent upon demands made by client's customers. In a supply chain, all suppliers, manufacturers, distributors and retailers have the same end customer. All of them will be successful, if they collaborate with each other in satisfying the demand. As mentioned earlier, the competition is not between organizations but between supply chains. If one supply chain fails to meet the demand, another supply chain will overtake and satisfy that customer.

Contemporary Issues in SCM in Indian Companies

- Reduced inventory goals require flexible, high-velocity manufacturing strategies that can enable a quick response when unexpected changes in demand occur.
- Expanding distribution systems across the national boundaries and becoming global.
- RFID compliance projects emerge as industry requirement, but long-term improvements to enterprise planning are unclear and ROI is yet to be identified

- Enterprise performance analytics needed to help improve planning and optimize decision-making
- Rapid, low-cost development and delivery of new products using web-based collaboration and procurement
- Increased demand responsiveness requires a "demand-driven supply network" (transformation from "push" to "pull" operations) Collaboration and closed-loop planning environment necessitates clean, synchronized data.
- Disconnected demand, supply, and financial plans make it difficult to reconcile plans with reality, and to re-plan accordingly
- Multiple echelons and constraints in global, distributed supply chain requires incisive collaboration and instant visibility of critical planning data
- Increasingly complex supply chain processes impede best-practice decision-making and management of data transfers.

Marico: The Whole Nine Yards Industry (A Case-Study)

Company Profile: Marico is a leading Indian Group operating in Consumer Products, Aesthetics Services and Global Ayurvedics businesses. Marico's FY 2003-04 Turnover was about Rs. 9 Billion (USD 200 Million) from 12 brands - Parachute, Saffola, Sweekar, Hair & Care, Shanti, Mediker, Oil of Malabar, Mealmaker, Sil, Revive, Kaya and Sundari. Marico's distribution width and penetration is acknowledged as one of the best in the industry and is a leverageable strength. Every month, 46 million consumer packs are sold to about 1.8 million households through 1.7 million retail outlets spread across the country. Marico's distribution network covers almost every Indian town with a population of over 20,000 (www.maricoindia.com).

Business Situation: Six years ago (Year 2000), Marico's top team took serious note of the fact that Marico had under performed. It was dependent on just two brands, Parachute and Saffola, for its lion's share of profits. Competitors like Hindustan Lever and Dabur had put its margins under pressure. Marico reacted with a series of line extensions, most of which sank without a trace, leading to a lot of discontentment within the organization.

To add to its woes, Hindustan Lever Ltd, had strengthened its presence in the hair oils segment with its acquisition of the 'Coco Care' brand from Recon Oil Industries. Analysts we led to believe that Coco care was a threat to Parachute and that the distribution muscle of HLL would prove just too dangerous for Marico.

On assessing the situation, Marico officials pinpointed a lack of visibility and promptness in the secondary sales and off take (read 'demand') information reaching the Company. Marico were still taking supply chain decisions based on its sale to distributors. The data was available on a 10-day or monthly frequency and was insufficient. There was a need to get secondary sales data at a higher frequency and granularity. In short, the company needed a software package to capture secondary sales data or distributor sales data and feed it into its SAP R/3 ERP (Enterprise Resource Planning) system. This meant 'forward integration' with Distributors, Super Distributors, Wholesalers, and stockists. It was at this juncture that Marico was confronted with a critical technology-business decision: Either build or buy the required system for better SCM. Because by then the company has realized that better SCM was the only means to combat with competitors in safeguarding and enhancing his share of market.

MIDAS-Marico Industries Distribution Application Software

The aim of the project was to enhance the responsiveness of the company's supply chain. A more responsive supply chain would help a company of Marico's kind (an FMCG or Fast Moving Consumer Goods company) to reduce costs and enjoy better sales and inventory management. But to do so, Marico had to base its supply chain decisions on secondary sales.

In an ideal scenario, to be able to accurately forecast demand, an FMCG company's supply chain decision should be based on the off-take (retail sales). However, this is seldom possible. Today, most supply chain decisions are based on secondary sales, whose data is captured by most SCM (Supply Chain

Management) applications.

In order to provide the off-take data readily and on a continuous basis Marico's IT team went around scouting for a distributor automation solution and discovered quite a few readily available packages. They went with one package, which came closest to meeting its needs and understanding its business, and customized it.

Marico selected "STOCKY", a product developed for distributors, by Botree. It was developed on Delphi with MS Access as a backend. Marico bought licenses for the package and went about with the customization. Eventually after taking private labeling rights from Botree, STOCKY was renamed MIDAS, and rolled out at selected distributor points.

Since the distributor community works like one big brotherhood, the company created a selected list of the leading distributors, called "Greenball Distributors", who stand as examples to their smaller counterparts.

During the course of implementation Marico faced no resistance from its target community, but there was increased skepticism. This might have happened because many distributors had seen other principles, like Marico, fail in their attempts at launching similar initiatives. But the Greenball distributors were open to the idea. So with the influential distributors on their side and by ensuring a successful implementation, Marico convinced the smaller distributors about the benefits of the solution.

Marico also made efforts to see that the package was relevant to the distributors. Stocky Midas was customized to a multi-user, multi-company product so that distributors could employ separate staff to manage products coming in from multiple companies. All the distributors had to do buy was the hardware, the PC and modem. Marico foot the bill for the software license.

The other hurdle Marico faced was in convincing distributors already running an automation package to switch over to Stocky Midas. Typically, some distributors used local software, which was tailored around their respective businesses and the availability of efficient local support. The company had to spend a lot of time convincing them that in the long run, the rugged Midas was superior to the local brew. Most distributors eventually saw the light; with the few who didn't, Marico terminated its business relations.

Eventually, all hiccups were overcome because of one of the most potent tool any company could use: Communication. The communication began with a personalized letter sent to each distributor by Marico's MD, a week before the rollout started. The letter explained what the company was implementing and why it was necessary for both the distributor and Marico. The letter set the tone of the relationship; it was like a partner talking to another. This way the distributors realized that even the top brass at Marico was committed to the project, and felt involved in the whole exercise.

Then, when the rollout actually started, the company realized that because most of its distributors were computer illiterate, each of them needed at least a week's training. The company tackled this problem uniquely. Marico figured out that a distributor and the TSO (Territory Sales Officer) understood each other's language perfectly." So Marico built teams comprising of a mix of technologists (from Marico), implementers (from Botree), and a few select TSOs. The technologist & Implementers taught the technology; the TSOs convinced the distributors and spent time understanding their issues and solving their problems. The TSOs, of course, were trained on Midas before they were sent out on this exercise. Botree provided the technology content for the teams.

At its peak rollout stage, Marico would evangelize up to 40 distributors a month. While the rollouts continued, bugs were discovered and features added/deleted until a final stable version of Midas was arrived at in about two months" time. Marico automated 330 distributors over nine months. These were the company's A Class distributors, who took care of about 75 percent of the company's business volumes.

The second phase involved hooking these 330 distributors to the company's SAP system. When the second phase of the project started, 200 distributors were already automated. This phase involved the creation of a middle layer to glue distributors' systems with the company's SAP systems. This took about six months to develop and roll out. The whole setup went live from April 2002. Today, distributors log on to the Marico site once daily, and select the "upload-download" command. Their data is automatically uploaded to Marico's system through the middle layer and SAP data downloaded to the distributors". This download could include information on promotional schemes, new pricing and the like.

The middle layer and the Midas (Stocky) distributor automation system were collectively called MI-NET. Both phases of the two-year long project were completed by April 2002.

Benefits: Marico implemented MIDAS and Mi-Net and are enjoying the following business benefits:

1. Data is centrally available to everyone within the organization
2. Drop in distributor transaction processing cost.
3. Reduction in communication costs on inventory and order status follow-ups,
4. Improved Sales Force productivity
5. Improvement in forecast accuracy
6. Reduction in sales Skew
7. Reduction in planning cycle time
8. Reduction in late deliveries
9. Reactivation of lapsed outlets
10. Improvement in return on investment for the distributor
11. Reduction in the working capital requirement

August 3, 2002, was a memorable day for Mr. Satish Pendse. For it was on this day that the 36-year-old GM-Information Systems of the Rs 671-crore Marico Industries won the Lakshya 2002 Systems and IT award conferred by the National Institute of Industrial Engineering. Judged by the likes of Prof. Nori (CTO, TCS), Neeraj Bhai (CTO, IDBI Bank) and Prince Azariah (CIO, Reliance Industries)

STOCKY MIDAS has helped Marico by providing critical downstream information it needs to compete in today's connected economy. The STOCKY MIDAS software has helped Marico's streamline its supply chain and build closer relationships with its customers, thereby, making its supply chain more responsive, efficient, and profitable. Thus the SCM initiative undertaken by Marico Industries has provided a strategic edge in the contemporary era of competition to combat with the ever-growing competition.

Strategic Edge-Domino Effects of SCM Application

- Integrated manufacturing, product development, and supply chain resources to drive reduction in inventory levels. For Example: **Mahindra & Mahindra** succeeded in reducing inventory in the supply chain of finished goods from 18,992 tractors before implementing mySAP SCM to approximately 8,400 units in 2001(Vaid Neelima, 'Supply Chain Management in Mahindra& Mahindra', www.mahindra.com).
- Increased speed of delivering new products from design to store while reducing supply chain costs. For Example: **Mahindra & Mahindra** was able to improve its order fulfillment rates from 51 days before the implementation of SCM solution to 19 days as per its plan.
- Optimized product development and reduction in finished goods working capital costs .For Example: '**Whirlpool**, the electronic appliances giant has achieved significant results in its targeted areas of improvement by making an SCM initiative. "In the first full calendar year after their implementation of SCM software solution, they were able to deliver 92.6 percent across all of their brands and products, and their target was 93 percent. They were supposed to deliver a 10 percent reduction in finished goods working capital, and they came in slightly better than that on inventory. They had a goal of 5 percent total cost productivity year over year, and they were at 5.1 percent." Whirlpool believes that these results were made possible by the support of i2 BOS professionals during and after its implementation of i2 solutions' (Durables Supply Chain, The ET Knowledge Series, Supply Chain & Logistics, 2002).

- Compression and modularization techniques to improve the efficiency of the manufacturing process to drive higher inventory turns. For Example: A number of companies, such as **Dell Computer Company**, have been successful in implementing pull systems, which has had a dramatic impact upon their inventory turnover. Essentially, personal computers that are ordered via telephone, fax, or the Internet are assembled /produced after the order is received. Dell can frequently produce the customized computer in forty-eight hours or less and ship it to its customers. Such a strategy has a dramatic impact on finished goods inventory.
- Improved trade partner relationships to ensure that products are effectively positioned in front of customers. For Example: **LG Electronics India** has also concentrated on its supply chain from the very beginning and plans to use it as one of the ways to become a market leader in consumer durables. LG has realized savings of up to $0.48 million from its direct-to-trade initiatives. Modifications in the distribution system have also helped them in saving time and cost. LG claims this has already saved them $0.24 million in 2002 due to improved trade partner relationships.

Conclusion

How can an organization manage its supply chain more effectively? If it can foresee accurately what is going to happen in the future by taking into consideration all possible constraints and takes decision based on it. This will improve chances of gaining a competitive edge. Any supply organization, which participates and collaborates fully and effectively will be valued as trusted partners, and becomes strong link in the supply chain. To achieve, this, Indian Companies need to develop flexible supply chain processes that can adapt to the needs of various customer segments. They must also develop supply chain strategy, processes and supporting systems that confirm to current and future requirements. Good collaborative demand planning, optimized supply chain planning and realistic replenishment planning and trustworthy collaboration with the trading partners are essential to effective SCM. There can be much further improvements like efficient transportation planning to minimize cycle time and to have optimized delivery schedules, effective warehouse management to improve the order fulfillment.

References

Anderson, David L.Britt, Frank E., and Favre, Donavon J., 'The Seven Principles of Supply Chain Management, Logistics Management'. pp.100-105.

Donald J. Bowersox, David J.Closs, Theodore P. Stank, and Scott B. Keller, 'How Supply Chain Competency Leads to Business Success', Supply Chain Management Review, September/October 2000, pp. 70-73.

Durables Supply Chain, The ET Knowledge Series, Supply Chain & Logistics, 2002.

Pais Anil, 'Supply Chain Management for SMEs – A boon for achieving distinction', pp. 1-12.

Sahay, B.S., Supply Chain Management for Global Competitiveness, Macmillan India, New Delhi, 1999. pp.25-37

Vaid Neelima, 'Supply Chain Management in Mahindra& Mahindra', pp.1-10.

14

Reinventing the Supply Chain

Alok Jha and P. Sailaja

Globalization has accelerated the evolution of supply chain management (SCM) in the last decade. Supply Chains worldwide are increasingly becoming complex and are going through unprecedented change. As the global markets have become more customer-centric, the growth of the organizations would get hampered if the customer oriented planning is not kept in place, as, gone are the days when a system is managed. Now, the system manages (Ansoff, 1969; de Leeuw, 1982; Cooper et al., 1997). Looking at the current scenario, the authors drew their attention towards thinking about how to reorient supply chain process to match the customer centric markets. In this process, authors have touched upon transition of process oriented SCM to customer oriented SCM and reinventing the SCM.

Introduction

In the modern world the main focus of competition is not only between different companies but also between supply chains. As the satisfaction of the final customer is of utmost importance for the successfulness of the whole chain, effective management of those processes is crucial. As known, SCM entails coordination and configuration of the process that is necessary to make products available in a timely, reproducible and satisfactory manner. SCM is changing the viewpoint from which a business need to be managed by looking at the current capabilities of the organisation to deliver the goods to customer in a satisfactory manner while giving due regards to optimisation of the resources. In recent years, the supply chain has gained more importance with the cost of information going down and physical distribution costs going up.

With the advent of Liberalisation, Privatisation and Globalisation there is a tremendous pressure for change on Indian industries. Such continuous pressures for change have not only demanded the fitness of organisations to compete, but have created imperatives to reengineer the age-old ritualistic management systems. Now this is the era of customer oriented SCM rather than the process oriented which is evident by many business organisations' practices like DELL, Wal-Mart, Amazon.com, Dabbawalas etc.,

So as to appreciate the performance of above stated companies, it is imperative to understand what the consequence of SCM is on giving ultimate value to the Customer.

Customer Oriented Objective Planning

Objective driven process encounters the problems of mismatches with the outcomes. The general objective of Customer oriented supply chain management could be matching with the requirements of customers in terms of manufacturing and supply shcedule adherece, perfect order etc., If the objectives of SCM interms of customer orientation is done, if would be easy for the next steps to follow.

Delineation of Supply Chains Sub Processes

Once the objectives are in place, it is important to prioritise the primary and supportive process of SCM. A primary processes in other words could be, in-bound & out-bound logistics put together in production chains concern activities like receiving raw materials, material supply for production process, storing and conditioning the product, selling, delivery and service. The re-invention can be take place in the primary processes of Value Chain by Re-eingeneering the business process, in other words, Business Process Reingeneering. The non-primary processes like the financial, Personnel etc., play a secondary role. They should also be constructed to support primary processes.

Disintegration of SCM Sub Process

In order to give focused reorientation, all the sub processes of SCM needs to be separated like for eg., the process of recieving raw materials, supply of material during production process, transporting the fininshed good etc,. Here is where the Step 1 should again take an aggressive stake.

This disintegration of SCM has two prime goals:

1. Reduction of complexity. Disintegration aims to reach a structure of decomposed, though interrelated, processes with maximal internal cohesion and minimal external cohesion. This is done to have a focused appraoach for reengineering.
2. Developing a assessment to know how should be reeingneered in each aspect and what is the targeted change expected. According to Beulens, (1997) Delineation of SCM sub processes helps on one hand, to the reduction of complexity to achieve a process configuration with manageable complexity and on the other hand, its goal is to achieve a responsive output oriented supply chain infrastructure (Beulens, 1997).

Conducting the Restructuring through Business Process Reengineering

Reengineering involves defining, analysing, and recreating the Value Delivery Process (VDP) to create competitive advantage. An understanding of the VDP would result in a shared vision and strategy for future. Reengineering VDP means being willing and able to dismantle the current process in order to create a new redesigned process. There are basically six depth levers for reengineering: Structure, Skills, IT systems, Roles & Responsibilities, Measurements & Incentives and shared values which may be of the order of 100% improvements over the existing process. The process used for reengineering depends on the complexities and structures of the processes involved.

The various phases of BPR include Diagnostic phase, Process Analysis, Process Selection, Process Design, Evaluation arid Appraisal after the implementation process. The diagnostic phase, comprises of the study of the company profile, its objectives followed by structuring of the problem areas and identification of relevant processes. After the critical appraisal of the functions, identification and structuring of problems, the identified processes are to be mapped by using the modeling tools of BPR. This phase is labeled as Process Design Phase. In the next phase, the processes are to be evaluated. This can be done by some quantification effort to understand the implications of the slow response of the existing processes. After redesigning the process, the redesigned process is to be actually implemented. This is followed by the appraisal phase, in which a snap shot can be taken to understand and appreciate the benefits or shortfalls of the expected benefits.

Reengineering of SCM is not an incremental improvement strategy' but a philosophy that leads to improvement not associated with functional/departmental reviews, which focus only internally. The essence of reengineering is that management must not only control inputs but also significantly change the processes itself. Hence, transforming a business from an inward looking with a view of 'what we make will sell' to a flexible outward looking business 'what the customer wants us to sell' becomes the focus of reengineering. The integration attempts are initiated to a combination of actors such as competition and changing customers. Inquisitive minds throughout the organisation aid in reengineering. This holds especially true at the higher echelons of the organisation as these positions give a wider perspective seeking core processes and creating leaner structures. Hence, this becomes absolutely a must for SCM integration through reengineering.

Table 14.1 indicates the areas of change to be brought in order to reengineer and specific strategy pertaining to making the change happen.

The sequence of Value Chain Process is indicated and throught this picture which gives a snap shot of a process where the Customer is initiating the total process of Value Delivery based on which SCM should accordingly vary.

Table 14.1: Strategy for Reengineering the Supply Chain

Area of Change	Strategy for Reengineering the Supply Chain
Focus	° What customers want us to sell
Process	° Reduce non value adding activities ° Lead time/inventory reduction
People	° Top level commitment with a SCM ° An inquisitive management ° An Inquisitive work force ° Multi-skilled work force ° Positive attitudinal change
Technology	° Invest in technology ° IT a key (computers, communication)

Integration of the Sub Processes of SCM to Deliver More Customer Value

In order to deliver more value to the customer, it is imperative to understand the various factors that can influence a customer. The customer perception can be managed by adding more and more value to the customers at each and every aspect that builds perception in them. According to David Simchi-Levi, Philip Kaminsky & Edith Simchi-Levi, the various dimensions that influence customers' perception are:'

1. Conformance to requirements: Relating to Customer access
2. Product Selection: Degree of freedom to customize
3. Price & Brand: Cost Reduction which ultimately results in price reduction
4. Value-added Services: eg: Information service
5. Relationships & Experiences: Through CRM and Customer Experience Management programs.

References

David Simchi-Levi, Philip Kaminsky, Edith Simchi-Levi, Designing & Managing the Supply Chain, Tata McGraw-Hill, 2004, p.p 237-258

Supply Chain Management in the Global Environment, Nancy W.Nix,

Response Books, 2001, p.p 27-37
Supply Chain Management, John T.Mentzer, Response Books, 2001, p.p 61-74

15

Promotional Strategies of Mobile Telephone Service Providers

Mihir Dash and M. Viswanathiah

Introduction

The Markov brand-switching model is a relatively simple application of the theory of stochastic processes to consumer behaviour. In modeling brand-switching behaviour, it makes two simplifying assumptions.

The first assumption, called the Markov property, is that customers "forget" the past history of brands used, and only consider the current brand they are using when deciding whether to switch brands or not. Thus, at any point of time, the brand-switching behaviour of customers is not determined by which brands they have used in the past, the order in which they used past brands, and their past experiences with these brands. The only data relevant to their brand-switching decision is the brand they are currently using.

The second assumption is that one-period transition probabilities between states are constant at all points of time – i.e. the percentages of customers switching between brands in the next period are fixed.

Thus, if there are only two brands, say A (Airtel) and H (Hutch), the one-period transition probabilities are given by p (the percentage of customers currently using brand A who switch over to brand H in the next period) and q (the percentage of customers currently using brand H who switch over to brand A in the next period).

These one-period transition probabilities are represented in a one-period transition probability matrix as follows:

		Next period state	
		A	H
Current state	A	$\begin{pmatrix} 1-p & p \\ q & 1-q \end{pmatrix}$	
	H		

The one-period transition probability matrix is used to describe the evolution of the system over time. Thus, if $\pi_{A,t}$ is the percentage of customers using brand A at time t, and $\pi_{H,t}$ is the percentage of customers using brand H at time t, then the percentages of customers using the brands A and H at time $t+1$ is given by the matrix equation $\pi_{t+1} = \pi_t.P$, where $\pi_t = (\pi_{A,t} \quad \pi_{H,t})$ is the state vector at time t.

As the system described above evolves, eventually a "dynamic equilibrium" is achieved whereby the switching between brands does not alter the distribution between the brands. This is achieved when $p.\pi_A = q.\pi_H$, where π_A and π_H are the percentages of customers using brands A and H, respectively. Such a condition is called "steady-state." The steady- state distribution of the customers under the above conditions would then be given by

$\pi_A = \dfrac{q}{p+q}$ and $\pi_H = \dfrac{p}{p+q}$.

The steady-state distribution of the customers between the brands thus represents their long-run market shares, under the two assumptions above.

The game theoretic framework presents a simple method for evaluating and determining decisions under conditions of conflict. The simplest form of game is that of a "2x2 two-player zero-sum game," in which there are only two "players" or participants, each of them having to choose between only two possible alternative courses of action, in which the outcome is determined by the alternatives chosen by both of the players, and in which the "payoff" resulting to one player is exactly the reverse of that resulting to the other player. Such a game can be represented by a payoff matrix (conventionally representing payoffs to the row player):

		Player H	
		T_1	T_2
Player A	S_1	a	b
	S_2	c	d

where a is the payoff to player A when player A chooses strategy S_1 and player H chooses strategy T_1, b is the payoff to player A when player A chooses strategy S_2 and player H chooses strategy T_1, c is the payoff to player A when player A chooses strategy S_2 and player H chooses strategy T_1, and d is the payoff to player A when player A chooses strategy S_2 and player H chooses strategy T_2. The payoffs to player H are exactly the negatives of these.

Assuming that these are the only alternative courses of action available to the players, two possibilities may result. The first possibility occurs if one of the elements a, b, c, or d of the payoff matrix is simultaneously the least element in the row in which it lies and the largest element in the column in which it lies. Such an element is called a saddlepoint element. If a saddlepoint exists in the payoff matrix, then the strategies corresponding to the row and the column in which the saddlepoint lie are the optimal strategies for the row and column players, respectively. The strategies are optimal in the sense that, assuming that the other player does not change their strategy, neither player can increase their payoff by changing their strategy.

The second possibility occurs if no saddlepoint exists in the payoff matrix. In this case, no single strategy is optimal in the above sense for either player. Instead, both players must "optimally mix" the two strategies available to them, shifting between the two strategies in a fixed proportion. These "optimal mixing" proportions are given by

$p_1 = \frac{d-c}{(a+d)-(b+c)}$ and $p_2 = \frac{a-b}{(a+d)-(b+c)}$ for player A, where p_1 represents the percentage of the time player A should use strategy S_1 and p_2 represents the percentage of time of time player A should use strategy S_2, and

$q_1 = \frac{d-b}{(a+d)-(b+c)}$ and $q_2 = \frac{a-c}{(a+d)-(b+c)}$ for player H,

where q_1 represents the percentage of the time player B should use strategy T_1 and q_2 represents the percentage of time of time player A should use strategy T_2. The "expected value" of the game, i.e. the average payoff to player A is given by $Ev = \frac{a.d - b.c}{(a+d)-(b+c)}$. The average payoff to player H is just the negative of this quantity.

Several studies have used the Markov model to study brand-switching behaviour (e.g. Bass et al, 1984). Pfeifer and Carraway (2000) used Markov chains to model the switching of customers between different levels of decency of buying with the firm. In the context of valuing customer relationships, Rust et al (2001) suggested the use of a Markov process to develop a customer equity model that takes into account brand switching. Libai et al (2002) have also suggested the application of the Markov model between customer segments to estimate customer equity. On the other hand, Sun et al (2003) have studied the impact of promotions of brand-switching, but their approach was based on logit choice models, and they proposed the use of dynamical structural models for better results.

The present study is an extension of the authors' paper (2006), incorporating brand loyalty into the Markov brand-switching model. Thus, if the initial market shares of Airtel (A) and Hutch (H) are denoted by m_A^o, m_H^o, and the proportions of brand-loyal customers of Airtel and Hutch are denoted by θ_A, θ_H, then the long-run market shares may be expressed as

$$\pi_A^L = \theta_A . m_A^O + \frac{q}{p+q}\left((1-\theta_A)m_A^O + (1-\theta_H)m_H^O\right)$$

$$\pi_H^L = \theta_H . m_H^O + \frac{p}{p+q}\left((1-\theta_H)m_H^O + (1-\theta_A)m_A^O\right)$$

The steady-state distribution in the extended model is thus further dependent upon two additional sets of parameters: the initial distribution and the proportions of brand-loyal customers. The question arises as to whether these initial conditions would affect the promotional mix of the mobile telephone service providers.

Data and Methodology

The objective of the present study is to extend the Markov model by introducing brand loyalty, and to assess the impact of brand loyalty on the "optimal promotion mix." As with the authors' earlier study, the scope of the present study was limited to studying brand-switching behaviour between Airtel and Hutch among students in Bangalore. In particular, the study was designed to investigate the effect of promotional strategies on brand-switching, so as to determine the "optimal promotion mix" that Airtel and Hutch should offer for the student segment. The different promotional strategies considered for the study were: unlimited free SMS (denoted by S_1 for Airtel and T_1 for Hutch), unlimited free outgoing calls within home network (denoted by S_2 for Airtel and T_2 for Hutch), and full talk time (denoted by S_3 for Airtel and T_3 for Hutch).

The data was collected from a random sample of 100 students in Bangalore who were Airtel users and an independent random sample of 100 students in Bangalore who were Hutch users. Each respondent was asked whether they would switch service provider under each strategy combination employed by Airtel and Hutch. For each strategy combination the sample switching rates were computed, and the long-run market shares of Airtel and Hutch were computed using these sample switching rates in the extended Markov model, under different initial conditions. These long-run market shares were then considered as the payoffs in a 3x3 two-player, zero-sum game (after adjustment by deducting 50 per cent from them). The optimal promotional strategy mix was then computed using game theoretic techniques. To analyse the robustness of the optimal strategy mix, sensitivity analysis was performed, using the 95 per cent confidence limits in the switching rates. Finally, the results of the analysis under different initial conditions were compared to assess the impact of the initial conditions on the "optimal promotion mix."

Analysis and Interpretation

The sample estimates one-period switching rates between the brands under each strategy combination are given in Table 15.1.

Table 15.1: Sample Estimates of One-period Switching Rates between Airtel and Hutch under Each Strategy Combination

Percentages switching from Hutch to Airtel					Percentages switching from Airtel to Hutch			
	T_1	T_2	T_3			T_1	T_2	T_3
S_1	62	43	61		S_1	17	18	13
S_2	42	66	69		S_2	55	10	09
S_3	28	26	42		S_3	70	63	11

The resulting payoff matrix for Airtel is given in Table 15.2.

Table 15.2: Payoff Matrix for Airtel (base case)

		Hutch		
		T_1	T_2	T_3
	S_1	28.48%	20.49%	32.43%
Airtel	S_2	−6.70%	36.84%	38.46%
	S_3	−21.43%	−20.79%	29.25%

Strategies S_3 and T_3 are clearly dominated strategies, and the optimal mixing percentages for S_1 & S_2 for Airtel and T_1 & T_2 for Hutch are given by: p_1 = 84.49 per cent, p_2 = 15.51 per cent, and q_1 = 31.73 per cent, q_2 = 68.27 per cent. The expected value for Airtel is Ev = 23.025 per cent. This means that, in the base case, the optimal promotion mix for Airtel is to offer unlimited free SMS 84.49 per cent of the time and unlimited free outgoing calls 15.51 per cent of the time, alternating, while the optimal promotion mix for Hutch is to offer unlimited free SMS 31.73 per cent of the time and unlimited free outgoing calls 68.27 per cent of the time, alternating, and subsequently the expected outcome would be a 23.025 per cent shift in the long-run market share in favour of Airtel.

As the data used in the computations above was sample data, sensitivity analysis was performed to analyse the robustness of the above optimal strategies. In performing the sensitivity analysis, 95 per cent confidence limits were used. In the "optimistic case" (from Airtel's point of view), the lower 95 per cent confidence limit (i.e. $\hat{p}-1.96\sqrt{\frac{\hat{p}(1-\hat{p})}{n}}$) was used to estimate the switching rate from Airtel to Hutch, and the upper 95 per cent confidence limit (i.e. $\hat{q}+1.96\sqrt{\frac{\hat{q}(1-\hat{q})}{n}}$) was used to estimate the switching rate from Hutch to Airtel. In the "pessimistic case" (from Airtel's point of view), the upper 95 per cent confidence limit (i.e. $\hat{p}+1.96\sqrt{\frac{\hat{p}(1-\hat{p})}{n}}$) was used to estimate the switching rate from Airtel to Hutch, and the lower 95 per cent confidence limit (i.e. $\hat{q}-1.96\sqrt{\frac{\hat{q}(1-\hat{q})}{n}}$) was used to estimate the switching rate from Hutch to Airtel.

The payoff matrix for Airtel (in the optimistic case) is given in Table 15.3.

Table 15.3: Payoff Matrix for Airtel (optimistic case)

		Hutch		
		T_1	T_2	T_3
	S_1	38.12%	33.43%	41.67%
Airtel	S_2	3.31%	44.81%	45.84%
	S_3	−12.38%	−10.75%	41.39%

Again, strategies S_3 and T_3 are clearly dominated strategies, and the optimal mixing percentages for S_1 & S_2 for Airtel and T_1 & T_2 for Hutch are in this case: $p_1 = 89.95$ per cent, $p_2 = 10.15$ per cent, and $q_1 = 24.64$ per cent, $q_2 = 75.36$ per cent. The expected value for Airtel in this case is Ev = 34.585 per cent. This means that, in the optimistic case (i.e. if all conditions are favourable for Airtel), the optimal promotion mix for Airtel is to offer unlimited free SMS 89.95 per cent of the time and unlimited free outgoing calls 10.15 per cent of the time, alternating, while the optimal promotion mix for Hutch is to offer unlimited free SMS 24.64 per cent of the time and unlimited free outgoing calls 75.36 per cent of the time, alternating, and subsequently the expected outcome would be a 34.585 per cent shift in the long-run market share in favour of Airtel.

The payoff matrix for Airtel (in the pessimistic case) is given in Table 15.4:

Table 15.4: Payoff matrix for Airtel (pessimistic case)

		Hutch		
		T_1	**T_2**	**T_3**
	S_1	18.30%	6.60%	22.42%
Airtel	**S_2**	−16.70%	28.13%	30.40%
	S_3	−30.45%	−30.63%	15.37%

Again, strategies S_3 and T_3 are clearly dominated strategies, and the optimal mixing percentages for S_1 & S_2 for Airtel and T_1 & T_2 for Hutch are in this case: $p_1 = 79.30$ per cent, $p_2 = 20.70$ per cent, and $q_1 = 38.08$ per cent, $q_2 = 61.92$ per cent. The expected value for Airtel in this case is Ev = 11.055 per cent. This means that, in the pessimistic case (i.e. if all conditions are unfavourable for Airtel), the optimal promotion mix for Airtel is to offer unlimited free SMS 79.30 per cent of the time and unlimited free outgoing calls 20.70 per cent of the time, alternating, while the optimal promotion mix for Hutch is to offer unlimited free SMS 38.08 per cent of the time and unlimited free outgoing calls 61.92 per cent of the time, alternating, and subsequently the expected outcome would be a 11.055 per cent shift in the long-run market share in favour of Airtel.

The results of the analysis using the extended Markov model show that the optimal promotion mix is not affected by either the initial market share or the proportions of brand-loyal customers. However, there is an effect of the initial conditions in terms of the shift in market share.

The results show about 5 per cent variation in the shift in long-run market share between different initial market shares; the variation increases with higher levels of brand loyalty. The impact of Airtel's brand loyalty level on the shift in long-run market share decreases by 2-4 per cent with decreasing initial market share, while the impact of Hutch's brand loyalty level on the shift in long-run market share increases by 6-8 per cent.

Discussion and Conclusion

On the basis of the above analysis, it follows that Airtel, by alternating using the strategies of unlimited free SMS 84.49 per cent of the time (on average) and unlimited free outgoing calls within home network 15.51 per cent of the time (on average), can achieve on average a 23.025 per cent shift in the long-run market share in its favour, and that the best response of Hutch would be to also offer unlimited free SMS and unlimited free outgoing calls within home network alternating, but in the proportion 31.73 per cent and 68.27 per cent (on average), respectively. Moreover, the sensitivity analysis shows a difference of more than 10 per cent between the optimistic case outcomes and the pessimistic case outcomes, indicating a high degree of variation. The initial market share and level of brand loyalty was not found to affect the optimal promotion mix, but does affect the shift in long-run market share. The impact of brand loyalty is higher at lower levels of initial market share. More accurate estimates should be obtained in order to be able to calculate the mixing proportions accurately, and to assess the final impact of the promotional mix.

In a sense, these results concur with the practices of service providers. Airtel and Hutch do offer the promotional schemes described above, and vary the offers available month-to-month. The analysis above suggests that this should be done in a systematic, calculated manner. A possible approach would be to estimate market shares, levels of brand loyalty, and switching rates periodically, and to update the optimal promotion mix with current data. In this way, the estimates would be more accurate, and any changes could be detected and incorporated into the analysis. This would result in a more dynamic, reactive strategy.

There are several limitations in the present study, relating to the assumptions of the Markov model and the methodological simplifications employed.

To begin with, the Markov property is a very restrictive assumption. Consumer behaviour, and in particular brand-switching, involves several factors, especially the history of experiences with brands. The extended model incorporates brand loyalty, but does not completely resolve the limitations of the Markov property. At best the assumption of the Markov property could be justified by arguing that brand-switching behaviour is determined mainly by brand differentiation, marginalizing the role of past experiences with brands.

Another weakness in the Markov model is the assumption of stationarity. In reality, switching rates themselves would depend on several factors, and would change over time. At best these switching rates could be taken to be constant for the short-run, in which case a long-run analysis would be misleading. The long-run market shares could be interpreted as "implied" market shares, and could therefore still function as objectives.

Another limitation arises from the restriction of scope only to brand-switching behaviour between Airtel and Hutch, ignoring switching to and from other service providers. The preceding analysis can be generalized to more than two service providers. Similarly, the analysis can also be generalized to include more promotional strategies, and more synthetic promotional strategies. Some strategies may be redundant or inferior, as was the case with the third strategy considered, viz. full talk time. A more detailed study of what factors affect brand choice and brand-switching behaviour in students would enable a more realistic model of the same.

References

Bass, F. M., Givon, M., Kalwani, M.U., Reibstein, D., and Wright, G.P. (1984), "An Investigation into the Order of the Brand Choice Process," *Marketing Science*, 3 (Fall).

Dash, M. and Viswanathaiah (2006), "Sensitivity Analysis of Promotional Strategies of Mobile Telephone Service Providers I," *Submitted for publication.*

Libai, B., Narayandas, D., and Humby, C. (2002), "Towards an Individual Customer Profitability Model," *Journal of Service Research*, Vol. 5, No. 1, August 2002.

Pfeifer, P. and Carraway, R.L. (2000), "Modeling Customer Relationships as Markov Chains," *Journal of Interactive Marketing*, 14(2), 43-55.

Puterman, M.L. (1994), *Markov Decision Processes: Discrete Stochastic Dynamic Programming*. New York: John Wiley.

Rust, R.T., Lemon, K.N., and Zeithaml, V.A. (2001), "Driving Customer Equity: Linking Customer Lifetime Value to Strategic Marketing Decisions," Report No. 01-108, Marketing Science Institute, Cambridge, MA.

Sun, B., Neslin, S.A., and Srinivasan, K. (2003), "Measuring the Impact of Promotions on Brand Switching when Consumers are Forward-Looking," *Journal of Marketing Research*, Vol. 40, No.4.

16

Development of Inventory Control Models

Koilakuntla Maddulety

Concept of Inventory Control

As the term inventory control is rather loosely used to cover two functions, which are quite different and are related to each other only in that they both require the maintenance of adequate records of inventory as well as receipts and issues corresponding to these two functions, inventory control is interpreted as accounting control and operating control. The control of inventories is concerned with:

- The safeguarding of the undertakings property in the form of raw material, work-in-process and semi-finished as well as finished products and
- The proper recording of receipts and consumption of materials as well as the flow of the goods through the plant and to finished stock and eventually to the customers.

Operating control of inventories is concerned with maintaining inventories at the optimum level keeping in view the operational requirements and financial resources of the business.

Benefit of Effective Inventory Control

- Improvement of customer relations:
- Improvement of labour and community relations:
- Increase in effectiveness of key personal:
- Reduction in manufacturing costs:
- Reduction of purchased Material cost:

Because of above benefits the researcher has developed appropriate inventory control models to HLL after detailed study of present system and gap analysis.

Need for Project Report

The raw materials in Hindustan Latex Limited, is controlled by using general principles and methods. The HINDUSTAN LATEX stores personal are not using scientific methods/models for controlling raw materials' inventory. The general models are also not adequate for controlling/maintaining inventory to optimize productivity and profits. So, an attempt is made to study the inventory systems, its process and procedures for developing inventory control models at least for all processing materials, after classifying and analyzing entire raw materials.

Objectives of the Study

The important objectives of this study are:

1. To know and understand the present system of inventory management at Hindustan Latex Limited.
2. To examine in detail the inventory control methods.
3. To find out deficiencies, if any, in the inventory methods.
4. To design and develop effective inventory control methods, and to make necessary suggestions for improving the inventory planning and control.
5. To develop purchase order guide for purchase officer.
6. To develop buffer and reorder levels for all processing materials.
7. Totally to develop a good guide to inventory managing personals.

Methodology

The study was undertaken in the form of a comprehensive study. The most of the data has been collected from Kanagala unit of Hindustan Latex Limited, only few data collected from its parent unit Nirodh factory, and corporate office Poojapura, Trivandrum.

The secondary data was collected from the statistical information given by the accounts and the administration section. These sources are field source and document source respectively. Thus entire information and data was collected from following sources for the study:

The following data was collected by administering questionnaires to store staff, purchase staff, materials consuming department heads etc. The other details and information were obtained through personal discussion, interviews and through direct observations.

Secondary Data: The secondary data was collected from monthly, quarterly and annual stores report, purchase reports, consumption reports of consuming departments and from records of production planning and control departments.

As the time is limited, the universe of study is confined to Nirodh factory, Kanagala, a unit of Hindustan Latex Limited only.

But the scope of utility of this report is for two units of Hindustan Latex Limited, (Nirodh factory, Trivandrum & Nirodh factory, Kanagala).

Major Findings and Observations

The researcher found that there is no A-B-C analysis at stores inventory management. The analysis helps them to take cost reduction 'steps towards 'A' class materials those contributed to 74 per cent of total material cost.

The H-M-L analysis was also not available earlier. Now the researcher's H-M-L analysis helps them in handling of materials. Now they came to know that the high value items' handling should be highly cared.

As per observation there was no ordering cost calculation. The calculations help them in their purchase department management.

As per the observation there was no carrying cost calculations. The models calculations helps store managers.

Other observations

- There are good general principles and methods, which purchase & store departments are following. But these are not scientific. .For example, there is no E.O.Q calculations.
- Storing of materials highly systematic at stores.
- The stores documentation and its maintenance are excellent.

- They have formats like stores requisition, card-ex systems cards, material arrival note, material receipt note, etc., are scientifically derived formats.
- Feedback to user department from store department, regarding stock position of various materials are being given through computer control stock statement is very good.

Conclusions

1. The study is limited to only production processing materials (chemicals and packing materials). We have not included the production supporting materials like spare parts of machines, engineering items, electrical spares, office stationery, etc., on the basis of this limited project report, the HLL has to develop detailed reports which can include inventory control models, for entire materials.
2. As on date the HINDUSTAN LATEX LTD kanagala unit has no inventory analysis such as ABC, VED, or HML etc., other than this report. So on the basis of this report they have to develop analysis for entire inventory.
3. As on date the Hindustan Latex Limited Kanagala unit has not developed E.O.Q models even for single material, hence this report is more useful to them.
4. As on date the HLL kanagala unit has no scientific inventory levels, so this report helps them to maintain various levels of process materials, and to develop scientific inventory levels to remaining inventory.
5. Due to lack of HML analysis they (the HLL staff) are using same handling mechanism to highest value (Rs 2,400 per kg) chemical namely XXXX, and lowest value (Rs 10 per kg) chemical namely Sulphur. This shows that they do not have concept of attempting cost reduction methods more and more on high value materials. They do not know the logic of saving of 1 kg of XXXX is equivalent to saving of 240 kg of sulphur, because lack of HML analysis and lack of price awareness.
6. Same way due to lack of ABC analysis they are using same

methods and efforts to reduce materials cost to all the items. The all concerned employees (stores, purchase and user department) did not know logic of 10 per cent saving of 6 'A' class items (Rs. 38,44,790) is approximately equivalent to 99 per cent saving of 29 'C' class items (Rs. 38,44,790) at production process area.

7. The Hindustan Latex Limited production process is effecting frequently due to lack of vital items, which are included in 'C' class. As per the value analysis the item may be 'C' class but it is vital to production. Generally everyone thinks that the 'C' class item may not be given much preference, hence the vital 'C' class is effecting production frequently.
8. As on date there is no ordering cost calculation at Hindustan Latex Limited. This project report helps to calculate ordering costs.
9. As on date there is no carrying/handling cost calculations at Hindustan Latex Limited. This project report helps to Hindustan Latex Limited, to calculate carrying/handling costs.

Suggestions

1. The all packages and while dispensing the sub-packages of a material should be marked with its unit price, or at least symbol of 'H' in the case of high value materials for taking high-care while handling the high value materials.
2. High efforts and attentions should be given to save 'A' class materials or to reduce wastage of 'A' class materials.
3. The handling mechanism at various inventory movements should be atomized to the possible extent, and improve wherever possible.
4. All required inventory control analysis will be done for entire inventory, starting from raw materials to finished goods and spare parts of machines, engineering items, electrical items, stationery items, etc.,
5. Appropriate EOQ models should be developed to remaining production supporting materials.
6. Improved systems should be developed/adopted and

implemented in inventory management.

7. Expert consultants should be called to study entire inventory systems and to modify to suite the present environment.
8. The required analysis such as ABC, VED, and HML etc., EOQ models and various levels of inventories should be developed by computer system and operated by computer to maximum extent. Wherever a variable value of analysis or model changes, the outdated variable values should be replaced by new value of variable, automatically the model or the analysis out put value will change. The new models or analysis will be implemented immediately. In this way real time updating of models/analysis is to be done by computerization.

17

Green Logistics

K. J. Paulose

This paper aims at presenting an overview of Reverse Logistics and analyzing its impact on Ecology & Environment from the perspective of Green Logistics. Reverse Logistics in general and Green Logistics in particular are emerging concepts and hence the amount of published information on these subjects is limited. The author has made an attempt to collate available data. Where documentation was unavailable, some extrapolation has been made, based on the author's own industrial and academic experiences in the field.

Introduction

Until about a decade back, reverse logistics was centered upon the axiom: "There is money to be made by getting things back". The point of focus was the bottom line. Recently, however, the focus has shifted to ecological concerns, thanks to the increasing societal awareness, and enactment of stringent regulations related to environmental protection. The earlier definition of reverse logistics – "It comprises all the activities, to collect, disassemble and process used products, parts, materials and packaging in order to capture value" – has been expanded by adding " ...in such a way as to ensure a sustainable, environment friendly recovery/disposal".

Significance of Reverse Logistics

Reverse logistics (R.L.) is more than reusing containers and recycling packaging material. Remanufacturing, reuse, recovery and rectification are also included in the definition of R.L. Also coming under its scope are activities such as redesigning packaging to use less material, reducing energy consumption and pollution from transportation and minimizing the generation of waste (esp. non-biodegradable). In fact, a new concept called **'green logistics'** is emerging. Recycling and/or disposal of obsolete, excess, defective, damaged and unusable goods and packaging materials fall under the purview of green logistics. As mentioned earlier the emphasis is on the ecological aspects, rather than on the bottom line. Another aspect of significance is that recycling, rebuilding and remanufacturing can conserve a considerable amount of energy. Managed effectively, 'green logistics' can add more 'green' to the bottom line.

Some of the major considerations in favour of adopting green logistics are:

- Environmental laws and regulations are becoming more stringent and widespread (e.g. in Japan, EU, U.S.)
- Consumers are becoming more receptive to products made from ecofriendly/ biodegradable/recycled/recyclable material.
- Green logistics is a major weapon in the fight against environmental damage.
- It is a departure from conventional disposal techniques such as land filling and incineration.
- It encompasses the entire supply chain (not just the distribution channel)

Reverse Logistics Process

The reverse flow can be divided into two categories: (a) products, and (b) packaging. Return rates vary significantly from industry to industry. For instance, in the retail industry, customer returns are estimated to be around six percent whereas in magazine publishing they are of the order of 50-55 per cent. Typical return percentages across a spectrum of industries are given in Table 17.1.

The following are some of the industries where ecological considerations are of utmost importance in terms of green logistics:

- Automobiles (esp. components such as batteries and tyres)

- White goods (Home appliances)
- Brown goods (Electronic goods)

It is the non-biodegradable nature of such goods that make recycling/disposal an arduous task.

Table 17.2 shows common reverse logistics activities

Table 17.1: Typical Return Percentages

Industry	Percent
Magazine Publishing	50 – 55
Book Publishing	20-30
Catalogue Retailing	20-35
Electronics	10-15
Computers	10-20
CD_ROM's	20-25
Auto Parts	5-10
Consumer Electronics	5- 10

Table 17.2: Common Reverse Logistics Activities

Material	R.L. Activities
Products	Return to Supplier Resell Reuse Salvage Recondition/Refurbish Remanufacture Reclaim materials/parts Recycle Disposal
Packaging	Reuse Refurbish Reclaim Materials Salvage Recycle Disposal

Application of the concept of Green Logistics should ideally begin at the design stage. Care should be taken to ensure that non-hazardous/recyclable/degradable materials are used as far as possible in the manufacture of goods as well as packaging. Throughout the supply chain, the following principles should be followed:

1. Eliminate waste (and in scrap/surplus: obsolete items) to the maximum possible extent.
2. Wherever it is not possible to eliminate waste, minimize it.
3. Recycle/reuse whatever remains after the above two steps.
4. Dispose of anything that cannot be recycled or reused in an eco-friendly manner.

Cost Implications

As can be seen, all the R.L. activities listed above, excluding the first three (i.e. Return to supplier, Resell and Reuse), have significant ecological impact.

The exact amount of reverse logistics costs are not known to most organizations. It has been estimated that reverse logistics costs account for about four percent of the total logistics costs. In U.S., it is found that approximately 0.5% of the GDP is spent on reverse logistics activities.

It is to be noted that, according to research findings, companies following best practices in Green Logistics experience significant operating benefits compared to those with the worst or non-existent environmental programmes. Environmental performance improvement does generate financial incentives, in addition to addressing regulatory and ethical concerns.

There is a misconception that reverse logistics is applicable only to the 'outbound', components of the supply chain. However, the 'inbound' and 'internal' components are also equally significant, from the point of view of reverse logistics. How one handles inputs as well as works in process that are defective/obsolete/surplus matters as much to the organization as the handling of returns from customers.

Reverse logistics comprises the following steps:

- Gate keeping (to ensure that only 'certified' materials are returned)
- Collection
- Sorting out
- Recycling/Reuse/Resale etc.
- Ultimate disposal (e.g. incineration/land fill)

Global Scenario

Countries such as the US, Japan, and those belonging to the European Union (esp. Germany and the Netherlands) have enacted stringent laws related to processing of "**returns**". In most cases, the onus is on the manufacturers/marketers to ensure eco-friendly recycling/disposal of products and packaging sold by them. In India too, environmental concerns are gaining momentum, thanks to incessant efforts by advocates of the 'Green Movement'. Days are not far away, when manufacturers and marketers will be compelled by legislation as well as by societal pressure to go in for Green Logistics practices, especially in the handling of returns, irrespective of their cost-benefit implications.

The Netherlands have pioneered introduction of mandates with regard to the 'green' concept. For instance, third party reverse logistics providers are required to attain a recycling rate of at least 75%, in terms of total weight. The EU has issued a directive on waste from electrical and electronic equipment (WEEE) that sets criteria for collection, treatment, recycling and recovery of WEEE. It makes the produces (not users) responsible for financing these activities.

In the US, there are hundreds of environmental laws within individual states as well as by the federal government. They include mandates for recycling operations of both goods and packaging. In Japan, any product purchased by the government must, by law, have a specific content of recyclable materials.

Environmental Management System

ISO 14001 is the primary international standard for environmental management systems. It contains the following components:

- Identifying environmental impacts within manufacturing and other activities.
- Setting environmental goals, measuring performance, and reviewing progress.
- Establishing procedures for reducing and controlling risks and impact of its activities, responding to emergencies, and taking corrective action.
- Communicating policies and requirements, and training employees, contractors, and others at company sites.
- Maintaining records and documentation.
- Auditing compliance with regulations and performance of the management system.

Where Does India Stand?

India has been rather sluggish in enactment of environmental laws, especially those relating to handling of 'waste'. Although the Ministry of Environment and Forests (MoEF) has set guidelines for hazardous waste management, there is a lot of ambiguity in the matter. The issue of the 'Blue Lady', a cruise liner which has been brought to the port of Alang, Gujarat, offers ample proof of the government's lack of clarity in the matter. Even the draft laws under consideration shift the responsibility of environment friendly recycling to third parties, rather than the manufacturers themselves.

Basel Convention

The Basel Convention on the "Control of Transboundary Movements of Hazardous Wastes and Their Disposal" was opened for signature in 1989 and came into force in 1992. It is designed to reduce the movement of hazardous waste between nations, especially from developed to less developed countries. Though 156 countries are parties to the convention, a few (including the USA) have not yet ratified it.

The Basel Ban amendment of 1994 went a step further by banning import/export of waste for recycling. While India has ratified the Basel convention, it is yet to ratify the amendment.

Blue Lady Anchors, Quietly

Yet another ship with toxic waste has recently beached at Alang, Gujarat. The Blue Lady's owner admits that the ship contains asbestos. But the ship carries neither documents required as per international law, nor a complete inventory of its hazardous wastes, says Gopal Krishna of the 'Ban Asbestos Network of India'.

However, on 5 June, Justice Arijit Pasayat and Justice C K Thakker (vacation bench) at the Supreme Court permitted the Blue Lady to anchor at Alang, on humanitarian grounds. The court saw an interim report of the Technical Committee on ship-breaking, chaired by Prodipto Ghosh, Secretary of the Ministry of Environment and Forests.

The Blue Lady does not have the mandatory Form 7 documents from country of export required for hazardous waste shipments. Neither does it have a complete inventory of toxic wastes on board.

In allowing the ship in, the justices seemed to agree with the Technical Committee that if the ship is not anchored it would not be possible for the inspection team to visit the ship. In addition, experts from the Gujarat Pollution Control Board, Gujarat Maritime Board (GMG) and Central Pollution Control Board will undertake an inspection. These were also the officials who had inspected Riky, the Danish ship which was allowed to be anchored and dismantled illegally in 2005 and that matter is still before the court. (See report: The scrapping of Riky).

The media appear to have failed to take note of the fact that the apex court has allowed anchoring of the ship on humanitarian grounds and not on legal grounds. As noted earlier, in a similar episode in 2005, the Danish ship, Riky, was allowed into Alang and dismantled despite repeated diplomatic recall requests from Denmark. The apex court is hearing the Riky case and is yet to decide on the issue.

More recently, in 2005-06, the French aircraft carrier Le

Clemenceau was being allowed to enter Indian waters laden with toxic substances, till the French government recalled the ship from the high seas under intense public pressure and legal action in the French courts.

Scope for Further Studies

As stated earlier, not much research work has been done on Reverse Logistics in general and Green Logistics in particular. The **Centre for Logistics Management** at University of Nevada, Reno is one of the pioneers in the field. Dr. Dale S. Rogers and Dr. Ronald S. Tibben-Lembke of the centre have co-authored a book: **"Going Backwards: Reverse Logistics Trends and Practices"** (published by the Reverse Logistics Executive Council), which is considered to be one of the most authoritative works related to reverse logistics. Another significant contribution is by Prof. Ray Kulwiec: **"Reverse Logistics – The Green Approach"**.

Prof. Harold Krikke of the Tilburg University, the Netherlands has come out with several papers on the subject. Research on reverse logistics is also being conducted at the following universities in Europe:

- Erasmus University (Rotterdam)
- Aristoteles University (Greece)
- Eindhoven University (The Netherlands)
- Otto-von-Guericke University (Germany)

There is vast scope for further studies by both research scholars and application experts in this area, especially in the Indian context.

References

Krikke, H.R., Mandatory recycling of consumer electronics in The Netherlands: a role model for Europe?, Warehouse of the Future 2001, Distribution Business Management Association, Lancaster, PA.

Kulwiec, Ray, Reverse Logistics–The Green Approach, On the Move, Winter 2002, The Material Handling Industry of America, Charlotte, NC.

Rogers, D.S. and Tibben-Lembke, R. S., Going Backwards: Reverse Logistics Trends and Practices

18

Role of Ethics in Supply Chain Management

Kalavathi V

Introduction

Supply Chain Management is managing inventories in a coordinated manner among all the players on the chain to achieve a sustainable competitive advantage. The success of Supply Chain Management of an organization is dependent on the performance and reliability of its suppliers and also customers.

We have seen that in a globally competitive to survive and make profits, it is imperative for the companies to link all its upstream suppliers and downstream distributors into an integrated supply chain network.

Traditional supply chains typically include individual business units, separate product lines and little communication or connectivity among individual parts of the business, much less with customers or suppliers, except via EDI or other limited processes. True connectivity is about being networked, which is about being at the point where your customer, your enterprise, your supplier and your employees are all linked. When a customer clicks in and conducts a transaction, it's about the supplier knowing that there is an inventory to fill, the employee knowing that there is a customer relation to manage and the fulfillment center knowing that there is a delivery required. Having said that, it is prime importance to follow some ethical practices in their day-to-day dealings with their suppliers and distributors.

Supply chain management is a cross-functional approach to managing the movement of raw materials into an organization and the movement of finished goods out of the organization toward the end-consumer. As corporations strive to focus on core competencies and become more flexible, they have reduced their ownership of raw materials sources and distribution channels. These functions are increasingly being outsourced to other corporations that can perform the activities better or more cost effectively. The effect has been to increase the number of companies involved in satisfying consumer demand, while reducing management control of daily logistics operations. Less control and more supply chain partners led to the creation of supply chain management concepts. The purpose of supply chain management is to improve trust and collaboration among supply chain partners, thus improving inventory visibility and improving inventory velocity.

Ethics is a study of morals and moral choices .It focuses on standards, rules and codes of conduct that govern the behavior of individuals and groups. The role of Ethics assumes a prime importance as the success and effectiveness of entire supply-chain network rests on the foundation of inter-relationships between the various organizations forming the network .keeping this in consideration. An increase in number of organizations is attempting to develop closer relationships with their major suppliers and distributors and even their supplier's suppliers. Given the dependency of firms on supplier performance some organizations are adopting strategies that can help foster improvement, including greater information sharing between the parties.

It is however, necessary in today's environment to pursue this policy of Supply Chain Management through and sound and proper value system. The values of the organization in which Supply Chain Management is enforced, have to be identified on the basis of its own vision and mission. The working of organization must therefore be transparent and rooted in right behavior and cultures that is ethics. Modern experiments like Supply Chain Management and research have proved that sustained progress is possible only if the organization observes its norms of ethics and morality. Ethic is the expression of culture and traditions in harmony with effectiveness and efficiency of

Supply Chain Management, customer delight and organizational growth. It is to be remembered that "culture" always has ethical connotations. It is rooted in moral tradition and habits. These habits must be value based. It is only in such circumstances that growth becomes and rewarding experience, which can be sustained. It may be possible to accomplish growth by using doubtful tactics and manipulative practices but it will prove to be fragile. So, ethics should be visible and values pervade all the activities of Supply Chain Management startup from planning, designing till conclusion.

Building human relations and relationship management are main key variables in the success of Supply Chain Management in the present age. Respect for the individual enhances its capability for achieving endless growth and success in the Supply Chain Management system.

This paper has the details of research of the anticipated problems in Supply Chain Management implementation on the ethical value systems and remedies for the same. Some of the ethical factors which leads to achieve successfully without unethical manipulation and with efficient success of the system are attitude, openness, understanding, integrity and empowerment.

Attitude

"Attitudes are evaluative statements either favorable of unfavorable concerning objects, people or events. They reflect how one feels about something."

Everything depends on one's own attitude, how he feels and thinks about the new theory and the cultural environment of the organization he has to work with. So, to manage the complex sequences and relationship, Supply Chain Management depends on cross dept functioning. It also has ownership and responsibility for productivity and success of Supply Chain Management in the organization. This needs ethical values for proper functioning. Some of the actions pertaining to attitude with respect to ethics are:

- When there is and problem, which needs immediate solution

without waiting for instructions and permission, it needs and complete thorough knowledge of row Supply Chain Management works in the organization.

- Have to inform partners of business about the problem before they become bigger problems due to lack of attention.
- Have to be honest with respect to partners not only in the case of finance and also with respect to others issues such as customer problems, Human Resource problems, etc..
- Have to be and loyal, value the different perceptions and perspectives of others, be tolerant, see the positive side of other's motives and suggestions, trust in others, be kind.

Openness

The sharing of information forms the backbone of any supply chain. Hence lack of open communication which forms the weakest link in Supply Chain Management which can lead to break of supply chain. In Supply Chain Management, which is a continuous process from the supplier to the customer, if there is one weak link, it is the information passing and openness between various links. The partnership role needed in the Supply Chain Management requires more give and take between the partners of the chain. The acceptance of direct discussions about problems makes it more possible to find creative win-win solutions to the problems in the Supply Chain Management.

Good relationships work when there is mutual adaptation. All the partners in the chain can not get that openness and commitment needed in this complex process unless the needs and wishes of all the partners are taken into account. Winning all arguments is hardly and victory if the loser starts to withhold vital information, passively accepting everything that the leader says without him taking any initiative or using judgments or just goes through the motions and carrying out the tough decisions of the leader. Leaders in the process of Supply Chain Management, specially, need the full commitment of all the partners in the chain, followed by the action in order to make the supply chain function properly.

As supply chain management is rather recent theory especially in the Indian industry scenario, it becomes more diverse to encompass the range of specialties and talent needed to cope with the rapid change and increased complexities. Thus, all the partners in the chain are important, whether seniors or juniors, and there is a need to complement each other. They must create value, commitment, trust and openness in their relationship with each other. Thus, information must flow horizontally, vertically and in all other directions. One partner should know what is happening with the other partners of the chain. And real cultural transformation must occur inside and outside the company for any supply chain to succeed. Roles change, jobs change, and information must be shared, not hoarded. Implementing Supply Chain Management systems is costly, complex and labor intensive. The process isn't for the faint hearted-but the payoff can be lucrative.

Integrity

Effective leadership is generally associated with integrity. This may not always be true, but nevertheless the assumption remains. Few managers, however, try to wrestle with ethical dilemmas, and thus they deny responsibility for actions, which may see to be unethical. Evidence from research suggests that organization, like individuals, need the option of others to ensure that broader perspectives are applied to the understanding of problems. The growth of knowledge itself rests on this paradigm, for; when diverse opinions are discounted truth becomes illusive.

Now viewing Supply Chain Management implementations as and business initiative it is up to the top management to educate and engage senior management as early as possible in its planning stage. It should be remembered that small things should be done well. Small acts of decency and respect for others' knowledge, skills and aptitudes will prove the company's principles of fairness build an environment of respect, commitment and continuity to set its own ethical compliance. The top management should lead by examples and be supportive to all the team members who are involved in the Supply Chain Management process. The key is the totality of conduct, the overall orientation displayed over time by words and actions.

Understanding

In order for a supply chain management implementation to be successful strategic level and gross root level of change and understandings must be addressed. Strategic level denotes the up-front, initial effort involving senior executives, senior managers, a small cadre of employees, and often consultants, who provide an outside view. Gross roots change is the effort that drives change deep into an organization. It shares implementation and sustenance of the desired changes at the local level. This can be done through setting goals, performing measurements, providing coaching and feedback, and offering reward and recognition.

The main challenges facing any organization in building communities integral to supply chain management across teams, disciplines, time, space, and business units, and understand its working are:

- To design human process and information systems that not only make information available, but also help community members think together and the·right implications.
- To develop communities that work together and share knowledge while still maintaining enough diversity of thought encourages thinking rather than sophisticated copying.
- The management challenge is to create an environment that truly values sharing knowledge and helps understanding of systems and processes peruse.

Empowerment

Empowered employees satisfy customers. The leader who is the driving force and at the helm of affairs must be responsible not only for the management of the business but also for the organizations key assets-people. Organizations should eliminate fear, create an environment where people are truly unafraid to participate and where people become part of the solution.

Empowerment strategy must be built upon 'TRUST'. The trust is demonstrated in the way the top management interacts with employees, the extent to which they use their power and position fairly in the organization and efforts they make to ensure a balanced equitable organization.

Empowerment does not simply mean giving power to the employees. It is about changing the conditions under which the employees perform their jobs. This look for an organization identity change which is what the supply chain management calls for. This means that organizational change management is the most critical responsibility in an overall program of process improvement through Supply Chain Management. Thus 'Trust' helps to ensure that all concerned are working to achieve great success for the organization, attending to the relationship with suppliers, customers and among groups or teams of the Supply Chain Management.

The implementation supply-chain management is not about reinventing the business. From an organization point of view, supply-chain management concepts are especially tricky. Because they go against the mantra of decentralization, which many companies adopted to spur innovation among business units.

19

Supply Chain Management of Carpet Industry in Erode District, Tamil Nadu

K. Guruswamy

Introduction

Bhavani carpets known as "Bhavani Jamakkalam" in Tamil is one of the products having history of more than 100 years with little changes in design, specification appearance and its application. The author found that product has no much changes despite of modernity. It is very interesting to note that the product is manufactured only in few villages in and around Bhavani, a carpet city of Erode district of Tamil Nadu.

The historically renowned town of Bhavani is noted for its handloom carpets known for durability and aesthetic. Thousands of weavers are engaged in producing exquisitely designed carpet, which once attracted international buyers. More than 300 private carpet-weaving units and 25 carpet weaving co-operation societies are functioning in the region. However present condition of industry due to globalization is facing lot of challenges.

Objectives of the Study

- Study present status of carpet industry with respect to supply chain management
- To suggest steps to be taken for export and to develop as world class supply base
- To suggest models for supply chain facility and capacity location for expanding the business.
- To suggest-steps to be taken for co-ordination in the supply chain
- To identify ways and means to minimize the hardships if any,

faced by weavers, unit owners, societies, and all stakeholders

- To identify the crisis faced and tactics followed to overcome those in the past.
- Recommendations and suggestion for maximizing the overall value generated in the carpet Industry.

Industry Profile

15,000 weavers and indirect labors about 10,000 are engaging in production of Bhavani carpets in 25 societies and about 10,000 weavers in private sectors (self employed). The societies and private weaving units are located in the following villages, where agriculture is predominant occupation.

- Bhavani
- Anthiyur
- Ammapet
- Jambai
- Thalaiwaipet
- Kuruppanaican palayam
- Peria molapalayam
- Sethunampalayam
- Kadiampatti
- Sinthagoundenpalayam
- Paruvatchi
- Punnam
- Appakkudal
- Nagaloor and few more places in Namakkal district.

As per Assistant Director of Erode District hand loom weavers Co-operative societies Federations Ltd., total no of looms, manufacturing Bhavani carpets are about 4727 and their dept. has the administrative control of all societies regarding material price , sales prices, wages, rebate subsidies, cash credits, loans, welfare benefits recommendation etc.,

Approximate turnover of the industry is about Rs 100crores (estimate based on judgement) most of the societies are producing goods worth of Rs. 75 lakh to Rs. 400 lakh. Each society is having membership from 50 to 250, who are owning hand looms from single up to 10 numbers in their native villages. The members are spread over, living in and around the villages and most of the looms are located in the house itself and only few members have separate sheds.

Carpet Industry Profile

Type	No. of units	No. of looms			Sales value annual.
			Weavers	Indirect labor	
Societies	25	4,727	15,000	2,000	Rs. 45 crore
Private	300	3,000	10,000	1,500	Rs. 55 crore

Prominent Private Carpets Firms at Bhavani

- SPM Textiles
- Easter carpets
- Thilagavathy yarns
- Sivakumar Textiles
- Sri Kandhan Rugs Exports Pvt. Ltd

Comments of Various Stake Holders of Carpet Industry

Mr. C. Rajendran, Manager of Athiparasakthi Weavers Co-Operative Production & Sales.

- Carpet industry grows & steady growth is there
- Next generation is not opting weaving job
- Advanced technology in loom design is available at Salem
- Aged workforce, non remunerative prices, poor wages

A Weaver, Mrs. S. Palaniammal w/o Police Constable says that their additional income from handloom helps for her son to study B.Tech. She had invested Rs 5000 for shed and loom costs about Rs. 5,000.

Mr. V. Arumugam, Handloom officer who is over seeing the working of 15 co-operative societies of carpet

manufacturing says the following.

- Complete administrative control of societies regarding price, subsidies, wages, rebates, cash credits, loans, training programmes for weavers, quality control for the products are dealt by them.
- Loan is given at 9.5 per cent interest rate by State Govt.
- Out of 25 of societies, societies at 1.Jambai, 2.Periamolapalayam, 3.Bhavani koodal, 4.Madeswaran Bhavani, and 5.Sethnampalayam are working under loss.
- Currently demand is more than supply in the Industry.

Mr. Kadirvelu, Manager of Jambai-Society says the following

- Dyeing is to be done only through Government approved Dyers
- Below 50 years, no male employee is in their society
- They are able to get products through outsourcing with in 15 days
- Loss making society can not pay dividend or bonus. Lost 10 years no bonus is paid in their society.

Mr. M. Nagarajan, Manager of the Appkudal Society says

- Their 85 per cent business is mats with Karur exporters other than Bhavani carpets
- Their weaver (lady) is earning Rs 60 for the mats where as for the Bhavani carpet only Rs. 40
- Their Production by outsourcing is 65 per cent.
- Their society owns 60 cents of land, 30 cents with shed for looms
- The following benefits are paid to their employees
  - Pension scheme
  - Group Insurance – Rs 60,000
  - Bunkar bema yogna scheme
  - Med claim up to Rs.15000
  - Education allowance for wards- SSY(Shikshy Shayog Yojana) Govt. of India scheme
  - Health package scheme
  - Goggle – Rs. 190 – by Central Govt.

- o Eye testing Rs. 190 –by State
- o For T.B. Rs. 2200 for 5 years
- o Maternity Rs.500 only for 2 children

Mr. M. K. Mallaya Raj, managing partner, M. K. Sons (1914) Bhavani says as given below

- He is in the field for the last 70 years.
- From the Bhavani Jamakkalam manufacturer, now he owns Dyeing unit, yarn dealer trading, and spinning mill.
- He used to supply Bhavani Jamakkalam through out India. Price of Jamakkalam will be same as societies price margin is only about 10 per cent.
- Inventory of Jamakkalam will be negligible only.
- At present the sales is only about 1lakh after the societies entered in the business.
- He owns shop of 5,000 sq. feet dealing other business export of mats.
- Societies are the main hurdles for the industry.

Mr. M. S. Yakhub, Manager of M/s Sri Kandhan Rugs Exports Pvt. Ltd. Bhavani says that

- Bhavani Carpets are just surviving and says the carpets are not being exported. Bangladesh & China are giving double the subsidies than what our handloom sector gets.
- Bhavani Carpets total business more than Rs. 100 crore out of which private firms share is Rs. 40 crore.
- There is no export till now for Bhavani Jamakkalam.
- There were earlier hundreds of shops but now it is to only for 4-5 shops at Bhavani.

Packing forwarding assistant of Bhavani Weavers Co-Op Production & Sales Societies Ltd., carpets says that

- 50 per cent production goes to Maharastra state and at Sholapur. Their own shop is at Sholapur.
- Gujaraties and marvadies prefer Bhavani jamakkalam for their pujas, festivals, functions extensively.

Product Profile

Bhavani carpets are home furnishing products supplied to

- Army
- Star hotels in the north Indian towns
- Mosque
- Marriage halls

The hub of handloom carpet activity exquisitely designed, multicolored products are a specialty and hall carpets enjoys a good domestic market A few of societies are producing hall carpets on order from north India Pattu Jamakkalam (art silk yarn carpets produced only by highly skilled weavers), costs slightly higher.

Hall carpets width 6 feet to 16 feet and length any size available

- Cotton carpets – 80 per cent
- Agalic carpets– 20 per cent. Market is declining due to higher cost

Carpets sizes available in the market

- 34x72 inches
- 40x72 inches
- 40x78 inches
- 46x84 inches
- 52x90 inches
- 60x90 inches

Hall Carpets

- 6x10 feet
- 8x10 feet
- 8x12 feet
- 9x12 feet
- 10x10 feet
- 10x20 feet

As per customer requirement any size

Production Management

Weavers get Rs 50 per day for weaving one carpets measuring 3 x 6 feet. But the wages are too low as one has to work for at least 10 hours a day which is very difficult.

Many weavers including women, have shifted to power loom weaving sector and house furnishing mats, are earning up to Rs. 1000 per week. This resulted in shortage of hand loom weavers in carpet sector.

Wages for Weaving

Carpet 6 to 8 feet– Rs 2.18/sqft
8 to 10 feet– Rs. 2.27/sqft
10 to12 feet– Rs 2.56/sqft
52 x70 inches LabourRs 70/ Piece

Costing

- Manufacturing cost plus 15 per cent margin
- Govt. subsidies 20 per cent to 30 per cent Societies claim the amount during the sales of the finished product.
- Sales price is fixed by Govt. Official including for Traders
- Govt. approved dyers are only to be engaged used for dyeing the yarn which requires only 10 days lead time.
- Dyeing charges per bundle is Rs. 100
- Tar coning the yarn –1 bundle (100 pieces), Labour charges is Rs. 100

Forecasting

Marketing supervisors, inspectors of co-optex inform well in advance to the societies through co-operative societies federation, their requirement especially for the seasons of Diwali and Pongal.

Similarly small traders and consumers are also booking their orders throughout the year

Supply Chain Management

Close linkage and co-ordination of activities involved in buying, making and moving a product

Network of organization and business process for processing materials, transforming raw materials into intermediate and finished products, and distributing the finished products to customers

Drivers of supply chain management

- Facilities – Looms, Sheds, lightings, go down
- Transportation - mini auto/manual/bus luggage/cycle/moped
- Technology – 50 years no change in the looms working
- Information technology –Letters, couriers, phone , personal only
- Lead time for weaving - 15 days by member of societies
- Delivery - weakly once by members
- Maximum lead time 1 month

In the cycle ,according to demand and supply position, seasions (winter/ summer, festivel/ ordinary days) inventory at various processes will change. Yarn (r.m) to finished products lead time is - 1 ½ months.

"The carpets produced in Nagpur and Sholapur powerlooms have hurt the sale and production of the industry. (G.S. Raja of Bhavani)

Powerloom carpets are much cheaper than the hand loom products. However handloom carpets' life is definitely longer than its competitor.

Another factor is the wards of handloom weavers have started preferring powerlooms to get better wages. This trend had forced handloom carpet weavers to switchover to weaving of doormats, and floormats, which have good international market, including in the United States and Europe. Some are even directly export doormats and floormats.

S.V.L.Gopalan – a carpet merchant of Bhavani while admitting that the powerloom carpets have affected the sale of handloom products, finds a silver lining in orders from the police, the army, of state and central govt departments for the hand loom departments." ,details the in the Net .

Current Status of Marketing

Demand is in peak during Dec Jan/Feb, low in July /August and moderate throughout year.

50 per cent is supplied to Co-optex and balance to open market but the price is same as fixed by AD.

As per govt. policy, profit to be availed is 20 per cent. Co-optex will avail 14½ per cent profit.

Show rooms are at Bhavani, and Erode.

Sales price – Rs. 6/20 per sq. ft

Labor – Rs. 3-70/sqft

In 2005 – Increased of sales

In 2006 - Good demand

For dyeing Rs 110 of 4 ½ kg bundle

Pricing: Manufacturing cost plus 14 ½ per cent Profit for societies and 20 per cent for outsiders/ private.

Raw material prices

Count No. 6- 4½ kg	- Rs. 215/bundle
Count No. 2-10 4½ kg	- Rs 270/ bundle
Count No.10-4 ½ kg	- Rs 265/bundle

Raw material price is day by day changing.

Mr. Srinivasan, Production supervisor of co-optex design and production office, Erode says the following regarding marketing of carpets.

1. Dept. has given their 2 months requirement for Jan / Feb, 2007 for 16, 413 Carpets, value about Rs.31.2lakhs, but they expect only 50 per cent of their requirement from societies.
2. They are selling about 3-4 crore worth of Bhavani carpets per annum.
3. In recent past, they are able to get only 50 per cent - 60 per cent of their requirement from society.

HRD

Subsidy/Other Benefits in the Industry for Weavers

- Bonus – up to Rs.2500 in profit making societies.
- Free electricity – members as well as primary members
- Saving and security scheme.
- Pension
- Group insurance Bema Yogna scheme – up to Rs. 60,000
- Med claim up to Rs.15,000
- Education allowance for children
- SSY–Shiksha Shayog Yojana – CentralGovt

- Health package scheme
- Bore well compressor, motor- free supply by Central Govt.
- Free goggle by central Govt.– Rs. 190
- Eye testing by state Govt. – Rs. 190
- TB treatment– Rs. 1100 for 5 years
- Maternity – Rs. 500 up to 2 children
- 15. Work shed subsidy – Rs 7000/loom/family – by Central Govt.

Weaknesses

- Aged labour only continuing in weaving
- Resources under utilization
- No involvement
- Low productivity

During Nov. 2006, Bhavani union president put

- Demand 50 per cent hike in wages
- Demand 20 per cent in DA
- Last 13 years no rise in wages in spite of agreement 10 per cent increase in wages and D.A. every year
- Negotiation is still going on

Information System

Information System in the supply chain of carpet industry is taking place through phone, personal contact letters, and couriers serve the following activities.

- Decide when and what to produce, store, and move
- Rapidly communicate order
- Track the status of order
- Check inventory availability and monitor inventory levels
- Reduce inventory, transportation, and warehousing costs
- Track shipments
- Plan production based on actual customer demand
- Rapidly communicate change in product design.
- E-mail, Fax facilities are not found in the industry.

Suggestions/Recommendations

1. Govt. should fix the yarn price once in six months. If the yarn price is stable, it will be possible to produce carpets at a reasonable price.
2. The solution is to reserve carpets production only for handloom sector and at any cost power looms should not be allowed. But the technology of loom is to be improved definitely.
3. All welfare benefits should be given to the members of societies even the societies incur loss beyond their control.
4. Further in depth studies are required to safe guard the industry which is declining.

Future Potential/Opportunities/Future Plans

Textiles committee of central govt. is working on a programme to evolve new design for hand loom carpet production in the Bhavani area to improve their export potential.

A cluster programme is taken up the committee for the home furnishing units in the Bhavani area. A consortium of private units was being formed with a minimum of six members.

A series of training programmers would be conducted as soon as the consortium was formed.

A "Processing Park" project for select processing units in the Bhavani area was mooted.

Private sectors said if a college for the weaving technology was started, youth would come forward to join the industry.

Conclusion

In this case, the following key issues may be taken up for further research.

1. Is it worth for the govt. to give subsidies up to 30 per cent for the survival of this industry?
2. What other measures, Govt. can take for the growth of this industry?
3. Measures to be considered for more private firms to enter and participate in the industry.

References

Books Referred

Supply chain management, strategy, planning and operation by Sunil Chopra and Peter Meindl

Supply chain management, concepts and cases: by Rahul V. Altekar

News Papers - News

News about carpet weavers in The Hindu dated 15/11/06.

News about carpet weavers in The Hindu dated 16/11/06.

News about carpet weavers in Express news service dated 15/11/06

News about carpet weavers in Kaalai Kadir-Tamil news paper dated 16/11/06

News about carpet weavers in Thinamalar-Tamil news paper dated 16/11/06

News about carpet weavers in Thinakaran – Tamil news paper dated 16/11/06

Following persons are thanked for the co-operation extended to conduct the research

Mr. C. Rajendran, Manager, Athiparasakthi Weaver's Co-operative Production & Sale.

Mr. M. Nagarajan , Manager, Appakkudal Harijan Primary-cum-Industrial Handloom Weaver's Co-op Production & Sale Society Ltd., Appakkudal, Sakthinagar.

Mr. Kadirvelu, Manager, The Jambai Industrial Weaver's Co-operative Production & Sale Society Ltd., Jambai.

Mr. M.S. Yakhub, Manager, Sri Kandhan Rugs Export Private Ltd., Bhavani.

Mr. Srinivasan, Production Supervisor, Co-optex Design and Production Office, Erode.

Mr. M.K. MallayaRaj, Managing Partner, M.K. Sons, Bhavani.

20

Modern ERP Systems vis-à-vis Orientations in Modern Manufacturing and Operations

P.O. Subash

Introduction

The coming century has been named as the age of knowledge economy. Manufacturing industry is facing more and more challenges. Though different technical bottlenecks for modern manufacturing have been or are being investigated, the real bottleneck is, however, the lack of knowledge. Efficient acquisition and utilization of knowledge have been considered as the trump to win the competition in the knowledge economy.

The base of the knowledge economy is the knowledge industry that is supported by the production equipment and modes, science and technology, management philosophy, etc., produced by the modern manufacturing system and technology.

During the historical development of industry, human society has experienced three industrial revolutions. Currently, the world is undergoing a Hi-Tech industrial revolution with information technology as its main feature. The manufacturing industry of the next century will be characterized by intensively concurrent engineering based on information technologies such as digitalization, computer network, artificial intelligence and the like. The focus of enterprise production is shifting from quantity/quality to service including quality, price, and after service.

People are paying more attention to the individualization, involvement and responsive requirements of product. The management of the enterprise is being transformed from a centralized and independent model to cooperative and coordinated management, in which the creativity of people will be given full play. The 21st century's manufacturing industry will be green. It does not damage but preserves and beautifies the environment. It not only utilizes but also saves and renews natural resources. It will play an important role in the harmonious development of humankind and nature.

Let us try to understand the orientations the evolution pattern of modern industry from the past under various attributes.

Economy pattern: Large scale economy to Speed economy to Knowledge economy

Main production mode: Large scale production to Integrated production to Intensive production

Main production factor: Labor to Capital to Knowledge

Production process: Production flow line to Interchangeability Manufacturing to Automatic line to Integrated Manufacturing to Concurrent engineering to Distributed networks to Intelligent manufacturing.

Production features: Mechanization to Automation to Digitization & network

Key technology: Unit technology to Synthetic technology to Intelligent technology

Requirements to Products: Big batch to Diversification to Individualization to involvement and rapid response

Focus of Production: Quantity to Quality to Services (quality, price, after service, etc.)

Management: Centralization to Independent to Cooperative to full play of personal creativity

Relationship to natural Resource: Utilization of natural resource to Saving natural resource to Preserve & renew natural resource

Relationship to Environment: Damages environment to Pays attention to environment to Preserves & beautifies environment. The manufacturing systems for the next century should possess the features of agility, intelligence, rapid response and favor high quality products, small batch sizes, individualization requirements, consumer involvement, and environmental consciousness. The manufacturing systems characterized by the above features have been named as intelligent manufacturing systems on which extensive studies have been conducted.

Modern Manufacturing Systems and Production Modes

Over the past one or two decades, a great amount of effort has been invested by the industrial world and academia to explore the advanced manufacturing system and technology that will deal with manufacturing complexities originating from globalization of markets, stringent competition environment and overload of constraints on the manufacturing environment. And many manufacturing systems and production modes have been proposed. According to the literature published by CIRP and other manufacturing periodicals during the latest decade, nearly 34 modern manufacturing systems and production modes have been proposed. Some of the key systems are listed below

- GT (Group Technology)
- TQC (Total Quality Control)
- MRP-I (Material Requisite Planning)
- MRP-II (Manufacturing Resource Planning)
- FMS (Flexible Manufacturing System)
- JIT (Just In Time)
- CAPP (Computer Aided Process Planning)
- CIMS (Computer Integrated Manufacturing System)
- CDP (Customer Driven Production)
- BR (Business Reengineering)
- CE (Concurrent Engineering)
- EFM (Environment Friendly Manufacturing)
- LP (Lean Production)
- AM (Agile Manufacturing)
- MAMS (Multi-Agent Manufacturing System)
- VM (Virtual Manufacturing)
- LCE (Life Cycle Engineering)

- GM (Green Manufacturing)
- CM (Collaborative Manufacturing)
- RM (Remote Manufacturing)
- TPM (Total Production Maintenance)
- OAMS (Open Architecture Manufacturing System)
- IMS (Intelligent Manufacturing System)
- FE (Fractal Enterprise)
- ERP (Enterprise Resource Planning)
- SOPS (Self-Organized Production System)
- RMS (Reconfigurable Manufacturing Systems)
- GM (Global Manufacturing)
- NGMS (Next Generation Manufacturing System)

Some of the above manufacturing systems and production modes have been maturely applied to practical manufacturing areas and have dramatically reduced the lead time of products. Some are still undergoing investigation or conceptualization. Behind these manufacturing systems and production modes lies the continuous pursuit of design intelligence, manufacturing intelligence and management intelligence, or the enterprise intelligence as a whole.

Intelligent Mathematics for Modern Manufacturing System Modeling

In order to model increasingly complex manufacturing systems, numerous mathematical methods, especially the so-called non-conventional mathematical tools, have been widely used. Some applications of these mathematical methods in the manufacturing arena have achieved exciting progress.

- Expert System (Knowledge Based System)
- Pattern Recognition
- Graph Theory
- Similarity Theory
- Optimization Theory
- Game Theory
- Time Series Analysis

- Wavelet Analysis
- Computer Vision
- Natural Language Processing
- Knowledge Representation
- Heuristic Search
- Constraint Based Search
- Confidence Theory
- Qualitative Reasoning
- Reasoning Technologies
- Machine Learning
- Machine Proving
- Multiple-Valued Logic
- Fuzzy Logic
- Artificial Neural Network
- Petri Networks
- Immune Networks
- Genetic Algorithms
- Artificial Life
- Associative Memory
- Blackboard Architecture
- Multi-Agent Systems
- Non-Classical Control Theory
- Operations Research
- System Engineering
- Simulated Annealing
- Combinatorial Mathematics
- Fractal Theory
- Chaos Theory

In the practical applications, these methods are usually combined with each other to deal with planning, design, process control, and system integration, etc. Research examples can be frequently found in technical literature. The wide application of these intelligent mathematical methods or their combinations in manufacturing will definitely promote the development of manufacturing system modeling and provide new solutions to the complexities manufacturing.

Agent and Agent-based Manufacturing

Currently, the open architecture Multi-Agent System (MAS) has become the main research direction. Agents are now being widely discussed by researchers in mainstream computer science. Though there is not a universally accepted definition of agent, it does not prevent people from expanding the application space of agent technology. In practical application an agent is usually considered as a self-directed program object which has its own value system and the means to solve certain subtasks independently and then communicate its solution to a greater problem solving process, either on its own initiative or on request from other agents.

Any agent comprises of the following components

- **Knowledge processor,** a knowledge base system that stores and processes the necessary knowledge for an agent to play the role the agent society has designed for it.
- **Perception**, a channel for an agent to receive information from the external world.
- **Effector**, an interface for an agent to modify or influence the state of the agent community.
- **Communication**, a mechanism for an agent to exchange views with other members in the agent society.
- **Objectives**, a list of roles for an agent to play.

The MAS is an open and distributed system that is formed by a group of agents combined with each other through a network for cooperatively solving a common problem. The MAS has been applied in many areas. The modern manufacturing system, which is a highly decentralized system, is one of the typical representatives of MAS application. A great deal of research effort has been devoted to agent-based manufacturing. Some leading manufacturers and government agencies in the USA are claiming that agent-based manufacturing is the future for US manufacturing and agent technology is the fundamental technology for implementing the agile manufacturing vision

There is multifold advantage in using an agent-based approach for manufacturing. First, manufacturing information is stored and processed in a distributed manner as opposed to being stored in one large program. Second, it makes the incremental improvement of the manufacturing system possible through the learning and cooperation in agents.

Third, it provides a promising method for enterprise integration.

Intelligent Manufacturing Agent

In manufacturing, an agent represents an object with certain intelligence, which is either a physical object such as a worker, a machine tool, and the like or a logical object such as an order, a task, etc. In order to establish an agent-based manufacturing system, the model of the Manufacturing Agent (MA) must first be defined.

Procedure repository, inference mechanism, knowledge base, and perception processor constitute the knowledge processing unit for the MA. The self-learning, self-organizing, and self-adapting are the optimizers of the MA. The simulation expert provides behavior evaluations for the MA. Working memory stores the temporary data produced by the other parts of the MA. The communication mechanism manages the message exchanging tasks of the MA with the other members of the system. The coordinator coordinates the internal functions of the MA, meanwhile it receives the coordination requests from other MAs.

The main features of MA are:

- **Self similarity:** Every MA has a similar structure.
- **Self learning:** The MA has coordinated learning ability that contributes to an emergent improvement of the whole system behavior.
- **Self adaptation:** The MA has the ability to adjust its behavior intention according to different rules.
- **Self organization:** The MA can organize or configure its internal procedures to deal with different tasks.
- **Self maintenance:** The MA can monitor the state of itself and

keep itself in the most efficient condition.

Demands on Modern ERP

Conventional and ERP at present focuses only on converting an organization into an Enterprise and in the process creating higher collaboration and resource utilization. This is both an advantage and draw-back because the dynamics and orientations of modern manufacturing as discussed above drive systems requirements of organizations far beyond resource utilization. Certain amount of Artificial Intelligence has to be built into the very foundations of the ERP. How then can modern ERP systems be re-oriented. The answer to this question is that the following factors must be incorporated into ERP systems.

All ERP must be based on sound synergy of Manufacturing Architecture and System architecture. System architecture must incorporate modern trends in production which reduces Customizing time. This in turn demands that all manufacturing systems be built on some principles like lean manufacturing, Agent based, Virtual Enterprise or Holonic systems.

Next Generation ERP systems demand an OPEN ARCITECTURE SYSTEM which is flexible and can be re-oriented as and when the need arises. In an OAS it is easier for few key stake-holders to make changes on the software or even execute updation under an over all framework of procedures. There are several kinds of OAS systems being created in the market and many companies in the US rival SAP and their implementations by advocating the OAS architectures

Another demand on ERP is Predictive Analytics and managing Uncertainty: The Software must be able to make MDP (Multi Dimensional Predictions and Co-ordination). This involves quantitative adaptation on the part of the ERP and the ability to see through a maze of data and Information. The utility of an ERP in the production and Operations environment in the future depends on its ability to assimilate this feature in all its operational elements and dimensions and give guidance to production managers on an on-going basis not necessarily on demand as conventional Enterprise solutions do.

ERP must support Intuitive Functionality in its operations: Under the open Architecture the ERP becomes open to a wide network of data inputs 40% larger than conventional closed ERP architectures. It must create a collaboration of the enterprise based on intuition for better real time operations. Most managerial situations on a day to day basis leverage on this feature for operational efficiency critical to Modern operations. For example a supply of raw material might have been defaulted due to some reason and the software must communicate to all concerned in the enterprise about the default and also suggest possible remedies.

ERP must use Artificial Intelligence tools and procedures: ERP must integrate itself with neural networks and robotics. To make operations procedure lean robotics and other AI related tools are integrated into the manufacturing system. Another key factor is machine learning. ERP acts as an engine supporting the entire process of manufacturing and operations and must necessarily learn from the operations in the future. This learning must be incorporated into the decision making process and process integration processes. ERP must cease to be dumb and must act as an Engine constantly in AI processes like Learning.

ERP must provide CPFR and Supply Chain Visibility: Managing uncertainty using probabilistic models is another demand on ERP in the future. The entire supply chain is bound by uncertainty and random processes because of the kind of environment in which it operates. CPFR which stands for Coordinated Planning Forecasting and Replenishment is the onus of the modern ERP in general

ERP must be a constant Knowledge Generator and not just an Information processing tool: Conventionally organizations worked in the realm of data with some degree of processing. With advent of computing and Information systems organizations moved towards better understanding of relationships between data leading to Information based

Organizations. We are now in the era of knowledge economy and knowledge goes much beyond the precincts of information processing. ERP in modern times must involve itself in knowledge Engineering not only in manufacturing and operation functions but also into all areas of the Supply Chain. ERP must be able to create fresh knowledge and process the knowledge even further entering into the finesse of Knowledge management. This knowledge must be actively used in Production and Operations

ERP must have multi-language multi-currency capabilities: With globalization plants are being located around the world. Sometimes plants have to be located in other countries within a very short period of time. Country incompatibility would render an ERP redundant and with many such plant shifts likely to occur the ERP would end up becoming of very little operational use. Modern ERP must be prepared for multi-lingual capabilities of at least some key languages and even with translator software's. The base could still be the English language or any other language with guest country languages written in the English script. Needless to say all key international currencies must be supported by the ERP and their fluctuations in the international market accounted for automatically by the ERP even on a daily basis.

Faster Implementation of ERP and quick Integration: One of the problems with ERP is the long implementation times. 55 per cent of ERP implementations involve cost and time over-run. Even the best of the implementation methodologies under go over-runs. There are many reasons for such occurrences. If ERP implementations take excessive time ERP will become obsolete vis-à-vis business processes. ERP must scale and change itself from one or some reference points of business processes and there after synchronize itself. The production environment is changing at a fast pace in techniques and methodologies to remain competitive. ASAP was one of the techniques developed by SAP for faster implementations. Today there are companies that build Enterprise Spread Sheets that concur with existing IT systems of an organization.

Web enabling to Integration: Emerging manufacturing scenarios goes way ahead of what conventional ERP software's provide- web enabling. This means a ERP system can take advantage of a public system like the internet as and when it requires. There is a time lag faced in such transactions. Web integration on the other hand through a fire-wall systems helps ERP get inflow of internet information as–if internet were an integral part of an ERP. Such enabling is becoming a need of the hour. ERP must go beyond only Internet enabling and must also be amenable to enabling of various Intranets.

21

Government Procurement in Supply Chain Management

Deepthi B.S.

Introduction

The concept of the government as a sovereign power distinguishes governmental procurement from the commercial contracting processes. As a sovereign power, the government writes procurement through statutes, executive orders, regulations and political policies and procedures. The government can change the procurement act to its advantages. Policies and procedures provide for equitable adjustment, but the government reserves the right to contract changes. Size, purchasing power, and sovereignty give the skilled government acquisition or supply management official great power.

Steve Kelman, a professor at the John F. Kennedy school, Harvard University, and former head of the office of federal procurement policy, writes, 'Contracting management must be considered a core competency of federal organizations. This is different from the traditional view of contracting as a subsidiary administrative function. In the 21st century, contracting management needs to become one of the central concerns of senior political and career executives, viewed the same as other core competencies'.

Sources of Funds

At all levels of government, taxes paid by citizens and businesses or debt are used to purchase required goods and services. Normally there is no profit incentive to generate funds for ongoing operations. In executing their roles as funds stewards, both the legislative and the executive arms of government promulgate procedures to carefully control funds expenditures. These procedures give government supply managers considerably less flexibility than their industrial counter parts. Fixed budgets often stop the government supply managers from taking advantage of quality discounts and longer-term contracts.

Lead Time

Lead-time is another phase of government procurement and industry differs. The government, for other than business purposes, has added additional costs to its purchasing operation. The advent of government purchasing cards in recent years has significantly reduced the time and cost to process orders for common commercial items of relatively low value and complexity.

Regulations

The decision making processes of government agencies are governed by numerous regulations. The Federal Acquisition Regulation (FAR) is the primary regulation for use by all federal executive agencies in their acquisition of goods and services with appropriated funds.

At the state and local government level, state statutes are often implemented in "codes" of regulations. Likewise, counties, municipalities and special districts may also have ordinances and implementing regulations.

Public Review

The expenditure of public funds properly attracts the interest of taxpayers. Except for the relatively small amount of money spent in necessarily classified projects, government's expenditures are open to the public. This openness is the result of federal and state constitutions, laws and statutes, and the moral obligation of government. The process is generally required to be conducted in full public view and all actions are a matter of public record usually with only limited exceptions.

Web-based Government Procurement

The Internet has been accepted as a transaction medium. Public institutions have several goals, which are similar to those of most private organizations seeking to use e-procurement systems. However, public institutions are also constrained by the requirement to provide equal access to opportunities where public funds are used.

State and Local Government

State and local governments also have a great power in the aggregate. Managed competition drives efficiency and innovation. Public organization managers are required to look at their organization as a business and find and implement new and novel ideas to make it more cost effective.

The following is a typical process that frequently is followed:

1. The public agency identifies and documents the service requirements.
2. The public service organization is evaluated. If the organization is capable of accomplishing the required tasks and service levels, it will be allowed to participate in the solicitation.
3. The outside service providers are given the opportunity to provide proposals based on the service requirements.
4. The public service organization independently prepares a sealed bid to perform the service.
5. The best value, most qualified outside service provider is evaluated.
6. The public service organization bid is compared to that of the best outside provider.

Quality of Government Purchased Items

In industry, suppliers normally have a strong incentive to interpret specifications in a way that is fully satisfactory to buyers. In government purchases, it is essential that specifications be developed with great care and completeness to obtain materials of the desired quality. If the government is successful in arguing that the supplier deliberately made a substandard product, then the government has the recourse of defaulting or suspending the supplier from future work with the government.

Disputes

A dispute arises between the government and a contractor that the parties cannot resolve through negotiation. The disputes clause of government contracts (based on the contract disputes act of 1978) provides a legal framework for resolution.

Remedies

The government has a number of remedies that it may apply during or even after contract performance. The contract may be terminated for default. The government may debar, suspend, or declare ineligible an errant contractor to make sure that contracts are awarded only to responsible bidders.

1. Develop the business strategy, specifying requirements for what will be bought, and choosing an appropriate contract arrangement and incentives.
2. Select the right suppliers
3. Administer the contract once signed.

Code of Ethics for Government Service

1. Put royalty to the highest moral principles and to country above loyalty to persons, party, or government department.
2. Uphold the constitution, laws, and regulations of the United States and of all governments therein and never be a party to their evasion.
3. Seek to find and employ more efficient and economical ways of getting tasks accomplished.
4. Expose corruption wherever discovered.
5. Uphold these principles, ever conscious that public office is a public trust.
6. Never use any information gained confidentially in the performance of governmental duties as a means for making private profit.

7. Engage in no business with the government either directly or indirectly, which is inconsistent with the conscientious performance of governmental duties.

Concluding Remarks

Government contracting is clearly bounded by more rules than in commercial purchasing. The necessity to guard the public interest as well as the peculiar needs of the government dictate such rules. Both commercial and government procurement entities are concerned with buying the "right" quality, in the "right" quantity, at the "right" price and time, and from the "right" source.

22

Outsourcing in Supply Chain Management

Bhavya Singh

Supply chain management (SCM) is the process of planning, implementing, and controlling the operations of the supply chain with the purpose to satisfy customer requirements as efficiently as possible. Supply chain management spans all movement and storage of raw materials, work-in-process inventory, and finished goods from point-of-origin to point-of-consumption.

Outsourcing once a mere option has today become a competitive imperative. The growth of the Internet, customer revolution, use of mass communication, severe competition etc, has forced the companies to focus on core competencies instead of vertical integration. This means that original equipment manufactures (OEMs) must ideally contract out part or all of manufacturing, assembly, distribution, and support operations. What to outsource has historically been decided by the question, "Is it strategic to my business?" If the answer is yes, you would keep it. If no, farm it out. Today, companies are asking a different question: Is it my core competency? If no, then it is ripe for outsourcing, whether it is 'strategic' of not.

The 'trendsetter barometer' conducted by Coopers and Lybrand LLP, contraction shows that 83 per cent of America's fastest growing companies have turned to out-sourcing for one or more functions.

What is Outsourcing?

Outsourcing is defined as the contracting of one or more of a company's business processes to an outside service provider to help increase shareholder value, by primarily reducing operating cost and focusing on core competencies.

Automatic data processing Inc (ADP) defines, outsourcing as the contracting out of a company's non-core, non-revenue-producing activities to specialists. It differs from contracting in that outsourcing is a strategic management tool that involves the restructuring of an organization around what it does best – its core competencies.

Why Do Companies Outsource?

There are several reasons why outsourcing is becoming a habit. The simplest reason to outsource is to alleviate administrative burdens and focus on strategic areas.

As the companies move from non-outsourcing environment to an outsourcing environment the profile of the time spent by the executives on various activities change dramatically. According to the figure in a non outsourcing environment, executives spend 60 per cent of their time on administration matters, while 30 per cent on tactical issues and this leaves only 10 per cent of their time to focus on strategic matters. On the contrary when they switch to an outsourcing environment and outsource some of the activities they need to spend only 10 per cent of their time on handling administration issues, 30 per cent time to focus on tactical matters while 60 per cent of their time they can devote to thinking, strategizing and planning.

Some other reasons for outsourcing are:

Reduction in Cost: A company may emphasize cost savings for a variety of reasons, such as being in a poor financial position or because of a goal to increase profits.

Thus, there are a few situations in which a company can reduce its costs by outsourcing, but there are many more cases where this is not a realistic reason for outsourcing.

Focus on Core Function: A company typically has a small number of functions that are key to its survival while other functions or activities are required to be done but are non-core.

A company could even outsource a function that is considered key to the company's survival if it can find a supplier that can perform the function better-in short, only keep those functions that are core functions and which company can do better than any supplier. For example, a company may be the lost cost manufacturer in its industry, which allows it to maintain a large enough, pricing advantage over its competitors, that it is guaranteed a large share of the market.

Acquisition of New skills: This is the most common reason and is used for outsourcing those functions that require high skill levels, such as engineering and computer services.

Acquisition of Management Techniques: Outsourcing a function to a supplier just to gain access to the supplier's better management can be a viable option. It may also be possible to rent management from the supplier. This can be a good option in all functional areas, though it is more common in areas requiring high levels of expertise such as engineering.

Fast Growth Situation: If a company is rapidly acquiring market share, the management team will be stretched to its limit, building the company up so that it can handle the vastly increased volume of business. In such situations, the management team will desperately need additional help in running the company.

Avoidance of Labour Problems: If a company is constantly bogged down by labour problems which start affecting its productivity and performance, outsourcing becomes a viable option.

Handling Overflow Situations: A company may find that there are times of the day or year when a function is overloaded for reasons that are beyond its control. In these situations it may be cost effective to retain a supplier to whom the excess work will be shunted when the in-house staff is unable to keep up with demand.

Improvement in Flexibility: This is similar to using outsourcing to handle overflow situations, except that the supplier gets the entire function, not just the overflow business.

A company may decide to outsource a function simply because everyone else is doing it, too. Also, a large amount of coverage of outsourcing in various national or industry specific publications will give company management the impression that outsourcing is the trend, and they must use it or fail.

A company may find that it has a function that has bloated costs or inadequate performance. To shake up the function, company management can put the function out to bid and include the internal function's staff in the bidding process.

New Opportunities in SCM Outsourcing

In today's global economy, companies are making their best attempt at shedding their flab and becoming lean and trim. This new avatar can ensure a faster response, agility and better ability to handle pressure. These companies often find it much more cost effective to outsource rather than build a proprietary infrastructure. They believe in having no production facility, no warehouse, no loading dock, no boardroom – just office space, a handful of employees, and a great idea for a product or service and marketing strength.

The following strategic and competitive areas can be used to their full advantage if a supply chain management system is properly implemented.

- **Fulfillment:** "Ensuring the right quantity of parts for production or products for sale arrive at the right time."
- **Logistics:** "Keeping the cost of transporting materials as low as possible consistent with safe and reliable delivery."
- **Production:** "Ensuring production lines function smoothly because high-quality parts are available when needed."
- **Revenue & profit:** "Ensuring no sales are lost because shelves are empty."
- **Costs:** "Keeping the cost of purchased parts and products at acceptable levels."
- **Cooperation:** "Among supply chain partners ensures 'mutual success.'" development."

Outsourcing Process

1. Understanding company goals and objectives
2. A strategic vision and plan

3. Selecting the right vendor
4. Management of the relationships
5. A properly structured contract
6. Open communication
7. Section executive support
8. Use of outside expertise

A survey of outsourcing was conducted. This survey presents a snapshot of who is outsourcing, why and issues they look at. It is taken from the perspective of the outsourcing services user, the buyer. There were 195 respondents. They were with firms that have strong interest in outsourcing or are active in outsourcing. The survey was broad, both as to industry types and to mix of company sizes, and presents a solid overview of what is happening.

The objectives were to: -

1. Assess the state of logistics outsourcing from the perspective of the outsourcing buyer.
2. Measure outsourcing development.
3. Determine what companies see as future outsourcing of supply chains.
4. Identify key customer needs.

The following points standout from the survey finding: 42% outsource half or more of their supply chains. This is a significant percentage and shows the degree of outsourcing acceptance, development and penetration.

Firms see a 10 per cent increase in supply chain and logistics outsourcing over the next two years. This shows the continuing, positive trend for outsourcing.

Only 2 per cent cited technology as a reason for outsourcing. This finding runs counter to the perception of outsourcing to gain technology for supply chain integration, collaboration, visibility and other purposes.

Firms who have not moved into logistics outsourcing cite a range of reasons from adequate in-house resources (16 per cent), organizational resistance (8 per cent), and loss of control (6 per cent). There is likely a correlation with organization resistance and loss of control as a fear-factor in not outsourcing.

While the function or activity is outsourced is broad, 59 per cent outsource supplier management. This is a significant use of 3PLs and shows the maturation and application of outsourcing from transaction driven to process driven. It also shows recognition that supply chain importance and success begins with suppliers, who can be difficult to manage, especially those thousands of miles away.

56 per cent import some or all of their finished products or materials. This also shows the expanding opportunities for outsourcing of offshore logistics. With the continuing use of global sourcing, managing offshore suppliers and supply chains should grow in importance and need for outsourcing opportunities.

The criteria for selecting outsourcing firms follow general understanding. Interestingly, 53 per cent cite Organizational Culture Fit as a reason. This shows the need for outsource service providers to become partners with their customers and to become an extension of them.

Conclusion

According to Prahalad and Hamel (1990) core competencies are the functional strength of the company, which should be identified and cultivated to build new products and market opportunities. The basic idea is that outsourcing facilities a focus on the resources and activities that are regarded as core competencies so that the management could focus on strategic business areas. According to Pfeffer and Sutton (2000), there are two main problems inherent in the outsourcing of production.

23

Supply Chain Management: An Integrated Approach

A. Duraikannan, B.L. Sairam Subramaniam and S. Baskaran

Supply Chain Management

A *supply chain* is a network of facilities and distribution options that performs the functions of procurement of materials, transformation of these materials into intermediate and finished products, and the distribution of these finished products to customers. Supply chains exist in both service and manufacturing organizations, although the complexity of the chain may vary greatly from industry to industry and firm to firm.

The term "supply chain" first appeared in literature as an inventory management approach. Commercial businesses had been encountering a demand for greater levels of responsiveness and shorter cycle times for delivery and inventory of goods and services—placing, preparing, storing, and fulfilling orders. The notion of "the perfect order" required that the supply chain provide non standardized, quality products quickly and efficiently every time. Since holding of inventories can cost as much as 40% of their value, their efficient management is crucial.

Marketing, distribution, planning, manufacturing, and the purchasing organizations along the supply chain have traditionally operated independently. These organizations have their own objectives and these are often conflicting. Marketing's objective of high customer service and maximum sales dollars conflict with manufacturing and distribution goals. Many manufacturing operations are designed to maximize throughput and lower costs with little consideration for the impact on inventory levels and distribution capabilities. Purchasing contracts are often negotiated with very little information beyond historical buying patterns. The result of these factors is that there is not a single, integrated plan for the organization---there were as many plans as businesses.

Clearly, there is a need for a mechanism through which these different functions can be integrated together. Supply chain management is a strategy through which such an integration can be achieved.

Common Supply Chain Performance Areas

- Products and services
- Sales
- Cost
- Responsiveness
- Customer service
- Quality
- Delivery
- Cycle times
- Assets utilized
- Warehousing

Benefits of Supply Chain Management

Today's information-driven, integrated supply chains are strategic assets that support innovative warfighting capabilities—enabling organizations to reduce inventory, add product value, extend resources, accelerate time to market, and retain customers

Effective supply chain management can impact and improve upon virtually all business processes, such as data accuracy, operational complexity reduction, supplier selection, purchasing, and warehousing and distribution. Other benefits include:

- Quicker customer response and fulfillment rates.
- Greater productivity and lower costs.
- Reduced inventory throughout the chain.
- Improved forecasting precision.
- Fewer suppliers and shorter planning cycles.
- Improved quality and products that are more technologically advanced.

- Enhanced inter-operational communications and cooperation.
- Shortened repair times and enhanced equipment readiness.
- More reliable financial information.

Supply Chain Decisions

We classify the decisions for supply chain management into two broad categories -- strategic and operational. As the term implies, strategic decisions are made typically over a longer time horizon. These are closely linked to the corporate strategy (they sometimes {\it are} the corporate strategy), and guide supply chain policies from a design perspective. On the other hand, operational decisions are short term, and focus on activities over a day-to-day basis. The effort in these type of decisions is to effectively and efficiently manage the product flow in the "strategically" planned supply chain.

There are four major decision areas in supply chain management: (1) location, (2) production, (3) inventory, and (4) transportation (distribution), and there are both strategic and operational elements in each of these decision areas. The effort in these type of decisions is to effectively and efficiently manage the product flow in the "strategically" planned supply chain.

Location Decisions: The geographic placement of production facilities, stocking points, and sourcing points is the natural first step in creating a supply chain. The location of facilities involves a commitment of resources to a long-term plan. Once the size, number, and location of these are determined, so are the possible paths by which the product flows through to the final customer. These decisions are of great significance to a firm since they represent the basic strategy for accessing customer markets, and will have a considerable impact on revenue, cost, and level of service. These decisions should be determined by an optimization routine that considers production costs, taxes, duties and duty drawback, tariffs, local content, distribution costs, production limitations, etc. (See Arntzen, Brown, Harrison and Trafton [1995] for a thorough discussion of these aspects.) Although location decisions are primarily strategic, they also have implications on an operational level.

Production Decisions: The strategic decisions include what products to produce, and which plants to produce them in, allocation of suppliers to plants, plants to DC's, and DC's to customer markets. As before, these decisions have a big impact on the revenues, costs and customer service levels of the firm. These decisions assume the existence of the facilities, but determine the exact path(s) through which a product flows to and from these facilities. Another critical issue is the capacity of the manufacturing facilities--and this largely depends the degree of vertical integration within the firm. Operational decisions focus on detailed production scheduling. These decisions include the construction of the master production schedules, scheduling production on machines, and equipment maintenance. Other considerations include workload balancing, and quality control measures at a production facility.

Inventory Decisions: These refer to means by which inventories are managed. Inventories exist at every stage of the supply chain as either raw materials, semi-finished or finished goods. They can also be in-process between locations. Their primary purpose to buffer against any uncertainty that might exist in the supply chain. Since holding of inventories can cost anywhere between 20 to 40 percent of their value, their efficient management is critical in supply chain operations. It is strategic in the sense that top management sets goals. However, most researchers have approached the management of inventory from an operational perspective. These include deployment strategies (push versus pull), control policies --- the determination of the optimal levels of order quantities and reorder points, and setting safety stock levels, at each stocking location. These levels are critical, since they are primary determinants of customer service levels.

Transportation Decisions: The mode choice aspect of these decisions are the more strategic ones. These are closely linked to the inventory decisions, since the best choice of mode is often found by trading-off the cost of using the particular mode of transport with the indirect cost of inventory associated with that mode. While air shipments may be fast, reliable, and warrant lesser safety stocks, they are expensive. Meanwhile shipping by sea or rail may be much cheaper, but they necessitate holding relatively large amounts of inventory to buffer against the inherent uncertainty associated with them. Therefore customer service levels, and geographic location play vital roles in such decisions. Since transportation is more than 30 percent of the logistics costs, operating efficiently makes good economic sense. Shipment sizes (consolidated bulk shipments versus Lot-for-Lot), routing and scheduling of equipment are key in effective management of the firm's transport strategy.

Supply chain management is typically viewed to lie between fully vertically integrated firms, where the entire material flow is owned by a single firm, and those where each channel member operates independently. Therefore coordination between the various players in the chain is key in its effective management.

24

Technical Training of Employees and Supply Chain Management

A. Azad and K. Narashiman

Introduction

The nine major objectives of supply management are (Leenders et al, 2002):

1. To provide an uninterrupted flow of materials, supplies and services required to operate the organization
2. Minimize inventory investment and loss
3. Maintain and improve quality
4. Create relationships with competent suppliers
5. Set standards for supplies
6. Get supplies and services at lowest cost
7. Achieve harmonious, productive working relationships with other departments
8. Keep purchasing administrative costs low
9. Improve the organization's competitive position

This paper discusses the effect of technical training on the capabilities of the employees, which influences the above nine objectives in a manufacturing industry. There is a general agreement about the importance of training as a tool to help companies in the development of sustainable competitive advantages based on their human resources. Training is the most predominant activity among all activities of total quality management. The employees are trained in new technology applications, communication improvement, computer skills, customer service, ethics, human relations, quality and safety. Human knowledge, skills and attitudes are the sources of competitive advantage of an organization according to Wright, McMahan and McWilliams (1994), Kamoche (1996), Mueller

(1996), and Barney and Wright (1998).

In a rapidly changing society, employee training and development helps in maintaining a valuable and knowledgeable work force. Every organization needs to have well-trained and experienced people to perform their duties. As the job becomes more complex, the importance of employee development also increases. The rapidity of change as well as the high degree of tacit knowledge in the production process prevents firms from satisfying all their human resource requirements by hiring new employees (Loof and Heshmati, 2002). Consequently, the more innovative firms are, the more they will need to enhance the skills of their employees through training. This will enforce the advantage of the efficient firms and contribute to persistent heterogeneity in conduct and performance.

According to Bassi, Buchanan and Cheney (1997), an important study of the American Society for Training and Development pinpointed seven key trends that would influence HRD in the future:

1. Training
2. Globalization
3. Changes in organisational structure
4. The way work gets done
5. Impact of technology
6. Role of HRD professional
7. More attention to the workers

In learning organisations the employees are given the opportunity and tools they need to learn new skills. Technical trainers must change from thinking that training is the solution to every problem to thinking about what causes a human performance problem and how that problem may be solved or even how its causes can be averted (Rothwell, Hone, and King, 2000).

A survey of 1000 firms in Singapore about their adoption and implementation of advanced manufacturing technology (AMT) identified training as instrumental in reducing uncertainties in AMT implementation (Zhao and Co, 1997). Many manufacturing firms experience resistance whenever a new technology is introduced. Continuing education and training help to ease the resistance to AMT adoption (Beatty and Gordon, 1988). An organization could never realize such a change by simply hiring engineers and technicians with new technical expertise from outside (Chang, 1989). A long-term educational and training program should be designed and implemented to train the employees so that reallocation of the human resource for jobs requiring advanced technical expertise can be made possible.

Technical training may be understood to mean instruction intended to help people perform the unique aspects of a special kind of work and apply the special tools, equipment, and processes of that work, usually in one organizational setting (Rothwell and Benkowski, 2002). Technical training includes training people how to use technology and perform under unique conditions for which special expertise is necessary.

Technical training is important for three key reasons (Ruber, 1996):

1. Technical training has a significant economic impact on employers
2. It accounts for a sizable percentage of all training offered in the United States
3. Its importance is growing as organizations scramble to find, keep and leverage talent.

In a study of 42 firms in a variety of industries, Smith et al. (1995) found that the major drivers of training in organisations were 'workplace change and innovation'. More recent studies of training practices in organisations (Kearns & Papadopoulos 2000; Figgis et al. 2001; Johnston & Hawke 2002; Dawe 2002) also highlighted the importance of change and innovation as major factors driving workplace training.

From careful study of the literature it is concluded that there is a need for a detailed study of the effect of technical training on the capabilities of the employees which considerably improves the supply chin management in large scale manufacturing industries.

The objective of this work is to study the effect of technical training on the capabilities of the employees, which considerably improves the supply chain management in large a scale manufacturing industry. The employees are in the production supervisory cadres who have undergone at least two technical training programmes in the past two and a half years.

Survey Methodology

In order to measure the effect of technical training on the capabilities of the employees in manufacturing industries, a survey instrument has been developed. It is based on an exhaustive review of the literature, brainstorming with employees and a pilot survey among the employees. The instrument underwent refinements based on the pilot survey and the suggestions from the experts from the academic field and industry. The instrument has been designed to maximally capture the effect of technical training on the capabilities of the employees that influences the benefits expected from a good supply chain management.

The items in the questionnaire are jumbled and arranged in a random order in the instrument. The random sampling procedure was followed to get the responses. The respondents were approached personally and were explained the purpose of the project. The respondents were requested to indicate their perception of the effect of technical training on the capabilities of the employees in manufacturing industries with respect to each item on a seven point Likert scale. A total of 21 candidates were approached and all of them returned correctly completed questionnaires, yielding a response rate of 100 per cent. The high response rate was due to personal contact approach. The items on the questionnaire are given in Table 24.1.

Results and Discussion

Three regression models were used with increase in profitability, improvement in the turnover and reduction in various costs as dependant variables.

Table 24.1: Employees Perception

1.	Improvement in the turnover
2.	Extent to which training reduced inventory
3.	Increase in operating results
4.	Increase in profitability
5.	Extent to which the training was helpful in the introduction of new technology
6.	Extent to which the training was helpful in responding to internal changes
7.	Extent to which the training was helpful in responding to external changes
8.	Extent to which training supported the business needs
9.	Extent to which the training was helpful to becoming a reliable and preferred supplier
10.	Extent to which the training was helpful to understand the current societal trends that may impact the organization
11.	Extent to which training resulted in new initiatives
12.	Extent to which the training was helpful in change management
13.	Extent to which the training was helpful in continuous improvement
14.	Extent to which the training was helpful to solve business problems
15.	Improvement in business performance as a result of training
16.	Extent to which training resulted in achieving the company objectives
17.	Improvement in the competitiveness of the organisation
18.	Reduction of overhead costs
19.	Reduction in various costs
20.	Extent to which the training was helpful in removing improvement barriers in the industry

Contd...

21.	Improvement in relationship management
22.	Extent to which the training resulted in technical conflict reduction
23.	Extent to which training resulted in team building
24.	Extent to which training aided in creating quality culture
25.	Extent to which training assists in meeting quality assurance activities
26.	Improvement in the quality related activities
27.	Improvement in the quality of services
28.	Improvement in the quality of the product
29.	Extent to which training assists in adapting to new quality assurance initiatives
30.	Improvement in the quality of working
31.	Usefulness of training to become a multi skilled employee
32.	Increase in the flexibility amongst employees
33.	Extent to which the training was helpful in the creation of flexible workforce
34.	Reduction in defects in products
35.	Extent to which training reduced wastage
36.	Extent to which training reduced errors
37.	Extent to which training resulted in reduced rework
38.	Reduction in unproductive work due to training

The multiple regression analysis of the survey shows the influencing factors resulting in the increase in profitability. The major factors leading to the profitability are the increase in operating results, quality culture, team building, change management and conflict reduction.

The influencing factors resulting in the improvement in the turnover are shown in the regression analysis. The major factors leading to the improvement in the turnover are reduction in various costs, introduction of new technology, reduction in wastage, team building and reduction in unproductive work.

The influencing factors resulting in the reduction in various costs are shown in the regression analysis. The major factors leading to the improvement in the turnover are creating quality culture, becoming a reliable and preferred supplier, Competitiveness of the organization, Relationship management and Quality related activities.

Conclusion

The knowledge gained during the technical training in industries results in benefits in all areas of supply chain management. This work discusses the results of the analysis of the perception of the employees on various gains made due to the knowledge acquired during the technical training. The influence of different variables on increase in profitability, improvement in the turnover and reduction in various costs were analyzed. It is significant that profitability, turnover and cost reduction are influenced by change management, new initiatives, quality culture, team building and relationship management. Reduction in various unproductive activities has a direct bearing on the turnover. It can also be seen that quality plays a significant role in reducing various costs.

References

Barney, J.B. and Wright, P.M. (1998), 'On Becoming a Strategic Partner: The Role of Human Resources in Gaining Competitive Advantage', Human Resource Management, 37(1): 31–46.

Bassi, L., Buchanan, L. and Cheney, S. (1997), Trends that affect learning and performance improvement: A report on the members of the ASTD benchmarking forum, Alexandria, VA: ASTD.

Beatty, C.A. and Gordon, J.R.M. (1988), Barriers to the implementation of CAD/CAM systems, Sloan Management Review, Summer: 25-33.

Chang, C.H. (1989), A new perspective on realization of computer-integrated manufacturing, Manufacturing Review, 2(2), 82-91.

Dawe, S. (2002), Focusing on generic skills in training packages, NCVER, Adelaide.

Figgis, J. Alderson, A. Blackwell, A. Butorac, A. Mitchell, K. & Zubrick, A. (2001). What convinces enterprises to value training and learning and what does not? NCVER, Adelaide.

Johnston, R. and Hawke, G. (2002), Case studies of organisations with established learning cultures, NCVER, Adelaide.

Kamoche, K. (1996), 'Strategic Human Resource Management within a Resource–Capability View of the Firm', Journal of Management Studies, 33(2): 213–33.

Kearns, P. and Papadopoulos, G. (2000), Building a learning and training culture: The experience of five OECD countries, NCVER, Adelaide.

Leenders, Michiel R., Fearon, Harold E., Flynn, Anna E., and Johnson, P. Fraser (2002), Purchasing and Supply Management, 12th edition, McGraw-Hill, Boston.

Loof , H. and Heshmati, A., (2002), Knowledge capital and performance heterogeneity: A firm level innovation study, Int.J.Production Economics 76: 61-85

Mueller, F. (1996) 'Human Resources as Strategic Assets: An Evolutionary Resource-Based Theory', Journal of Management Studies, 33(6): 757–85.

Rothwell, W., Hohne, C., and King, S. (2000), Human performance improvement: building practitioner competence, Woburn, MA: Butterworth-Heinemann.

Rothwell, W.J. and Benkowski, J.A. (2002), Building effective technical training, Jossey-Boss/ Pfeiffer, San Francisco, CA.

Ruber, P. (1996), The high cost of technical training, Computer reseller news, 710, 27-28.

Smith, A, Roberts, P, Noble, C, Hayton, G & Thorne, E. (1995), Enterprise training: The factors that affect demand, report commissioned by the Australian National Training Authority and the Office of Training and Further Education (Victoria), Office of Training and Further Education, Melbourne.

Wright, P.M., McMahan, G.C. and McWilliams, A. (1994) 'Human Resources and Sustained Competitive Advantage: A Resource-Based Perspective', International Journal of Human Resource Management, 5(2): 301–326.

Zhao, H and Co, H.C. (1997), Adoption and implementation of advanced technology in Singapore, Int. J. Production Economics 48: 7-19.

25

Turning Returns Management into a Competitive Advantage

S. Chandrasekaran, Ashvini Ravi and G.Nirmala

Introduction

Many organizations and individuals have tried to define Returns management. It can be defined as all activity associated with a product/service *after* the point of sale, the ultimate goal to optimize or make more efficient the aftermarket activity, thus saving money and serving the purpose of competitive advantage. Other terms synonymous to Returns Management are Reverse Logistics™ (RL) are Aftermarket Logistics, Retrogistics, or Aftermarket Supply Chain. The reverse supply chain is also a term used in the industry. RL is not to be confused with forward logistics or getting the product to market commonly known as the forward supply chain. Types of activity common with reverse logistics includes: logistics, warehousing, repair, refurbishment, recycling, e-waste, after market call center support, reverse fulfillment, field service and many others.

Returns Problem

Certain important trends and developments in the future could make the returns or reverse logistics problem even worse in the future. The table below reveals that returns in hi tech industry can be as high as 20 per cent (Prasad, 2004).

One is the increase in low cost and low touch channels such as the web, catalogs and other direct to consumer mechanisms. Though these channels have their own advantages, they do come with some disadvantages too. Without demonstration of the product, answers to queries and the lack of tactility and other stimulation of the senses, customers could end up being more dissatisfied than otherwise would be the case. This might result in a higher rate of returns. Moreover, since these channels involve no physical outlet where the returns could be taken the whole logistics of the returns becomes a nightmare (Prasad, 2004). A significant impact of this on the corporate bottom line is inevitable.

Cost of Returns: The conventional returns-management model only takes into account those costs related to bringing the returns back into the system, along with the cost of warehousing and returns-request management. But the cost impact of returns extends far beyond that to such areas as customer-retention efforts, product reworking, redistribution, inventory maintenance, overheads allocated to other departments, Cost of disposal and Compliance with regulations such as WEEE (Waste from Electrical and Electronic Equipment) and RoHS (Restriction of Hazardous Substances) (Deker and Brito, 2003). This makes returns management or what is called reverse logistics, to be a much graver issue than it initially was taken to be.

Current Flaws in Returns Management

Typical returns-management solutions take a very general approach of digitizing, streamlining, partnering and outsourcing (McNerney, 2002). This is definitely not good enough in today's scenario, with all the hidden costs of returns management. There are numerous companies specializing in web services for Returns Management. While some specialize in pack and ship operation, others concentrate only on liquidation and asset recovery. Some companies are product specific, for example only focusing on pharmaceuticals or food. Some companies focus on auctioning while others focus on retailing. Thus there seems to be at best only a piecemeal and fragmented approach to returns management

Web Services for Competitive Advantage

A good returns management model should provide for contact centers, customer service, depot repair, field service, transportation and warehousing, spare parts management, replacement management, IT process management, recycling, refurbishment and warranty support. It should manage the entire returns process, should increase net asset recovery, match invoices for accurate return credit provide insight into purchase and return behavior, provide opportunities for up-selling, sale protection and cross promotion, help lower inventory holding costs at returns centers, should differentiate between tiers of buyers to customize user experiences, consolidates returns into one shipment back to the vendor and run manufacturer and extended warranty programs in a single centralized system (www.manh.com, 2006).

Also, a good Returns Management Model should provide a comprehensive return stream for improved cash flow, technology that's scalable and reduces costs, A fully integrated system that speeds up cycle times, a consistent process for improved business controls, diverse remarketing that increases salvage values and an adaptive transportation process that improves transportation effectiveness (genco.com, 2006). It is very important to formulate a model that takes into deliberation the above key factors. It is also essential to aggregate the sell-buy-returns data and understand the flaws and successes of everything surrounding the return.

Web Services and Returns Management: Web Services is the technology (black box) that was missing from many equations dealing with eCommerce. This is especially true for Returns Management. It gives consumers, manufacturers and channel partners a superior, proficient and cost effective approach to handle the predicament of returns.

Web Services requires a few basic things: Internet hardware, XML based software, connectivity, and development techniques. Those businesses that can deliver unmatched returns management services and those businesses that can provide the `infrastructure necessary for delivery will make money; those that can't, won't. Thus, Returns Management services represent a business fundamental that is a true competitive advantage over those that don't have a program. The technology used for Returns

Management was born out of a business need, not a business "need" born out of technology (Smith, 2006). Returns Management must integrate effortlessly into existing supply chains both technologically and culturally. Web Services provide the perfect information exchange mechanism and the most efficient and cost effective data analysis engines when used to manage products and information coming back. Web services collects, encrypts, converts, interprets and communicates.

Conclusions

The proliferation in e-commerce has in turn catalyzed a massive returns threat. The low contact nature of the web seems to increase customer dissatisfaction, and therefore returns. Web services, by its very nature, have innate synergy to returns management. Though there are many web services based models, the one suggested here has tried to integrate the plethora of variables involved in the process. The model promises to be a flexible one which can be adapted to the needs of different products, verticals or business size.

References

Best Practice Guide to Reverse Logistics, LIS (Now part of Red Prairie) White Paper, Sourced from http://www.idii.com/wp

Directive 2002/96/ec of the European Parliament and of the council of 27 January 2003 on waste Electrical and electronic equipment (WEEE), Official Journal of the European Union, 13/2/2003.

Electronic Waste Processing: Manufacturers Running Out of Time, Vinay Asgekar, Allison Bacon, Nigel Montgomery, Gerald McNerney; March 26, 2003

Getting Strategic Value From Returns, Nigel Montgomery, John Fontanella, Marc McCluskey, April 12, 2004

Going Backwards: Reverse Logistics Trends and Practices. Rogers and Tibben- Lembke. 1999.

Prasad Thrikutam, Sandeep Kumar, Turning Returns Management into a Competitive Advantage in Hi-Tech Manufacturing, 2004.

Reverse Logistics – A Framework, Marisa P. de Rommert Dekker and Brito Erasmus Research Institute of Management (ERIM), 30 May 2003.

Reverse Logistics Is the Icing on the Customer Fulfillment Cake, Gerald McNerney, AMR Research, July 29, 2002

Rogers, Dale S, Tibben-Lembke, Ronald, An examination of reverse logistics practices Journal of Business Logistics, 2001

Service Providers tackle e-product returns, Internet week, June 2000.'

26

Logistics Management in Central Public Enterprises in India

R.K. Mishra

Public Enterprises (PEs) face the challenge of improving their rate of return on investment. The operating and financial leverages play an important role in lifting the rate of return. The DuPont matrix points out the role of logistics in contributing to a higher rate of return. The logistics costs have shown the tendency to increase rapidly. The total logistics costs as percentage of Gross Domestic Product (GDP) increased from Rs. 2,50,000 crore in 1987 to Rs. 8,00,000 crore in 1994. These costs have had the tendency to steeply increase thereafter. In percentage terms, these costs constituted 10 per cent of the GDP in 1987 and 12 per cent in 1994. [1] The infrastructural bottlenecks have only added to the woes during the period 1994-2007. The logistics costs can be easily estimated at 20 percent of the GDP amounting to Rs. 8,00,000 crore with a GDP of Rs.40,00,000 crore at current prices (the recent estimates show that India has become a one trillion economy. [2] Assuming that the country requires Rs. 1,00,000 crore for achieving 1 percentage rate of growth in GDP and that the investments in logistics could be reduced to 75 per cent of its present level, it could be surmised that reductions in logistics costs can unlock huge resources for development purposes resulting in the increase in the rate of growth from the present 9 per cent to 11 per cent as Rs. 2,00,000 crore are expected to be released by toning up the effectiveness of the logistics management.. This paper lists the decision areas for better logistics management and examines the scope of introducing e-commerce to the inventory management in PEs.

Logistics Management holds the potential of lifting PE

performance to new levels. These enterprises have to meet the challenge of globalization and competitiveness. With the onset of economic liberalization, these enterprises may become multi-locational and multi-product and the reorganized structure may have a substantial chunk of their base in countries other than India. That the logistics management holds an olive branch for success on the financial front could be seen from Table 26.1.

Table 26.1: Trends in PE Performance for the Period 2001-02 to 2005-06

(Rs. crore)

Parameters	2001-02	2002-03	2003-04	2004-05	2005-06
Turnover	478731	572833 (19.65)	630704 (10.10)	744307 (18.0)	832584 (11.86)
Net Profit	25978	32344 (24.5)	52985 (63.8)	64963 (22.6)	70288 (8.2)
Contribution to Exchequer	62866	81867 (30.22)	89035 (8.75)	110604 (24.22)	125384 (13.36)
Dividend	8068	13769 (70.66)	15288 (11.03)	20718 (35.5)	22886 (10.46)
Investment	324614	335647 (3.39)	349994 (4.3)	357939 (2.27)	399057 (9.8)
Net worth	225472	241864 (7.26)	291828 (20.66)	341595 (17.05)	412737 (20.82)
Inventory	52175	58282 (11.5)	59705 (2.0)	73642 (9.0)	90164 (7.0)

Source: Government of India, Department of Public Enterprises, Background paper for the Conference of Chief Executives of Public Enterprises, pp. 8-9.

The following areas are emphasized for better decision making and logistics management:

1. Product Design.
2. Plant Location.
3. Choice of Markets/Sources.
4. Production Structure.
5. Distribution/Dealer Network Design.
6. Location of Warehouses.
7. Plant Layout and Logistics including Transportation.

8. Allocation Decision.
9. Production Planning.
10. Re-look at the purchase procedures and systems paving the way for e-tendering.
11. Inventory Management-Stocking Levels.

Inventory Management and Application of e-commerce

Inventory constitutes a major segment of investment and thereby also impacts greatly the return on investment. Inventory comprises raw material stocks, work-in-process, stores and spares, finished goods and, supplies and miscellaneous goods. Table 26.2 provides data about value of inventory, inventory-production-sales turnover ratio, and inventory in terms of number of days/cost of production/turnover.

Table 26.2 shows that PEs stocked inventories to the tune of 179 days production/turnover as on 30.3.1970 which has declined to 47 days production/turnover as on 31.3.2006. In advanced countries such as Japan, Just-In-Time (JIT) inventory concept is being practiced which is also known as zero level inventory. Giving due regard to the nature of the Indian economy and uncertainties of timely procurement, we may still provide for inventory build up of 30 days production/turnover. In other words, investments in inventories could be brought down by about Rs. 24,000 crore. Assuming 30 per cent as inventory carrying and holding costs, this may result into a saving of about Rs. 8,000 crore. Together, these two may improve the operating and financial leverages considerable and also lift the rate of return on investment to greater levels

Both the enterprises producing and selling goods, and enterprises rendering services were involved in overstocking. However, the enterprises involved in producing and selling goods were responsible for heavy overstocking. Within this category enterprises belonging to heavy engineering, medium and light engineering, minerals and metals, fertilizers, chemicals and pharmaceuticals, steel, transportation equipment, consumer goods, agro-based industries, coal & lignite and power distinguish themselves for indiscriminate overstocking. The contract and construction enterprises had this feature in the case of enterprises rendering services.

Table: 26.2: Inventory Management

Year ending	Value of inventory (Rs. crore)	Cost of prodn/ turnover (Rs. crore)	Inventory in No. of days, cost of prodn/turnover
31.3.1970	892	1,714	179
31.3.1975	2,698	8,118	121
31.3.1980	6,223	20,110	113
31.3.1985	12,639	49,804	93
31.3.1990	21,868	96,118	83
31.3.1991	24,938	1,06,283	86
31.3.1992	27,341	1,19,432	84
31.3.1993	32,580	1,31,958	90
31.3.1994	32,773	1,37,713	87
31.3.1995	33,770	1,59,425	77
31.3.1996	37,477	1,95,105	70
31.3.1997	40,815	2,06,658	72
31.3.1998	41,661	2,18,940	69
31.3.1999	44,404	2,78,720	58
31.3.2000	52,414	3,54,446	54
31.3.2001	50,717	4,25,100	44
31.3.2002	52,175	4,31,362	44
31.3.2003	58,282	4,66,444	46
31.3.2004	59,705	5,13,334	42
31.3.2005	73,642	6,26,427	43
31.3.2006	90,164	6,94,128	47

Source: Department of Public Enterprises (Government of India, New Delhi), Public Enterprise Survey: Vol. IV, 2005-06, pp 56- 57.

We now propose to examine as to how the application of e-commerce could bring down the inventory levels. In the general scheme of things, a new plan of action has to be designed as follows:

1. Detailed purchase requisition.
2. Indenting.
3. Calling the tenders.
4. Tender analysis.
5. Placement of orders with the vendors.
6. Transportation of goods.
7. Receipt of the goods at factory gate.
8. Inspection.
9. Storage.
10. Payments to vendors.
11. Insurance.
12. Administrative costs including management, development & training costs.
13. Inventory control.

Generally, all the above mentioned activities in PEs, are undertaken manually. The completion of inventory cycle ranges from 100 to 300 days. The application of e-commerce is expected to bring down the cycle time substantially and consequently the inventory costs. Now, the purchase requisitions are made by the user department involving the man on the ground to the head of the department. The entire process takes about 15 days time. Installation of computers with all the functionaries in the user departments, could bring down not only the paper work, .avert the situation of loss of papers, but also resolve the problem on the real time basis through e-mail and tele-conferencing. Suitable packages may have to be developed for this purpose. Similarly, indenting could be transacted very fast. In fact, both the activities of detailed purchase requisition and the indenting could be combined.

PEs float open tenders, general tenders, limited tenders and rush tenders. All these again are handled manually. A whole lot of executives come in picture. Depending on the importance of tender, the Tender Committee finalizes the deal. The Tender Committee comprises executives from the user department, finance department and stores and spares department. The

Committee is headed by the chief of stores and spares department. The finalization of tender requires several sittings, revisions and re-revisions. The introduction of e-commerce is likely to facilitate this activity and result in its quick completion. Activities 5 through 11 could involve an extensive use of e-commerce. The relationship with vendors is likely to become more positive as not only the payments could be arranged in time but also the report about the inspection of goods. Similarly, the movement of goods could also be tracked continuously.

The logistics management provides a clear solution to the problem of reducing lead time in the procurement of inventories in public enterprises. Mishra [3] has found both the administrative and technical lead time to be very high in the case of public enterprises in general and in select enterprises studied by him in particular. The horizontal report by the Committee on Public Undertakings (COPU) had similar observations to offer. [4] Though these studies were dated, the conclusions continue to remain valid. Viewed from the context of the. composition of inventory, it may be mentioned that in the case of both the raw materials inventory and stores and spares inventory, the administrative and technical lead time tend to be very high. The application of e-commerce in the case of inventory control relating to these two constituents of inventory ought to bring down both their levels of holding and investments therein. The only requirement is to design a flawless e-commerce system, which can cover entire gamut of operations.

The inventory control function can receive a great facilitation through e-commerce. To begin with the insurmountable problem of the preparation of the vocabulary of materials can easily be done through computerization. In many PEs the items stored are as many as more than 3,00,000. The computerization helps in identifying the location and the rate of use of materials for the purposes of reordering. The optimal inventory computation requires the application of some universal concepts such as the Baumol's model. In terms of this model, the annual usage of the product is calculated and also the inventory carrying and ordering costs are estimated. Expressed as formula, it is

$$EOQ = [2\ DO / ic]^{1/2}$$

where, D is the annual usage, of the product, O is the ordering cost and. "ic" is the average carrying cost representing the *cost* of insurance, go-down rent, obsolescence and interest charges. A study of the various items in stock would show that even' A' category items are in huge numbers. Any system of manual control makes it very difficult to optimize inventory. Once the inventory levels are .worked out through appropriate software, checks and balances could be installed and the system upgraded.

However, the use of e-commerce comes in very handy in the situation of exigencies such as stock-out of a vital item and the unavailability of the decision makers at one place. For instance, the failure of a blast furnace in the case of the steel plant may require an instant decision about its partial or full replacement amounting to a cost ranging from Rs.500 crore to Rs.1500 crore. Any decision on this would naturally the involvement of the managing director, general manager (finance), general manager (production) and general manager (materials).

Summing Up

An intensive application of e-commerce is bound to reduce the .cost of logistics and shore up the quality of logistics management. Not only the red tape and delay in decision making will be reduced but also the quality of decision making will improve. The participative process in decision making will bring about holistic solutions. It is said that inventory management has become a den of corruption due to lack of transparency. The introduction of e-commerce has the potential to bring down the corruption levels. As a consequence, the rate of return will touch new and probably more satisfying levels. The potential of logistics management need to be tapped to improve the profitability, resource position and value addition to the GDP. [5]

Notes

1. Raghuram R, 'Logistics Management: An Introductory Note', Vikalpa, V 01.17, No.I, January-March 1992.

2. See: Economic Times, May 2, 2007, Hyderabad, p. 1.

3. Mishra, R.K, Problems of Working Capital with Reference to Select Public Enterprises in India', Somaiya, Bomaby, 1975.

4. Government of India, Committee on Public Undertakings, New Delhi, 1967.

5. Department of Public Enterprises (Government of India, New Delhi), Background Paper for the Conference of Chief Executives of Public Enterprises, pp. 8-9.

27

Role of E-Business in Supply Chain Management

J. Suresh Reddy

Introduction

As we move from industrial age to the information age, a new distinct set of global competitive realities is emerging. In present information era, competitive price and high quality are necessary but not sufficient determinants of business success. Speed-to-market and quick flexible customer response is increasingly pivotal.

The rapid succession of cost, quality, delivery speed and agility as strategic imperatives reflects the continuous search for differentiating capabilities that provide firms with competitive advantage in the market place. In information age, delivery speed alone will not be sufficient for market success. To be successful in market, companies need to offer high quality customized products with less prices and faster service. Supply chain management is a powerful technique to address this challenge, which enables manufacturers to model analyze and revamp their essential business processes.

E-Business: E-business is the execution of business transactions over the Internet. C.S.V. Murthy defined e-business as "A market place where businesses are using Internet technologies and network computing to securely transform:

- Their internal business processes (via intranets)
- Their business relationships (via extranets)
- The buying and selling of goods, services and information (via e-commerce)"

E-Supply Chain Management: A marriage between supply chain management and e-business can be termed as e-supply chain management. According to Patel and McCarthy (2000), companies like Federal Express and Ingram Micro have leveraged e-business for differentiating their services from competitors, and increasing their competitive advantages. E-business implementation does offer a great potential of enhanced supply chain efficiencies.

Supply chain transactions that involve e-business include the flow of information, product and funds. Organizations conducting e-business can perform the following supply chain transactions over the net.

- Providing information across the supply chain.
- Negotiating prices and contracts with customers and suppliers.
- Allowing customers to place orders.
- Allowing customers to track orders.
- Filling and delivering orders to customers.
- Receiving payment from customers.

The internet, however, is the first channel that makes it possible for information located at a central source (the seller's web server) to be available to anybody, because it is a public channel. Some companies have used electronic data interchange (EDI), but EDI information is only available to those customers that have a dedicated EDI link to the seller.

Today, companies are using the internet to conduct a wide variety of supply chain transactions. For example, Dell displays all its product information over the internet. Customers are able to identify all options available for a personal computer (PC) they want to purchase along with the price of the configuration they select. Companies like eBay allow people to auction products over the internet.

Companies with an e-business allow customers to place orders over the internet. A customer can order PCs at Dell.com and books at Amazon.com. Federal Express allows customers to track their packages over the internet. Companies like Netscape and Shockwave.com fill and deliver orders over the internet through downloads of electronic products. Most companies involved in e-business allow customers to pay over the internet using their credit cards.

Use of internet has enabled companies to realize several supply chain related benefits.

- More collaborative, timely product development through enhanced communication between functional departments, suppliers, customers and even regulatory agencies.
- Reduction of channel inventory and product obsolescence owing to closer linkage across the supply chain and better insights into demand signals to drive product schedules and ultimately achieve build-to-order capability.
- Reduction in communication costs and customer support costs with more interactive, tailored support capability inherent with internet technologies.
- New channel capabilities to reach different customer segments and further exploit current markets.
- Ability to enhance traditional products and customer relationships through customization driven by internet connectivity and interactivity.

An effective e-SCM would be expected to have the following components:

- Supply chain replenishment: - web enabled customer ordering across the extended enterprise.
- E-procurement: - web enabled requisitioning, sourcing, contracting, ordering and payment.
- Collaborative planning: - facilitating buyers and sellers to come together to forecast demand and plan supply of goods and services.
- Collaborative product development: - e-business facilitating development to a product idea through shared information and knowledge across organizational teams.
- E-logistics: - leveraging web-enabled processes to manage the warehousing and transportation activities.

Impact of E-business on Supply Chain

An e-business offers potential opportunities to a firm for

gaining competitive advantage and it is having a significant impact on supply chain performance. To make supply chain more competitive e-business providing the following revenue enhancing and cost reduction opportunities.

An e-business allows a supply chain to exploit the following revenue enhancing opportunities:

1. Offering direct sales to customers: An e-business allows manufacturers to enhance revenues by bypassing intermediaries and selling directly to customers. For example, Dell computers sell Personal computers (PC) on-line directly to customers. As a result, Dell is able to enhance margins because it shares no margin with other supply chain members.
2. Providing access from any time and from any location: An e-business attracts customers who may not be able to place orders during regular business hours because it is always open for placing orders. E-business also allows a firm to access customers from any part of the world.
3. Aggregating information: An E-business allows a firm to increase sales by offering information regarding a very large selection of products. For example Dell offers customers a very large selection of computers and peripherals.
4. Customization: An E-business allows firms, to offer customized products to the customers. For example, Dell allows customers to customize their computers by using the options available on the Dell web site (www.Dell.com).
5. Speeding up time to market: An E-business allows firms, to introduce new products much faster than physical channels. An E-business, introduces a new product by making it available on the web site. A new product can be made available as soon as the first unit is produced. This is the evident in the computer industry where Dell often introduces new products earlier than its competitors using traditional channels.
6. Implementing flexible pricing: An E-business can easily alter prices over time by changing one entry in the database. This

ability allows an E-business to maximize revenues by setting prices based on current inventories and demand. For example, Airlines make last-minute low-cost fares available on the web on routes with unsold seats.

An E-business allows a supply chain to gain profit through effective utilization of the following cost reduction opportunities.

1. Reducing product handling with a shorter supply chain: An E-business allows manufacturers to reduce handling costs because of fewer supply chain stages.
2. Postponing product differentiation until after an order is placed: An E-business allows firms to manufacture customized products. Firms will manufacture the core products and waits for the customer order, which significantly reduce the inventories handling cost.
3. Decreasing delivery cost and time: If a firm can put its product in a form that can be downloaded. The Internet will save the cost and time for delivery. For example, downloading music from Amazon.com is eliminating all costs associated with transporting CDs.
4. Reducing facility costs: An E-business can reduce facility costs by centralizing all inventories and decreasing the number of facilities required.
5. Reducing processing costs: An E-business can lower its order fulfillment costs because it does not have to fill an order as soon as it arrives, where as retail store must staff its sales counters when more customers are shopping. At an E-business, maintaining a reasonable buffer of unfilled orders reduces the peak load for order fulfillment and thus reduces resources requirement and cost.
6. Decreasing inventory costs through aggregation: An E-business can aggregate inventories because it does not have to carry inventory close to the customer. The ability to reduce safety inventory without hurting product availability can significantly increase supply chain profitability.
7. Improving supply chain co-ordination through information sharing: an E-business can easily share demand information

throughout the supply chain to dampen the Bullwhip effect and improve co-ordination. [Bullwhip effect, in which fluctuations in orders increase as they move up the supply chain from retailers to wholesalers to manufactures to suppliers. The Bullwhip effect distorts demand information within the supply chain, with different stages having a very different estimate of what demand looks like].

Implementations of an E-business in supply chain also have some potential disadvantages. They are:

1. Customers that require a short response time may not use the Internet to order a product, because physical products cannot be downloaded.
2. Inventory aggregation leads into the higher transportation costs.
3. Setting up an E-business requires a large initial investment in the Information technology (IT) that will support it.

Conclusion

Firms have been using an E-business to provide information across the supply chain, to negotiate prices and contracts, allow customers to place and track orders, allow manufacturers to receive orders and receive payments from customers. Supply chains have been using an E-business to enhance revenues by selling directly to customers, providing 24-hour access. Providing customers with a customized shopping experience. Supply chains also been using an E-business to reduce costs.

Supply chains that have used an E-business successfully are able to move several supply chain activities from the push to the pull phase and postpone product differentiation until after a customer has placed his/her order. Successful B2B supply chains have used an E-business to lower their transaction costs for processing order and exchange information to better match supply and demand

References

B.S. Sahay; "Supply chain management for global competitiveness"; Macmillan, 2000.

David J.Bloomberg, Stephen Lemay and Joe B.Hanna; "Logistics"; PHI, 2002.

G. Raghuram and N.Rangaraj; "Logistics and supply chain management"; Macmillan India Limited, 2001.

Gattorna JL and Walters DW; "Managing the supply chain"; Macmillan Business, 1996.

Martin Christopher; "Logistics and supply chain management"; 2nd Edn; Pearson Education Asia, 2003.

Robert B. Handfield and Ernest L. Nichols, Jr; "Supply chain redesign"; Pearson Education (Singapore) Pte. Ltd, 2003.

Sinchi D. Levi, Kaminsky Phillip and Simchi-levi-E; "Designing and management of the supply chain"; Mc GrawHill, 2000.

Sunil Chopra and Peter Meindl; "Supply chain management"; Pearson Education Asia, 2002.

28

Value Stream Mapping as a Tool of Effective Supply Chain Management

Manimala. K

Introduction

The value stream mapping method is a visualization tool oriented to the Toyota version of lean manufacturing. It helps to understand and streamline work processes using the tools and techniques of lean manufacturing. The goal of VSM is to identify, demonstrate and decrease waste in the process. Waste being any activity that does not add value to the final product. VSM can thus serve as a starting point to help management, engineers, production associates, schedulers, suppliers, and customers recognize waste and identify its causes. As a result, VSM is primarily a communication tool, but is also used as a strategic planning tool, and a change management tool.

In order to do this, the value stream mapping method visually maps the flow of materials and information from the time products come in the back door as raw material, through all manufacturing process steps, and off the loading dock as finished products.

Mapping out the activities in the manufacturing process with cycle times, down times, in process inventory, material moves, information flow paths, helps to visualize the current state of the process activities and guides towards the future desired state. The process usually includes the physically mapping of the "current state" while also focusing on the "future state" map, which can serve as the foundation for other lean improvement strategies. The wastes identified in the organization by value stream mapping are Overproduction, Transportation, Unnecessary Inventory, Inappropriate Processing, Excess Motion Defects, under utilization of Employees' Minds/Ideas.

The Value Stream Mapping is carried out in a fertilizer enterprise, Karnataka Fertilizers and Chemicals Limited (KFCL) for effective lean management. The tool is used to identify the wastes in the organization and to reduce them.

The study performed at KFCL is as follows:

- A thorough description of the supply chain in KFCL is done.
- Based on this description, an analysis of the entire processes is done.
- Based on the analysis, a current state map showing the current flow of materials and information needed is drawn.
- Based on the findings in the analysis, problems are diagnosed and changes are suggested.
- A future state map representing the improved manufacturing process in KFCL is shown.

Current State Value Stream Mapping of KFCL

The current process in KFCL is studied and analyzed by using VSM as follows:

- Natural gas is supplied by GAIL from tatipaka through specially designed pipelines. And naphtha is supplied by HPCL, Visakhapatnam. Supply of natural gas is a continuous process. GAIL gives the lowest tariff of Rs.298 per MSCM for Tatipaka-Kakinada section. So the raw material cost is less for KFCL. The GAIL informs the company about the amount of natural gas it can supply per year, and raw material consumption is planed accordingly. The consumption of naphtha will be increased according to the supply of natural gas.

Materials and Stores

- When it comes to other raw materials and other material requirements of KFCL firstly, an indent will be raised. And it is also released on online system. The indenter will ensure the requisition for purchase would be complete in all respects. The indenters will ensure to take a note of the present stock status of the materials and accordingly raise PR's.

- Then selection of vendors is done.
- Enquiries are sent to vendors. The modes of sending enquiries are mailing, through post and fax.
- After sending enquiries to vendor, the purchase department will call the tenders on the basis of technical suitability, price, delivery period and absorbing freight.
- The next procedure is to receiving quotations. Purchase department will analyze the quotation and make the short list of suitable vendors.
- The vendors will be selected. The list is sent to higher approval to raise the purchase order. Then the order is made to the concerned suppliers. The lead times for different materials will be different.
- The items ordered by purchase department are received by the receiving section at stores. The supplier delivers the items along with orders.
- The consignment will be collected from nearby transport office.
- All the items which are sent by the supplier are checked thoroughly. If there is any damage then the supplier is informed. Accordingly, the supplier will take action.
- Then the goods are brought to KFCL store. Then the concerned department will be informed and are asked to check the quality of the items. If the items are approved and accepted then goods receipt note is made.
- The purchase order to goods receipt (GR) lead time will also differ depending on the materials ordered. If some items are rejected then goods discrepancy note (GDN) is made.
- After the GDN is prepared, the supplier will be informed and the rejected items will be sent back.
- The quality approved items are stored in the bins. The bins are given numbers. Every item has its own code and each code has 8 digits. The first two digits is their respective group code, and then there will two zeros following the group code, which is followed by a number (serial wise).

- The stored items are checked frequently. A note is prepared in order to check the items stored and they have to be verified before the dead line. All these process is done manually. Since the stores have lot of items, the time taken to count and check the items is more. After checking, certain measures are taken to preserve the items. They make sure that the packing's are correct and Metal items are lubricated from time to time, in order to prevent them from rust.
- The stores maintain maximum inventory. Maximum inventory = pre-order level + safety stock.
- When the pre-order level is consumed, the stock is ordered. They maintain one month safety stock.
- The three previous years lead times are taken and a lead time analysis is made, depending upon this analysis (i.e., purchase requisition to purchase order and purchase order to goods receipt) a lead time (i.e., purchase requisition to goods receipt) is fixed for every item. According to that they plan to order the items needed.
- The materials will be sent to the concerned department from stores on request.
- The stores department conducts ABC and FSN analysis in order to classify items according to their consumption rate and to know the costs incurred on the items and accordingly plans their inventory. The previous three years FSN analysis is studied, and plans to reduce their non moving items accordingly.
- SAP is used in stores to conduct ABC analysis. It can be generated for any number of days. They consider 365 days for generating the report. The system considers the day of generating the report by default and works backwards.

Procedure for Identification and Disposal of Surplus/Obsolete Items

Surplus/obsolete items are identified after studying FSN analysis report every year in the month of April/may. Subsequently action will be initiated after committee's approval for disposal of such items through e-auction, normal tendering, through website, circulation to other fertilizer industry. Two efforts have been made for disposal but the response was not satisfactory because surplus/obsolete items are mostly engineering spares which are made specific to the equipment and special consumable materials which have lost self life.

Production Plant

- The supply of natural gas is a continuous process. When the plant is shut down for a short time then, they burn the natural gas. But when the plant is shut down for a long time then KFCL intimates to GAIL to stop the supply of natural gas for that period.
- Natural gas is used as a primary input to ammonia plant. Then a series of steps are involved in the ammonia plant, which produce liquid ammonia. This liquid ammonia is transferred into the urea plant where after a series of processes, the liquid ammonia is turned into prilled urea.
- The available capacity of ammonia plant is 297000 MT/Yr. the uptime of ammonia plant 1 is 92.8 per cent and that of ammonia plant 2 is 89.4 per cent.
- The Cumulative shutdown hours from Apr'05-Mar'06 for ammonia plant 1 is 628.59 hrs and Cumulative shutdown hours from Apr'05 - Mar'06 for ammonia plant 2 is 925.96 hrs.
- The cycle time for one MT of ammonia for plant 1 is 76.12sec and the cycle time for plant 2 is 73.03 sec. (these cycle times are calculated by taking the average production of ammonia in plant 1&2).
- The available capacity of urea plant is 495000 MT/Yr. the uptime of urea plant 1 is 90.65 per cent and that of urea plant 2 is 89.65 per cent.
- The Cumulative shutdown hours from Apr'05-Mar'06 for urea plant 1 is 819.00 hrs and Cumulative shutdown hours from Apr'05 - Mar'06 for urea plant 2 is 905.91 hrs.
- The cycle time for one MT of urea for plant 1 is 39.61sec and

the cycle time for plant 2 is 44.67 sec. (these cycle times are calculated by taking the average production of urea in plant 1&2).

- The shut down is planned annually once in KFCL. If there are any repairs or installations then those works will be done. When one plant is shut down then another plant works, so that the production wouldn't stop. Both the plants will be shutdown for about 10 days.
- This shutdown period will be planned at the time of March or April. The shutdown will be for about 20 days in plant 1 and 20 days in plant2. This shutdown is very much useful in order to reduce the wear and tear of the machinery, since the machines work though out the year without stopping.
- The plant utilizes 130 per cent of its capacity.
- At an average the plant produces 4000MT per day, which is equal to 80,000 bags.
- After the urea is prilled and is ready for transfer to the bagging plant, then a sample of urea and other chemicals are taken every four hours and their quality is checked. In lab four people work in 3shifts.
- Biuret is the main impurity in urea. It is limited to 1.5 per cent according to the fertilizer control order. The total quality checking will be done in about 11/2 to 2 hours. A report is made and will give to the concerned department.
- If anything goes wrong then the urea will be diverted into silo instead of going to the bagging plant.
- The silo is located between the urea plant and the bagging plant. At the tran:fer house there is a flip gate, where the urea can be diverted into silo whenever required. The capacity of silo is 30,000MT and when necessary, the urea can be sent from silo to the bagging plant.
- For bagging of urea high density polyethylene bags are used and stored at the bagging plant. The bagging plant has an area of 1000 m^2 for the storage of bags. The trucks directly come to the bagging plant. A safety stock of 1, 00000 bags are stored at the bagging plant. Everyday 7 to 8 tons of bags come

to bagging plant. And it takes one hour to unload a truck. Two EOT cranes each of capacity1 ton are used for this purpose.

- 193 employees work in bagging plant. 144 are staff, 20 are supervisors, 5 are engineers and others are contract workers.
- The prilled urea comes from the process plant to the bagging plant through conveyors. In an average 180tons of urea is transferred to the bagging plant in an hour. The conveyor which passes from plant 1 to the bagging plant is 350 m. and its speed is 1.2m/sec, the time taken for the conveyor to travel from the process plant to the bagging plant is 4.86 min.
- From there the urea falls onto another conveyor, BC-04 which is also 350m in length and its speed is 0.8m/sec. The time taken for the urea to travel on this conveyor is 7.29 min.
- If there is any problem in the bagging plant or with the distribution then the urea is diverted into silo. From BC-01 the urea falls on to the BC-02 which is directed to silo. Its length is 250m and has a speed of 1.6m/sec. the time taken for the urea to enter the silo is approximately 3 min.
- From silo the urea is sent to the bagging plant on requirement through BC-03 conveyor, which is of the same length and speed of 0.8m/sec. The time taken for the urea to travel from silo to the bagging plant is 5.2min.
- When the conveyor enters the bagging plant, the urea falls onto the BC-05, & travelling tripper. Discharge of BC-1 will fall on belt conveyor, BC-4. BC-4 will discharge urea to belt conveyor, BC-5. Travelling tripper, TT-2 is over-ridden on belt conveyor, BC-5.
- There are 8 bunkers in the bagging plant, each of capacity 50MT. TT-2 is a 3 way tripper. By suitably operating TT-2, they can feed urea to bunkers (B1-B8) according to operating requirements.
- A composite sample is taken every hour from the bagging plant and is sent for quality checking.
- They have 8 bagging streams. Any stream can be taken on line according to the loading programme. A stream has the following equipments: bunker, electro-magnetic machine,

electro bagging machine, wooden slat conveyor, stitching machine, bag turner, stream of conveyors and bag diverters for handling the stitched bags, lorry loaders and wagon loaders.

- Bunkers are provided with load cell to sense the levels. Electronic bagging machine is positioned below each bunker. Each bunker has two independent bagging machines. In total there are 16 bagging and stitching machines, with a capacity of 1200 bags/hr/stream.
- Spilled urea from each bunker is collected by their respective spillage hoppers. They will discharge the urea on belt conveyor BC-28 & BC-29 will fall in buck elevator boot. It will discharge the spillage urea to bunker number 8.
- The HDPE bags are brought to the bagging machines by two workers. The time taken for the worker to bring the bags to 1st bunker is about 5min and 8th bunker is about 1min. A trolley is used to bring the bags.
- The cycle time for one bag of urea is about 6-8sec, where only the bunker, bagging and stitching machining times are included.
- Since, the bagging is a strenuous process; the workers will be taking 21/2 hr break in their 8 hr shift, ½ hr break each. There will be few extra workers, when one member takes break then another member comes and join the work, so that the work wouldn't be stopped.
- Filled bags are moved by a slat conveyor for stitching the open mouth, and then the bags are turned from vertical position to flat position. These flat positioned bags are conveyed by conveyors to wagon loader or lorry loader to the requirement. There are 8 lorry loaders.
- There are three platforms in the bagging plant. And when the conveyor is moving there are diverters which divert the bagged urea onto the required platform as per to the loading programme. The capacity of each platform is about 6000MT. all these platforms are connected by a railway track, wherein it becomes easy for the rake to come into the bagging plant

and get loaded.

- The trucks have a capacity of 10MT and 17MT. the time taken for loading a 10MT truck is about 15min and 17MT truck is about 25min. generally, one to two workers will be working to load the trucks.
- There are four type of wagons - Covered CG 24MT, CRT 27MT, BCT 55MT and BCN 55MT.
- There are 4 automatic travelling loading machines and 2 mobile roller conveyors are used for loading.
- The time taken for a worker to take the bag from the conveyor into the wagon is about 5-6sec. to fill a wagon 25-30 workers will be working. The time taken to fill a rake is about 8 hrs.

Distribution

- The head office takes the work order and reviews it. It fixes up where the urea has to be sent and in what quantity. Then that is sent to the distribution office at the company. Where they prepare the truck and rake plan. To make this plan they use the least cost module. They calculate the cost incurred for taking the bagged urea, both by trucks and by rake. The loading and unloading charges at different places and all the other costs involved are taken into account.

This map shows the process which takes place at the distribution department. It shows the relation between sales and the customer.

- Then the officer concerned makes an order to process plan which takes about 4days, then process to truck in, 1day and then the trucks in and truck out plan, which takes less time. According to the distribution plan, the trucks and rakes are ordered. Rakes from central railways and trucks from transport unions.
- Trucks are loaded in a certain manner which enables easy checking. Rakes are randomly checked, where two wagons are unloaded, checked and loaded again.
- Some materials go to the dealers directly but some go to the ware houses where the bags are stored and from there the

bags are sent to the dealer.

- Sometimes, the bags will be moved from one warehouse to another to meet the immediate requirements of the market.
- Some dealers will be given credit and some pay directly. The bills are prepared accordingly and sent to dealers or the customers and they pay according to that.

Wastes Identified in KFCL

Physical Counting of Inventory: The inventory in the stores is physically counted. This is a very painful and time taking process, since the inventory in stores is about 41,220 items. Every time an employee adds or removes an item, there is a risk of introducing inventory variance.

Maintenance of Inventory: At stores the inventory maintained is at maximum level. Whenever the inventory comes to safety stock, the materials are ordered, taking the material lead times into account. Therefore, the number of items in stores is more. And KFCL prefers to incur cost on maintenance rather than making loss during the sudden shutdown of the plant. But incurring cost on few items is not a problem but there are many items in the store, and every year incurring so much on maintenance of items is definitely a huge investment.

Increase in Number of Non Moving Items: The increase in value is Rs.0.612cr as 201 items got added into non moving category after crossing non moving logic period of three years during sep,05 to feb,06. Although efforts have been made for disposal in the financial year 2005-06 the response was not satisfactory because surplus/obsolete items are mostly engineering spares which are made specific to the equipment and special consumable materials which have lost self life.

Transportation Costs: All the trucks used at KFCL are outsourced. They are tied up with many unions, and get the trucks as per to the demand. This costs them more. KFCL distributes urea to many places in A.P and also in other states. Whenever there is an increase in the price of petrol and diesel, the transportation costs are also increased. Sometimes the trucks do not come in time. And they cannot send all the urea through rakes as it costs them more.

No Truck Tracking System: KFCL uses hundreds of trucks for distribution. The company doesn't know anything about the truck once it goes out, till it reaches the destination place. Many a times there has been a problem that the truck goes to the wrong destination, and the reason being the truck drivers being uneducated and do not understand the address. Often, the lead times taken by the trucks are more. Because of these reasons, the waiting time of customer is increasing which results in customer dissatisfaction.

Checking of Bags: In KFCL, when the bags are loaded into the trucks and rakes, they are physically counted, to make sure that the correct numbers of bags are loaded into them. There is not much problem with the trucks, because the trucks are weighed before loading and after loading. But the problem is about loading of rakes. After loading the wagons, the wagons are randomly checked i.e., two wagons are selected randomly, they are unloaded, checked and then loaded again. This involves more time, labour and also there are chances that the other wagons may have excess bags.

No Information Flow: Although all the area offices and other departments of KFCL are connected through SAP, still there is no proper information flow. Unless until, the dealer or the customer calls and complaints that they didn't get the urea in time, the distribution office does not know and also they are unable to track in time where the fault has happened.

Warehouses are not connected Through Sap: The warehouses are not connected through SAP. All the area offices and KFCL are connected through SAP. Area officer will go and check the warehouses once in a season. He will ensure optimum utilization of multiple warehouses at same location. The inventory status will not be updated unless until the area in charge will go and check the warehouse. If anything is necessary then, the warehouse agent will call up to area officer, and inform him. They review the quarterly joint warehouse inspection reports and initiate necessary remedial actions.

Future State Value Stream Mapping: The current state value stream map is very well observed and wastes have been identified in the organization. The wastes identified in KFCL can be solved by implementing few measures. A future state map can be achieved by taking the following recommendations or suggestions into account:

Reduction of Administrative Lead Times: The administrative lead times can be reduced by ensuring that their suppliers are well connected to the company through SAP or by other mode like internet wherein the general transactions and sending of quotations can take place very fast. This helps the departments (connected through SAP) to go through quickly and compare the quotations and select the vendor accordingly. This helps to reduce the time taken for receiving quotations and the negotiations.

Automatic Vehicle Locator System

The automatic vehicle locator system can be used to track the trucks of KFCL.

An Automatic Vehicle Locator System uses the GPS, GSM and SMS technologies to enable businesses to keep track of their fleets of vehicles. The system provides management with accurate information through MIS reports and can be interfaced with ERP and JIT systems to increase and monitor employee productivity and efficiency.

There are multiple benefits of using AVLS

- Better route planning and vehicle utilization
- Benefits in utilizing Just-In-Time systems for ordering raw materials
- Better Storage and Warehouse management
- Monitors drivers' irregular behavior: route deviation, unscheduled stops, long breaks enroute, over-speed, etc.

Use of Barcoding System at Stores and Bagging Plant: To conduct efficient and accurate cycle counts, the company can use mobile computers with integrated barcode scanners that allow the operator to automatically identify items, and enter inventory counts via keypad. The software then transmits data to a database on a host system which can generate inventory reports. The barcode system can be used in bagging plant. The barcode labels can be attached to the bags, which help to know the number of bags loaded. If this methodology is used at the warehouses, then it becomes easy for the company to know the transactions and the inventory levels at warehouses.

Implementation of Vendor Managed Inventory: KFCL is spending more money in the maintenance of its inventory. In order to reduce the cost spent on inventory, vendor managed inventory system (VMI) can be followed. VMI, in which the buyer of a product provides certain information to a supplier of that product and the supplier takes full responsibility for maintaining an agreed inventory of the material, usually at the buyer's consumption location.VMI makes it less likely that a business will unintentionally become out of stock of a good and reduces inventory in the supply chain.

Reduction of Non-Moving Items: The number of non moving items should be reduced in the inventory. They have to consider the FSN analysis seriously and should prepare plans according to that. Proper study of consumption of materials or items should be made, which help them to order the items according to the requirement. Maintaining more than safety stock also makes the company incur more cost on the inventory. Therefore, the consumption rate of items should be thoroughly gone and the consumption of items should be studied at least for the last three years, which help in analyzing the inventory status, consumption value of items and reduction of non moving items.

Own Transport: KFCL uses hundreds of trucks for distribution purpose. But all the trucks are owned by private agencies. Therefore, the cost spent on the trucks is more. KFCL can start its own transport, which helps in save a lot of money in the long run. KFCL need not own hundreds of trucks but at least few number of trucks, for distributing to the near by area dealers or warehouses, and gradually can increase the number of trucks owned, which will prove to be very advantageous in the long run.

Own Warehouses: KFCL utilises many number of warehouses within A.P and outside A.P. KFCL stores it's urea in these warehouses and distribute to the dealers from the warehouses. The rental charges paid by KFCL to all the warehouses are more. Generally, warehouses are built in villages or near by towns. Therefore, KFCL can plan to build small warehouses first and then gradually improve the number of owned warehouses. Since, all the warehouses are rental, the company is unable to pressurise the warehouse agents to use computers at the warehouse. Since, the warehouses are not connected to the plant, the plant will not know, the daily activities which are going at the warehouses. Since, the officers will go and check once in a season, they may not know what is happening at the warehouses.

And also by connecting the warehouses through intranet, the company will know the day to day inventory status report and also about the sales and the lead times. This will be very helpful to the company in analysing the sales and to plan up their stock at warehouses.

Conclusion

Value Stream Mapping is the tool that can be used to drive the continuous improvement activities in the organization to a successful conclusion. To transform an organization into a Lean Enterprise it is necessary to have a vision, something to guide the activities of many continuous improvement teams as they implement changes using the lean enterprise tools. The Value Stream Mapping planning tool is what solidifies the vision. The Value Stream Plan is the tool that makes that vision understandable and achievable. Using the Value Stream Map as a guide and the Value Stream Plan to manage resources, continuous improvement is focused and concentrated to achieve maximum gains from resources available, achieving success for the Lean Enterprise.

References

Books

- Basics of Process Mapping by Robert Damelio
- Designing and Managing the Supply Chain Management by Simchi-Levi, D., Kaminsky, P., and Simchi-Levi. E.

Journals

- Indian Journal of Fertilizers
- KFCL Manuals

Index

Index